D1316692

Bureaucracy

Bureaucracy

Guy Benveniste

University of California, Berkeley

boyd & fraser publishing company
san francisco

Guy Benveniste

Bureaucracy

Manufactured in the United States of America.

Library of Congress Catalog Card Number: 77-75390
International Standard Book Number: 0-87835-059-4, paper
0-87835-063-2, cloth

2 3 4 5 6 * 9 8

For Karen

As for us, we hardly know what to think of the pro-digious changes that are taking place around us and even within us. New powers, new constraints; and the world has never been less sure where it was going.

Paul Valéry, 1931

Contents

Preface

The bureaucratic phenomenon is with us, and everyone complains about it: "they" are never able to do things right; "they" do not care about anything; "they" are immobilized in red tape; "they" spend our taxes; each year, "they" get bigger and bigger; all "they" do is push papers around; "they" control the market; how can you expect to do business in that situation?; it's big fish gobbling up the small fry!; I hate my job — I am just a number; "they" always check on you; if you miss out, out you go. . . .

These complaints or their equivalent are heard in the United States, in Western Europe, in the Soviet Union, in Third World countries, in China, everywhere. The last quarter of this century will be remembered as the bureaucratic era. Bureaucratic organizations prevail, and most social activities take place in bureaucracies. People are born, work, play, and die in bureaucracies, and most everyone, at one time or another, complains about the way bureaucracies function.

This book attempts three tasks:

— First, it explains why the bureaucratic phenomenon has reached crisis conditions: how uncertainty creates excessive fear, and fear results in protective strategies. These protective strategies are the games that are played in and out of bureaucracies.

— Second, it reviews the first remedies: how organization development came about; how accountability, evaluation, and planning were supposed to help, but how decentralization does not take place.

— Third, it looks into the future and examines new institutions which are needed to make bureaucracies function effectively.

This book is intended for students of politics, economics, sociology, medicine, law, engineering, social work, public health,

xi

journalism, education, etc., who work with or use bureaucracies. I am a professor of education, and I wrote this text because bureaucracy is probably the number one issue in education. We may have the best program and the best curriculum. If the teachers or professors have to play games, if they are unable to perform because of bureaucratic nonsense, our program and curriculum will go by the wayside. Today, everyone has to be concerned with bureaucracy.

This book assumes no previous knowledge of organization theory. I present what theory is needed as we go along, chapter by chapter. I provide references for further reading and introduce the interested student to the relevant literature.

To a limited extent, this book expands arguments that first appeared in my *Politics of Expertise* (Benveniste 1972). Readers particularly interested in the subject of experts and planning may want to refer to that text.

I am indebted to many, as are most authors. I owe special intellectual debts to a number of persons who have helped me in different ways: Bo Anderson, Douglas Ashford, Charles Benson, Irene Blumenthal, Robert Biller, Judith Balderston, Burton Clark, Michel Crozier, Ladislav Cerych, C. West Churchman, Sandra Elman, John Friedmann, Bertram Gross, James Guthrie, Albert Hirschman, Alice Ilchman, Warren Ilchman, Arnold Meltsner, Ivar Nelson, Karen Nelson, Jennifer Nias, Philip Selznick, W. Richard Scott, Jean-Claude Thoenig, Martin Trow, Kathleen Unger, Dwight Waldo, Harold Wilensky, Aaron Wildavsky, Alan Wilson, and Morris Zelditch, Jr.

I wish to thank all the students in my course in organization theory who reviewed an earlier version of the manuscript, and in particular Carl Bernard, Susan Chandler, Peter Finnegan, Edward Graef, Harold Jenkins, Margo Kennedy, Nilo Sarmiento, Louise Stoll, Raymond Yu, and Mary Lou Zoglin.

I also wish to thank Joan Killeen, Ann Nishizawa, and Jo-Ann Work for producing the manuscript, and Joan Parsons and Jack Taylor at Boyd & Fraser for editing and publishing the book.

I was fortunate to be able to write this book while administering a $998,000 grant from the Agency for International Development (AID) to The Regents of the University of California. The topic of the grant research was the financing of education in Third World countries and was not directly related to this book. But my administrative role, which took about thirty percent of my time, kept me in touch with bureaucracy. It also allowed me to spend summers writing and provided supporting services which I hereby acknowledge. I hasten to write that AID and Berkeley have not been my principal sources of empirical evidence.

I am solely responsible for all errors and omissions, and if readers find a Gallic flavor to the sentence structure, they are on the right track; I was born in Paris.

GUY BENVENISTE
Berkeley, California

Scheme of the Book

This book assumes that there is a universal culture of organizations that transcends political or economic ideologies of the left or of the right. We assume that control, rewards, punishment, careers, promotions, corruption, errors, and fear exist anywhere modern bureaucratic structures are established. We also assume that there is a universal culture of organizations that stresses task orientation and goal attainment (making a profit or fulfilling plan objectives); which espouses efficiency, coordination, and rationality of decisions; which rejects what is spontaneous, disorderly, or accidental; which emphasizes what is systematic, thorough, and painstaking; which endorses verification, control, and formalization; which rejects amusement, pleasure, and delight for their own sake; which applauds risk-taking but rarely encourages it; which rejects hedonism in the organization as sheer fantasy; which assumes that organizational survival is the only relevant goal to be pursued. These are universal traits of bureaucracy as we know it.

Yet we also know that cultural and political differences affect bureaucracy. If we go from nation to nation or from culture to culture, we find that the laws, the structures, the economy, or the customs modify the prevalent patterns of bureaucratic behavior.

In France, we are told, there is a general fear of face-to-face relationships which helps explain the French hierarchical and centralized model of bureaucracy (Crozier 1964, Grémion 1976). If people will not confront each other, they need a superior to adjudicate their conflicts. In Asian nations, other cultural patterns dominate, such as deference to status, which greatly limit upward communications. In Latin America, personal and family ties provide informal linkages that may have more significance than official relations. In parts of Africa, participation in decisions is reinforced by traditions of open discussion. Yet these particular cultural differences do not alter the more fundamental, universal characteristics that we described. It is not surprising that the current American literature on comparative organization pays scant attention to these differences (Etzioni 1961; Heydebrand 1973; Landesberger 1970; Perrow 1967).

Bureaucracy does not work well. Why? Because of excessive fear; because too many people in organizations are afraid of losing their jobs, afraid of jeopardizing their careers, afraid of being caught in an error, a scandal, or a bad move. Instead they pursue defensive strategies, which hurt their consumers and their clients who, in turn, complain and fight back, thus increasing the fears of those who are already in fear. The main argument of this book is very simple: if we want to improve the effectiveness of bureaucracies, we have to reduce the level of fear that exists within them. We may have to create new institutions that will protect clients, organizations, and people in organizations.

This book is divided into three parts. In the first we deal with the current bureaucratic crisis. In the second we review current remedies. In the third we present new approaches for thinking about the future of bureaucracy.

This book is concerned with large organizations, both public and private. We are concerned with their functioning, how they serve clients, and to what extent the people in them enjoy their tasks. We are not concerned (except in the next to last chapter) with political and ideological issues. We do not discuss who owns the means of production or who exploits whom. Instead, this book is concerned with a crisis phenomenon which afflicts most large organizations in both socialist and capitalist economies.

In addition, this book presents the elements of a theory of organization. Chapters one and two review much of the current conceptual apparatus in order to enable the reader to comprehend subsequent arguments. While we do not have, as yet, a comprehensive theory of organization to explain what is happening, we do have theoretical notions about the nature of social power, the way it is legitimated into authority, and the way rewards and punishments are used to control members of organizations. These notions permit us to explain why the members of organizations behave the way they do. I say this because it is useful to keep in mind that what happens in organizations, the bureaucratic phenomenon we complain about, *does not take place by accident.* There are important factors that make people behave as they do, not because they have peculiar personalities, not because they are good or bad, courageous or weak, but because they are controlled to behave in a specific way.

The Crisis

What do we mean by uncertainty? We mean that individuals in organizations are often unsure about how to behave, which way to go. They are afraid that their sub-unit or their entire organization will be involved in an error: the service they provide will not be wanted or they will provide a needed service at the wrong time. They know that certain errors can be severely punished: organizations or portions of organizations can be abolished, individuals can find themselves without employment, and even those protected by civil service regulations or union contracts fear a disruption of their careers and worry about being shunted off into unpleasant and undesirable assignments.

To avoid such problems, they pursue defensive strategies. We call these strategies "games" (Berne 1964). Games are sets of ulterior transactions, repetitive in nature, with a well-defined payoff (Berne 1972, p. 23).

Clients also play games to counter unsatisfactory relations with bureaucracies. Similarly, large organizations play games among themselves and with their clients. They pursue these strategies to avoid the consequences of large-scale errors. Among these games is planning. Planning is a game in the sense that it is one of several strategies that organizations use to protect themselves. Interorganizational planning serves the important function of rationalizing policy-making. But it also has ulterior functions. It is a conscious attempt to reduce uncertainty by preventing errors.

This book begins by tracing the development of ideas about organization and uncertainty. The first chapter discusses modernization, Durkheim's theories of social integration, the function of the market, and the growing importance of rationalization exercises. We also review parallel developments in the sociology of organizations.

The second chapter focuses on control: how organizations control individuals — or more exactly, how individuals are controlled while pursuing careers in organizations. We also examine how organizations control each other and the way individuals are affected by these external controls. This chapter provides the basis for understanding the games that are played.

In the next four chapters we analyze the defensive strategies. The chapter on the games clients play shows that clients have few defensive tools with which to protect themselves. The chapter on the games organizations play focuses on client control, planning, and organizational spread. The following chapter deals with the serious business of protecting oneself inside the organization. Lastly we discuss corruption and examine the effect of corruption on organizational uncertainty.

The Current Remedies

The second part of the book deals with current remedies: organization development, accountability, decentralization and participation, and the ombudsman. Planning is not included among the remedies; it is, rather, a game. But not all games are bad and not all remedies are good. We will show how planning has some utility in reducing uncertainty and how accountability can exacerbate uncertainty. The difference between games and remedies is one of intent. Games have ulterior functions. Remedies are understood to serve the purpose they are intended to serve. Organization development, accountability, participation, and the ombudsman are all conscious efforts to deal with the bureaucratic crisis brought about by increased organizational uncertainty. Planning is somewhat different because planners do not perceive their role in this context.

In these four chapters we present, as succinctly as possible, an outline of the social forces that bring about these remedial efforts and their consequences for organizations. My purpose is to provide enough information and a clear line of reasoning to permit us to weave together a theory about what might be done to reduce uncertainty and possibly also reduce patterns of organizational behavior that are neither effective nor pleasant.

Models and Ideas about the Future

So far the book is conventional. Part three departs somewhat from current convention to present material about possible futures. As Moore pointed out (Moore 1966), there is utility in being interested in what happens next. Utopian constructions are used to explore the realm of the possible. They can, if the purposes are made explicit, also provide a heuristic tool for comprehending the present and the past.

A central value is pursued in this last part of the text. It is related to social power. Excessive fear in organizations means that excessive power is used to achieve purposes. To use ordinary language, the stick is too long and the carrot insufficient. Therefore, we wish to reduce the stick and improve incentives for professional performance.

Chapter eleven presents three central ideas about the future of bureaucracy. These are ideas about ways of reducing uncertainty so as to eliminate or reduce excessive fear, which is dysfunctional. The first idea is to reduce uncertainty by centralizing and planning. This has been tried in centrally planned socialist economies. The second idea is to reduce uncertainty by making the system simpler and by adopting austere styles of life with small-group self-sufficiency. The third idea is to reduce uncertainty by establishing new institutions whose function is to correct the consequences of errors.

Obviously there does not exist any "grand" or final solution to the current bureaucratic crisis. Bureaucracy will change gradually as small incremental steps are taken to adapt this human institution to new conditions. But these elements — reducing uncertainty by correcting errors, strong centralized planning, and adopting austere life styles — will be discussed more and more in coming years.

In chapter twelve we turn to the current discussion about centralized socialist planning versus "small is beautiful." We discuss the experience of the Soviet Union to highlight the pitfalls of excessive centralized planning. We then proceed to contrast that pattern with one presented by writers in quest for simplicity, small-size enterprise, and a "human" technology. We regretfully conclude that while much can be done to simplify modern life, there exist sharp limitations to this approach.

The last chapter is utopian. It presents a complex model of professional institutions designed to correct errors and reduce uncertainty. It is an insurance scheme whereby a set of institutions called the Professional Governors protects the careers of individuals in organizations, another set called the Councils protects organizations, and a third set, the Professional Courts, protects the interests of clients and the public at large. These institutions are administered by Professional Boards whose function is to raise the revenue for the scheme and to adjudicate between conflicting claims.

* *
*

part one

The Crisis

one

Uncertainty

At the outset of one of his books, economist Robert Heilbroner has posed the question: "Is there hope for man?" (Heilbroner 1974, p. 13).

He asks whether we can imagine a future as dark and cruel as the past — or even worse. Is the human condition deteriorating? Do we already sense the impending catastrophe?

> That such a question is in the air, hovering in the background of our minds, is a proposition that I shall not defend by citing bits of evidence from books, articles, and the like. I will rest my case on the reader's own response. . . . (pp. 13–14)

We begin with the same premise. Some readers may wonder how we know there is a crisis, how we know that today's large organization is worse than it was, say, one hundred years ago. Is corruption worse? Are people more unhappy? Are services deteriorating? Is this pessimism justified?

If we conduct a careful historical comparison we will probably find areas where today's organizations have clearly improved and other areas where the contrary has happened. But that is not the point. The significant issue is that a lot of people sense that something is wrong, that organizations are not doing well. It has become politically fashionable to attack bureaucracy as an evil. For example, a leading writer on organizations describes the views of John Gardner, a man who has had considerable experience in government and private life, who was a member of the cabinet of President Kennedy, and who later initiated Common Cause, the consumer policy organization:

> John Gardner has, for years, attempted to awaken the world regarding the "dry rot" that is slowly engulfing and enveloping organizations. He has predicted the eventual collapse of our society because of the collapse of its institutions. (Argyris 1970, p. 1)

This is strong language indeed, but I do not believe it is too strong. I remember a Belgian city administrator who once visited Berkeley. His statement was typical:

> We reach a stage where making decisions becomes too difficult, too expensive. So many new agencies and pressure groups have to be involved, so many conflicts have to be resolved, coordination and participation become excessive burdens: *nous devenons immobilisés* [we are becoming immobilized].

This book does not attempt to prove empirically that conditions are deteriorating in the bureaucracy. But it develops a line of argument that helps to explain why it is reasonable to assume that all is not well.

The Cause of the Crisis: Modernization

Let me argue that the invention called "organization" is less able to cope with worldwide problems than it was one hundred years ago.

Why?

Because the environment in which every large organization operates has become so complex and therefore so uncertain that organizations do not function well.

The environment of an organization includes many other organizations. The world system of organizations is less able to function effectively because the institutions created to coordinate and adjust all these organizations are inadequate. National and regional planning have not failed, but planning is not sufficient. Markets are not functioning well either; government regulations are not sufficient.

Economic growth and modernization imply differentiation and specialization — the more economic growth the more differentiation. As the system of production and consumption becomes differentiated, a need for *conscious* communication, coordination, and mutual adjustment emerges. Such interchange is called "articulation." The earlier instruments of articulation (market information, prices, forecasts, contracts, etc.) were, and still are, imperfect. What happens is always slightly or even radically different from what was expected. As economic growth spreads worldwide, interdependencies between units of production and consumption become more numerous, complex, and intense, and involve partners who are increasingly distant and diverse. The existing instruments of articulation become more imperfect, and the level of environmental uncertainty in which organizations operate rises.

As the larger environment becomes more uncertain, organizations respond in a variety of ways. They attempt to control or seduce the environment; they become submissive and feel threatened; they attempt to use rational instruments to force the environment into more predictable patterns; they create internal structures adapted to certain external changes; they expand because they are afraid of remaining small. As they become larger, they become more impersonal and rule-ridden, and make many more errors.

These remedies are insufficient. Conditions in bureaucracies continue to deteriorate. More people become aware that the task is performed with difficulty. Clients complain about impersonal treatment, about getting the "runaround," about the stupidity or ineptness of those with whom they deal. The crisis accentuates, and we do not really know what to do about it.

Exchanges: Markets

Modernization depends on role specialization and differentiation. In a traditional society fewer roles exist. Except for sexual role divisions, labor is largely undifferentiated. For example, at the turn of the century in tropical Africa, men performed numerous tasks: they cleared bush, made fences, set traps, hunted, and, when necessary, fought their neighbors. Women fetched water and wood, made pots and baskets, sowed, weeded, and harvested (Kimble 1962, p. 23). Such a society is fairly predictable. Exchanges take place, gifts are made, people know their roles and what is expected of them. In these situations, most of the uncertainty is caused by external factors: weather, accidents, illness.

In contrast, a modern society is highly differentiated. In fact, modernization is usually defined by structural differentiation and by the need for integration and articulation of exchanges (Smelser 1964, p. 259). Work is specialized and depends on others. For example, in 1965 the United States Department of Labor used as many as 35,550 different occupational titles; that is, different occupations in the economy for which a name had been invented (U.S. Department of Labor 1965). With specialization and domain restriction (I work in this area, you work in that one) comes the need for articulation: I do something, you do something else, and we exchange what we need from each other.

What are the mechanisms of integration and articulation? We can think of many: laws, regulations, and customs (the fact that we know to stop at red lights to avoid collisions); nonverbal understandings (in Mexico you move your index finger rapidly from right to left and back to express "No, I do not want this"; the young boy who shines shoes leaves you immediately); and exchanges: the actual transactions that tie us together, the messages we send, the goods we sell and buy, the love we give and receive, the contracts we sign, etc.

Exchanges and Integration

Émile Durkheim, the French sociologist, suggested that exchanges result from mutual dependencies which bind the social system together. Organic solidarity, as he called that form of integration, is based on differences. The division of labor itself is the mechanism of integration:

> Higher societies can maintain themselves in equilibrium only if labor is divided. . . . Law and morality are the totality of ties which bind each of us to society, which make a unitary, coherent aggregate of the mass of individuals. (Durkheim 1933, pp. 397–98)

For Durkheim, the division of labor did not result from economic causes although higher productivity was a consequence. He focused on the social functions of organic solidarity. Different people were able to co-exist because they needed each other, in an acute struggle for existence:

> The oculist does not struggle with the psychiatrist, nor the shoemaker with the hatter, nor the mason with the cabinet maker, nor the physicist with the chemist, etc. Since they perform different services, they can perform them parallelly. (p. 267)

But while the division of labor serves to integrate society, it also generates uncertainty. If we think of a world system of production and consumption, the exchanges between all who produce and all who consume serve to integrate the world system. But the more that diversification takes place, the more new technologies are invented, and the more interdependence exists, the more organizations need to know about the characteristics of this integration. Otherwise, they may make serious errors of judgment. A service may not be available when it is needed, or an organization may provide a service for which there is no demand.

For example, you go to school and train to be a teacher, but the day you graduate, there are no jobs for teachers. This is an error of judgment caused by an error of articulation, an error about the availability of employment. Such errors are severely punished. In our example you do not find a job. In the case of organizations, they may lose their markets or be displaced.

In a relatively well understood economy, the economic world Durkheim knew, it is possible to talk about the integrative function of the division of labor without further specification. Economic integration takes place largely as a result of market mechanisms. Durkheim assures us that there is adequate awareness of the process of integration. The hatter makes hats in response to the need for hats. People tell him about their wants and he meets them. From time to time the hatter may produce too many hats or ugly hats. But Durkheim did not think this was a problem, and he dismissed the phenomenon. Such instances are "pathological"; they are irregularities like forgetting to eat or a break in the equilibrium (p. 271).

Durkheim's book *The Division of Labor in Society* was first published in 1893. At the time, the "unseen hand of the market" was considered a natural phenomenon. People believed in the market and so no one was to blame if the market was fickle and changed overnight.

The unseen hand of the market carries with it a good deal of uncertainty, but this is akin to the uncertainty of the weather. Just as the peasant in a traditional society knows how cruel events can be, the mercantilist learns about the uncertainty of the market. A prudent and diligent businessman behaves and reacts like a prudent and diligent peasant. Both blame their misfortunes on arbitrary conditions. Peasants, organizations, and individuals are punished if the weather or the market behaves erratically. But everyone understands about good and bad luck. As long as the rate of change is relatively slow, organizations cope: if the system is sufficiently stable and repetitive, these punishments are taken as a way of life. They do not cause secondary problems.

Conscious Perception of Uncertainty

When the rate of change accelerates, when technology makes it possible to convert local into international markets, it is no longer possible to anticipate events and Durkheim's hatter begins to worry more and more about what is going to happen next. The hatter wants to know if the price of felt is going to change; if one should buy stock now or later. He wants to know if he should move into new synthetics, if there is a market for them. He wants to know the new trends in bonnets. Articulation becomes a conscious function within the organization and within society. Planning is born.

Changes took place in the public sector as governments increasingly began to provide collective goods (such as education, health, welfare, etc.) and intervened to regulate economic life. Public policy required a better understanding of the consequences of actions or omissions. The hidden hand of the market began to be guided.

As these changes emerged, new theories about decision-making and planning were invented. In the nineteen-thirties and forties important advances were made in the theory of decision-making and choices under uncertainty. Contributions came mostly from mathematicians and economists. The dates of these publications are related to the changing nature of the system of economic interaction.

Frank Knight, an economist, wrote a pioneering work about risk, uncertainty, and business decisions in 1921 (Knight 1921). Work on the mathematics of games continued in the thirties, but it was not until the forties and fifties that a widespread literature on decision-making and uncertainty emerged (Bowman 1958; Carter 1962; Luce 1957; Oza 1965; Raiffa 1968; Schackle 1952; von Neumann 1953). These works provided logical explanations of the way decision-makers behave. At the same time, in the early fifties, the computer became available commercially. The combination of new ideas about problem-solving together with the possibility of handling large volumes of data by computer ultimately provided more powerful tools of analysis.

By the early sixties, a new science of management decision was recognized (Simon 1960). These developments were useful in their own right, but they also provided palliatives which delayed and disguised for some years the great difficulties that were emerging in the administrative world. They served organizations in a manner similar to the "hidden hand" of the market. They provided legitimation to protect decision-makers: "How can you blame me for this error? We programmed the decision in our computer and our choices were based on the best data available at the time."

John Maynard Keynes' *General Theory of Employment, Interest and Money,* published in 1935, provided a new rationale for government intervention in the economy — thus eradicating the notion that nothing significant could be done about business cycles (Keynes 1964). Kenneth Arrow's classic, a search for a rational theory of collective social choices, appeared in 1951 (Arrow 1963). His intellectual predecessors had published their works on welfare economics in the late thirties and early forties (Bergson 1938; Kaldor 1939; Lange 1942).

Even though welfare economics did not provide any definitive answer to the question of optimal collective choices, there is little doubt that these and other works, combined with the practical experience of World War II, radically altered the practices of government and private management.

Uncertainty and Rationalization Exercises

Starting in the fifties, organizational uncertainty began to be treated systematically by several writers. The notion that it is possible to control physical and social systems has its foundations in Norbert Wiener's work on "cybernetics" — a term coined by Wiener to describe the field of control and communication theory (Wiener 1948). Several intellectual trends began to emerge:

— the notion of planning and policy coordination;

— the application of systematic thinking, such as the theory of games, to policy choices;

— the introduction of system analysis and control theory in management practice;

— the attempt to rationalize budget control by the use of program budgets.

These approaches are all rationalization exercises: they are conscious attempts to use rational, logical thinking to deal with problems of organizational articulation — both internal and external.

These ideas were a response to increasing uncertainty, and offered the first techniques for dealing with it. We will discuss some of these remedies at great length later on, but it is useful, at this point, to examine some of the limitations of rationalization exercises and of planning in particular.

Rationalization exercises are only useful when the problem is formulated in such a way that there is sufficient information to yield a solution. Suppose you want to know how many spare parts you should store for the machinery of a complex production line. You cannot ask the question in a vacuum. You cannot ask how many spare parts are needed because there is no logical way to answer your question *unless you specify certain conditions you want to meet*. The problem has to be formulated as follows:

— We know the probability that each component of the production line will break down (based on past experience).

— We decide what length of breakdowns is permissible — say, we do not want any machine to be out of commission for more than twelve hours because of lack of spare parts. (This is a specification.)

— We decide the maximum amount of money we want to invest in spare parts. (This is also a specification.)

— On the basis of these givens, we can find out if there exist one or more solutions for the optimal stock of spare parts.

Many problems are not amenable to rational thinking because it is not possible to say what the specifications are. If you ask me what the best investment for education in your school system is, I have to ask you what the specifications are. What is the maximum you want to invest? Do your neighbors know what they want to spend? Do you know if education is to be used to prepare for employment or for intellectual development? Is there a consensus about that? I will also point out that I do not really know the consequences for education of spending different amounts for different services. Since neither of us can answer all of these questions adequately, we have difficulty with rationalization exercises applied to education.

In general, we find that rationalization exercises are valuable:

— when goals — or objectives — can be easily specified. (We want to have a man or a woman on the moon in five years. That is specific. We want "good" education. That is vague.)

— when there is knowledge, i.e., a theory of the relations between what is done and what happens. (We have theories about gravity, propulsion, and the movement of the moon in relation to the earth; we have less adequate theories about the relations between what teachers do and what happens to pupils.)

— when we can measure important components of the inputs, process, and output variables. (We can measure the payload lifted by a rocket; we can only approximate a measure for a characteristic labeled "reading ability.")

— when there exists a consensus about goals, process, input, and output variables within the relevant community. (If half the population defines good education as vocational training and the other half as liberal education, you may have a problem specifying output measures unless everyone agrees to have two educational streams.)

This last point is most important. What it says, in effect, is that if we can agree about the future, we can make it less uncertain. But to make it less uncertain we need a consensus. People have to see things the same way. How do people reconcile their differences? Through the political process. Therefore, all rationalization exercises are influenced by the political process and they, in turn, influence politics.

As we will see in the following pages, politics and planning are closely linked together. But before we discuss the recent evolution of our ideas about planning, let us agree that rationalization exercises are important in the context of rising levels of external uncertainty if and when:

— they provide ways of thinking about decisions involving many variables as long as goals are agreed to and are clear and measurable, and as long as we know what it is we are doing; and

— they provide a logical way to discuss the articulation of components of a system, and this logical discussion is acceptable to all concerned so that a willingness to cooperate emerges from this knowledge.

Beyond this, they do not reduce the effects of uncertainty.

Planning

The most important early contributors to the sociology of planning are Florian Znaniecki and Karl Mannheim. Znaniecki published *The Social Role of the Man of Knowledge* in 1940 (Znaniecki 1965). In this work, he recognizes the importance of uncertainty: when unexpected changes disturb established patterns, there is a demand for advisors (p. 33). Knowledge and its use impose requirements. The advisor must have access to knowledge which is *believed* to be useful; therefore, the advisor needs *credibility*, he must have a special role of his own. For example, in traditional society he may be an elder — even a retired elder. Or he may be a member of a religious order; a priest who "interprets the mysterious signs of gods and foretells the future, [one who] advises people what gods to address and what methods to use for their propitiation" (p. 34).

Znaniecki underscores the importance of "men of knowledge" in an uncertain world. He wants intellectuals to take this role; otherwise the role is assumed by ideological fanatics. Znaniecki elaborates two functions which recur frequently in the literature on planning: that of defining the ends, i.e., the values, and that of studying the means to these ends. First, he says, we need to agree about what we want to do, what our values are. This is the role of sages (read intellectuals). Sages help us agree about what is desirable. Once we know where we want to go, planning can be used. What Znaniecki is telling us is actually quite simple: when there is much change in a world fraught with uncertainty, a central responsibility for intellectuals exists: inventing a consensual ideology which serves to orient collective action. If we all agree about what to do, planners can help us do it. Otherwise, other forms of leadership will emerge. Znaniecki was particularly concerned about the rapid rise to power of Adolf Hitler. He saw that intellectuals could be seduced or controlled by a dictator, and he noted that whenever a totalitarian regime takes over, intellectuals are asked to validate the truth of the new ideology, as happened in Hitler's Germany (p. 81).

Karl Mannheim's contribution also reflects the events of the thirties. His writings on planning are concerned with the danger of totalitarian regimes. But there is a fundamental optimism in his work; he is hopeful that an elite of planners, divorced from attachments to the politics of the left or of the right, can provide a "third way" between laissez-faire and total regimentation. Such a "third way" would also be beyond fascism and communism (Mannheim 1965, p. xvii).

Mannheim believed that planning would emerge because its time had come. He wrote that there are "converging forces which were moving events in the direction of planning" (p. 31), and as we now know Mannheim was correct. Social and economic planning became an important strategy in the post–World War II period in both capitalist and socialist countries. By 1965, Albert Waterston, writing from the vantage point of the International Bank for Reconstruction and Development, could list 136 countries and territories that had an approximation of a central planning agency (Waterston 1965, pp. 644–52). The time "had come" swiftly.

As soon as planning spread, a literature about planning also flowered. First, there were attacks motivated in part by ideological considerations (at that time planning was still associated with totalitarianism). Hayek's *The Road to Serfdom* (Hayek 1944) and Jewkes' *Ordeal by Planning* (Jewkes 1948) revealed these sentiments. These authors feared planning because they thought that planning would lead to control of the economy by a small central elite. Planning would destroy competition and result in state monopolies which would then control the state: "The state itself becomes more and more identified with the interests of those who run things than with the interests of the people in general" (Hayek 1944, pp. 197–98).

Planning meant that a small group of planners would impose what they thought best on the rest of society, and the only way to carry out their plans would be through force (p. 223). Hayek also argued that the idea of planning was born in Germany during World War I and had taken root in Nazi Germany. The Nazis were dedicated to socialist organization and the ultimate supremacy of the state. Therefore, planning could not be apolitical. It implied ideological conformity and the abolition of individual freedoms. It went hand in hand with totalitarian rules. Where Mannheim had argued that planning was the way of finding an alternative to total laissez-faire or total regimentation, Hayek and Jewkes saw it as the quickest road to regimentation. They thought it would bring about the transformation of the state. These apocalyptic visions were shattered by the reality of Western planning, which did not seem to bring all the evil consequences that had been predicted. Instead, the consequences turned out to be simpler and more predictable (Millett 1947). The first sobering sociological study of planning was published by Phillip Selznick in 1949 (Selznick 1966). This classical study of the Tennessee Valley Authority (TVA) dispels the romanticism of Mannheim and the gloom of Hayek and Jewkes. Selznick reminds us that planning does not alter the facts of social power. It is not the planners who impose their ideology on others but the existing power structure which imposes its ideology on planners. As Znaniecki had seen much earlier, the "men of knowledge" are not inviolate. They can be bought or at least co-opted.

Planning for the TVA was intended to be rational and democratic. But the existing power structure had quickly co-opted the planners:

> My conclusion was not merely that T.V.A. trimmed its sails in the face of hostile pressure. More important is the fact that a right wing was built *inside* the T.V.A. The agricultural program of the agency was simply turned over to a group that had strong commitments, not only to a distinct ideology, but to a specific constituency. (p. xiii)

Since Selznick's pioneering study three opinions about planning have emerged: the first states that planning is so dominated by politics that it is useless; the second holds that planning contributes to the rationality of political decisions; and the third emphasizes the importance of planning in reducing uncertainty by helping to establish a consensus.

Planning Is Useless: Some authors agree that planning makes little difference and is sometimes a waste of effort. Charles Lindblom, an economist, belongs to this group (Lindblom 1965, p. vii). "Reasoned" coordination, as he calls planning, is no more reasoned than political bargaining because, in most instances, there are no agreed criteria upon which to reason. When there is conflict about values, goals, and priorities, there are no criteria to initiate analysis; therefore, the "reasoning" of planners is arbitrary (pp. 182–91). Intellectuals cannot provide a blueprint of what is desirable. Therefore, the social order is not altered by planning, because the existing power structure is not changed. Decisions are based on mutual dependencies. In politics this means log-rolling. You vote for my bill and I will vote for yours. Mutual adjustment means that I understand your needs and your power, you understand mine, and we both agree on a desirable outcome.

These authors agree that there is much change and uncertainty, but they suggest that the way to cope with change is through market exchanges and political action. To understand what is happening, one must look at the political process. Analysis and policy research are important but if you want to understand how the American Congress or the Bureau of the Budget deals with the budgetary process, you are not going to understand much by looking at it in terms of planning. But you will understand a lot in terms of politics. The important authors in this group include Aaron Wildavsky (Wildavsky 1964, 1975), Naomi Caiden (Caiden and Wildavsky 1974), and Ida Hoos (Hoos 1972).

Other authors have focused on the problems of implementation. Planners attempt the impossible because they do not have the means of solving problems. Planning is wasted motion because nothing much can happen. No one can take responsibility for the whole of public administration of large cities or for an entire nation. There are too many vested interests, too many pressure groups, and too many problems for planning to succeed. Most plans are futile exercises. They gather dust on shelves.

These authors agree that there is much change and uncertainty but they do not expect Western planners to reduce uncertainty; planners simply do not have the means of compelling politicians or organizations to follow their prescriptions. In socialist economies, however, the plan must be observed and so it makes a difference. In capitalist economies planning has not yet succeeded because planners are co-opted by the political process. The relevant authors in this group in addition to Selznick are Martin Meyerson and Edward C. Banfield, who studied planning in Chicago (Meyerson and Banfield 1964). Lastly, and along a slightly different line, we must also mention works such as Harold

Wilensky's study of intelligence failures (Wilensky 1967). As Wilensky points out, intelligence failures (i.e., disregarding relevant knowledge on decision-making, even though the knowledge is at hand or can be obtained) occur frequently. In other words, another source of planning failure is the fact that politicians and administrators do not listen to facts when they do not want to.

Planning as Rational Politics. In a politicized world where decisions are made to please politicians or pressure groups, some authors stress the advantages of rationality, systematic thinking, coordination, and coherence maintenance. Heirs of the tradition of Saint-Simon and Auguste Comte (who wrote together in 1822 a *Plan of the Scientific Operations Necessary for the Reorganization of Society*), these authors assume that rationality is preferable to irrationality (Bross 1953; Fishburn 1964; Hitch and McKean 1961; Novick 1965).

This literature is often normative; that is, it describes what planning can and *should* be — how to achieve the "one best way." These authors are close to the traditions of scientific management.

The best-known theorist of normative planning is Yehezkel Dror (Dror 1968, 1971a, 1971b). He proposes a list of eleven phrases of analysis for "optimal" policy-making: (1) processing values; (2) evaluating future events; (3) setting priorities; (4) assessing resources; (5) establishing strategy; (6) examining alternatives; (7) predicting costs and benefits; (8) selecting the "best" alternative; (9) motivating the execution of policy; (10) executing policy; and (11) evaluating policy (Dror 1968, pp. 312–18).

Writers such as Dror argue that some thinking, however limited, is better than none. Even purely political decisions can be improved if the facts upon which they are based are more accurate, complete, and fully analyzed. Analysts contribute in two ways:

— If goals are unclear, knowledge of the available means provides the basis for distinguishing those goals that can profitably be pursued from those that are impossible to achieve. Analysts help the political process by clarifying the possible alternatives.

— If goals are specified, analysts determine the preferable or even the optimal use of resources to achieve them.

In other words, planning reduces uncertainty by improving

both political and administrative processes. Planning is not politics; it is instead the pursuit of rationality and efficiency in a turbulent and confused arena. Politics always prevails but politics is improved:

> Analysts at the Bureau of the Budget can and should play the role of efficiency advocates. . . . They are in effect "partisan efficiency advocates" . . . the ultimate decision maker has to balance their voice against political, tactical and other considerations. (Schultze 1968, p. 96)

Some authors go further and suggest that analysis should also be tempered by a sophisticated awareness of political reality. They blur the differences between technique and politics (Meltsner 1976).

Planning and Uncertainty. These authors also focus on the role of planning in reducing uncertainty. Michel Crozier (Crozier 1956) sees planning as a mechanism for adjusting to social change by avoiding traditional crises and responding to the needs of a rapidly changing environment (p. 148). Other early authors include Bertram Gross (Gross 1967), Stephen Cohen (Cohen 1969), Robert Bogulsaw (Bogulsaw 1965), this author (Benveniste 1972), and Jean-Claude Thoenig (Thoenig 1973).

We discuss planning at greater length in chapter four, but let me briefly review some of the arguments presented in *The Politics of Expertise* (Benveniste 1972):

— Rationality serves to legitimate an image of the future around which a consensus can be created. Planning is a process that allows an elite (planners, the "Prince" who hires them, the relevant implementers of the plan, the representatives of organized pressure groups) to settle, on the basis of a rational argument, the future courses of action of many different organizations. Therefore, planning can only succeed to the extent that there is an agreement about what to do in the future.

— Reaching this agreement need not involve everyone concerned. There exists a multiplier effect in planning — or, we might also call it a bandwagon effect. Once there is a general belief that the plan will be implemented, everyone begins to act as if it were going to happen. In doing so, those who act as if it were going to happen bring about implementation. The logic of planning requires that the participants in the agreement be those whose commitment makes it credible.

— The choice of methodologies used in analysis and planning, by its very nature, favors some political groups and hampers others. The analysis sets the stage, the timing, and the language of future negotiations. A study by Lautman and Thoenig shows that those departments in the French Ministry of Labor concerned with the application of labor law have more trouble with the planning process than those departments concerned with well quantified objectives — for example, those concerned with accelerated manpower training; it is easy to quantify manpower training and hard to quantify the policing of labor codes (Lautman and Thoenig 1966, pp. 140–42). Therefore, planning is linked to politics from the start.

— Planning alters the possibilities of participation in policy-making. Those who have access to data, those who can speak the language of computers, who can hire experts and produce research results, will have a greater voice than those who can only express their dissatisfaction. Therefore, planning alters the political process.

— Planning is a fragile human invention. It only reduces uncertainty to the extent that there is sufficient agreement about what to do in the future. Short of having an absolute totalitarian tyranny, planning is limited in scope.

— To succeed, planning has to be limited. One cannot plan everything. One cannot have an agreement about everything. Therefore, planning *partially* reduces uncertainty.

— Planning reinforces centralization and strengthens the executive branches of administration to the detriment of elected bodies such as school boards, parliaments, and the U.S. Congress. Planning tends to give more power to organized corporate units. It tends to disregard clients and beneficiaries — not because planners dislike them, but because the time pressures involved in any planning exercise do not allow sufficient consultation. To the extent that elected bodies or affected parties object to planning or oppose it, constraints are imposed on what can be planned and how much uncertainty can be reduced.

— Planning, like all scientific endeavors, is based on previous assumptions. Any scientific analysis begins with assumptions about the relevant "givens." If, for example, we want to discuss the price of commodities, past price data serves as a starting point. But past price data is partially the result of a given distribution of income. In other words, when analysts use past price data, they also assume that past distributions of income are "given." All policy research and analysis carries similar kinds of assumptions. They are unavoidable. Therefore, planning tends to be conservative in the sense that the more the future is decided in advance, the more current limitations are projected into the future. This pattern suggests inherent time limitations in any planning exercise.

— Planning is sometimes used to mystify, to give the impression that something is being done about a problem when, in fact, nothing is being done except studying it to death. This is called trivial or utopian planning. Such planning is sometimes necessary, but more often it merely gives a bad name to the planning profession. To the extent that trivial or utopian planning is practiced, it becomes more difficult for planners to reach a consensus about the future; therefore, the games played within planning constrain the ability of planners to generate confidence and reduce uncertainty.

— To summarize: planning has emerged at a time of turbulence and rapid change. By itself it is not an effective social invention for reducing organizational fears. Uncertainty remains and prevails. Other social inventions are needed.

Developments in the Sociology of Organizations

The history of ideas in the sociology of organizations can, for all practical purposes, be placed into three periods or stages of development (Etzioni 1964, pp. 20-21).

The first stage emerged at the beginning of the century and is best known as scientific management. In this stage, the environment (the market) is taken for granted, but the problem is to improve the performance of the organization. We must find the "one best way" to do things. Given the peculiarities of human beings (they get tired, their span of attention is limited), we must find the most efficient way to arrange the task so that wasted motions, fatigue, etc., are kept at a minimum. The best-known author of this school is Frederick W. Taylor (Taylor 1911). The intellectual contributions in this field come from engineering and physiology: human-machine system analysis. An important aspect of this school of thought is that the "one best way" is "natural" since it is a science based on technical and physiological characteristics.

The second stage was set by the "human relations" school. It too is concerned with the "one best way," but it injects sociological and physiological variables. According to this school, people are complex: they have personal wants and aspirations, they dream, and they are influenced by their peers. The focus is still the organization; the environment is taken as given. Therefore, if we want to understand what happens in the organization, we must pay attention to informal processes.

People respond to their own wants and to the pressures of informal groups in which friendships, status, and peer norms have as much, or more, influence than formal hierarchical lines of command. To find the "one best way," we must take this reality into account. The foremost works in this field are by Elton Mayo (Mayo 1924, 1933) and the study of the Hawthorne plant of the Western Electric Company in Chicago (Roethlisberger and Dickson 1939). As this research proceeded, it illuminated the importance of uncertainty. Why do workers respond to group norms about rate busting? Because they are worried about the depression; they are worried about uncertainty, and the informal group provides them with protection.

The third stage is called the "integrative" school. It finally abandons the quest for the "one best way" and recognizes the complexity of organizations, in both their formal and informal aspects.

A major breakthrough emerges in the work of Herbert Simon in the nineteen-forties; he is no longer concerned with the "one best way" (Simon 1957). Simon is interested instead in uncertainty and how people make decisions. He realizes that, in practice, decision-makers rarely, if ever, find the best solution to any

problem. Even rationality is "bounded" in at least two ways:
(1) any problem has to be formulated within time and space
boundaries — you cannot trace the effects of a decision into the
infinite future; and (2) the costs of searching for a solution
cannot increase indefinitely. Simon argues that, in practice, the
search for a solution to a problem tends to end as soon as an
adequate answer is found. But this is not necessarily the "best"
solution:

> The central concern of administrative theory is with the
> boundary between the rational and the non-rational aspects
> of human social behavior. Administrative theory is pecu-
> liarly the theory of intended and bounded rationality — of
> the behavior of human beings who satisfice because they
> have not the wits to maximize. (Simon 1957, p. xxiv)

What Simon is saying is that organizations are human inventions, and that rationality is created in the mind. Reality, however, is much more complex; therefore, we have to think of
organizations as social devices that never quite fit reality. Since
reality is never completely understood, there is always some uncertainty. Choices are never completely predictable. The study
of organizations is not the study of a theoretical, rational ideal,
but rather the study of human behavior in situations filled with
ambiguity.

Another breakthrough appeared in the work of Michel Crozier, a French sociologist interested in uncertainty, particularly
the perceived uncertainty of actors in organizations and how it
influences their behavior (Crozier 1964, 1970, 1974). In a study
of the French Tobacco Monopoly conducted in the nineteen-
fifties, Crozier focused on the way social power is linked to uncertainty (Crozier 1964, pp. 145–74). He pointed out that power
emerges from unbalanced relations, an idea that had been made
explicit a few years earlier (Emerson 1962). Social power emerges
in a relationship if A needs B more than B needs A. If I need you
and you do not need me, I am going to be running after you asking you to help me. You will have power over me because I am
dependent on you. The more dependent I am, the more power
you have.

For example, if uncertainty threatens you and I can reduce

this uncertainty, I will acquire power over you. Crozier's study reveals that in the Tobacco Monopoly the maintenance workers have more power over production workers than do line supervisors, because the production workers need the help of the maintenance workers for the functioning of the equipment. When the equipment breaks down, the production workers do not reach minimum production targets and suffer a financial penalty. They have to work harder to catch up. If the breakdown lasts longer, they are reassigned, causing anxieties, loosening friendship ties, etc. Therefore, production workers care about maintenance, and the relations between production workers and maintenance people are relations of dependency. The maintenance people reduce the uncertainty arising from breakdowns. This case illustrates a link between uncertainty and power.

Specialized knowledge and skills provide a source of power. The maintenance workers keep tight control on their knowledge and the tricks of the trade. They make sure that blueprints are not generally available and scorn any attempt of production workers to do their own repairs. They intensify the production workers' need for their special skills. The production workers seek the reassurance that maintenance workers give them; they go out of their way to seek their help and to form an "alliance" with them. Thus, the maintenance workers come to have more power over production workers than the latter's own supervisors. The supervisors are hierarchically above the production workers and are therefore supposed to have more authority and influence, but the real dependency of the production workers derives from that aspect of the task they cannot themselves perform. The maintenance workers acquire their influence because they reduce the uncertainty associated with the workers' tasks (p. 109).

Crozier's book was published in the United States in 1964. Three years later, James D. Thompson published *Organizations in Action,* which conceived of complex organizations as open systems. Thompson was interested in both the organization and its environment. He thought of organizations as systems open to an uncertain environment. Thompson listed three kinds of uncertainties that affected behavior within the organization:

— First, the generalized uncertainty of the environment, which results from the absence of a general theory of cause and effect. If one does not know how things work, one cannot recognize alternatives; one has no grounds for claiming credit or escaping blame. In short, there is no pattern for self control.

— Second, the consequences of organizational links; i.e., what is done in the environment and how it influences the organization. Even if one knows how things work, the environment may be uncooperative, and the organization will try to regulate the way the environment affects it.

— Third, the internal uncertainty of the organization due to the interdependence of its own components: how what is done in marketing affects production and the extent to which these effects are predictable. Even when the environment is predictable, the organization needs to achieve internal self-control through subordinating each component to a centralized structure (Thompson 1967, pp. 159–60).

Thompson only alludes to the consequences of excessive uncertainty. For example, he writes that when the future is too uncertain, members of the organization will avoid taking responsibility; they will *tend to avoid discretion* (p. 119); that is, they will not act within all the degrees of freedom the position allows. They will sharply limit their behavior to areas without risk. Thompson shows that when there is no knowledge about what to do or how to make a decision, members of the organization still have to justify what they decide. They may, as he suggests, flip a coin, find solace in elaborate trend charts, or rely on precedent. They need a justification, and they may therefore *find protection in rules.* He also points out that the more the environment is uncertain, the more there will be factions and *conflicts* within the organization about what to do (p. 129). But beyond this description, Thompson does not attempt to discuss the consequences of rising levels of uncertainty. His principal contribution is the formulation of the idea that organizations are problem-solving institutions that have to be designed to adapt to changing and uncertain environments. Yet his contribution is important because it leads to a discussion of the ways in which organizations cope with an uncertain environment.

Thompson's work also belongs to a larger literature of the

nineteen-sixties, which focuses on the ways in which organizations adapt to rapid changes. This is called Organization Development. This literature argues that organizations must be designed to adapt to rapid change and uncertainty. Such design usually means:

— *more scanning and intelligence about the environment:* if the environment is changing all the time, the organization has to find out ahead of time what will happen.

— *flexible internal structures:* if the task has to change, the internal structures of the organization have to be able to change rapidly;

— *more planning, both internal and external:* plan what markets to enter and plan what structures are needed internally to achieve new output configurations.

— *more internal communications:* create organizations made of overlapping components with individuals serving in several components (linking pin); create internal trust.

— *new management styles:* participation, collegial cooperation, and conflict resolution through team participation.

Some of the best-known authors in Organization Development are Douglas McGregor (McGregor 1960, 1967), Rensis Likert (Likert 1967), and Warren G. Bennis (Bennis, Benne, and Chin 1969; Bennis and Slater 1968).

In the late nineteen-sixties and seventies, social scientists became increasingly interested in the notions of change and uncertainty. For example, in 1969 Professor Dwight Waldo organized a series of panel presentations on the theme of Public Administration in a Time of Turbulence (Waldo 1971); the tenth John Dewey Society Lecture focused on The Unprepared Society: Planning for a Precarious Future (Michael 1968); and researchers published studies on the characterstics of organizational environments, examining whether they are complex or simple, stable or unstable, changing rapidly or slowly (Emery and Trist 1965; Jurkovich 1974; Segal 1974); inquiring about what factors affect the perception of uncertainty (Duncan 1972); studying the characteristics of the environment that affect performance (Child 1972; Osborne and Hunt 1974), and examining whether the structure of the organization is adapted to the demands of the environment (Lawrence and Lorsh 1967; Saroff 1974; White 1969, 1971). The focus of these works is on environment, organization, and the way in which the organization adapts to change.

Conclusion

The problem is now clearer: worldwide modernization is altering the environment of organizations; uncertainty is increasing. In this first chapter we surveyed recent developments, and saw how the notion of the hidden hand of the market was unsuited to rapidly changing technological societies, how rationalization exercises were introduced to cope with uncertainty, how planning emerged in the forties and fifties, and how organization design sought to find more flexible adaptive models.

* *
*

two

How
Organizations
Control

In this chapter we focus on control and examine why people in
organizations do what they do. We acquire a better sense of
organization control, and we review concepts that help explain
how uncertainty and control limit discretion, risk-taking, and the
ability of organizations to cope with change.

First, we discuss power, authority, orders, rules, and budgets.
These are instruments of control. Then we turn to a broader view
of the incentive system. Individuals pursue careers; organizations
are stepping-stones for a career. We examine how the incentive
system of organizations accommodates career objectives. We discuss output measures and how they are related to evaluation and
control.

Output measures lead to a discussion of the difference between
goals, outputs, and outcomes. We begin to see how certain controls distort behavior. We contrast control by output measures
with professional control. We conclude by examining how uncertainty affects the incentive system and the kinds of strategies that
individuals pursue.

Before beginning, let me clarify a number of issues. First, this presentation is based on social relation theories. It says little about the psychological or political makeup of people or of situations. This omission does not mean that personalities or ideologies do not matter. To the contrary, we all know that people fight for convictions. But if we want to understand organizations — *qua* organizations — if we want to understand the relations between people in positions of authority and their minions, we must leave aside issues of personality or ideology. Later, in real life, we leave nothing aside. Once we understand how organizations influence or control behavior, we may complete the real picture and think in terms of specific people in specific situations.

Second, there is an important distinction between what is said by members of organizations and what you and I, as analysts, think about what is said. We must distinguish between what the organization claims and what we can infer about reality. We do not have to take anything for granted. We know that organizations do not think or speak outside the minds of their staffs. In every organization there is a formal (official) rhetoric about what is going on. There may also be many informal explanations. As analysts we are not bound by rhetoric, nor are we bound by the informal explanations. We may not be able to think differently; we may lack intuition or imagination, but that is another problem. We do not start by assuming that the management's definition or the union's definition of the organization is the best explanation. We can invent our own.

Third, I am presenting this material to suit my purpose, which is to deal with control and ultimately with the relations between uncertainty and control. If the reader wants a more conventional textbook on the sociology of organizations, I recommend Etzioni's little paperback *Modern Organizations* (Etzioni 1964) or Blau and Scott's *Formal Organizations* (Blau and Scott 1962). These books provide a systematic review of definitions of organizations and of the concepts used to analyze them. Victor Thompson's *Modern Organizations* (Thompson 1961) describes many of the problems of bureaucracy covered in this text.

Organizations

Organizations are composed of individuals. With each position, there exists a definition of the way one ought to behave in the organization. This is called a role. People play their own roles and expect other people in the organization to play theirs. The organization too is defined by boundaries. We can determine who belongs to the organization and who does not. Teachers, principals, and students belong to the organization called school. The teachers are paid; the students are not; yet both are members of the organization. Each has a role to play. The organization is always characterized by the fact that it has goals. Goals are ends the organization claims to achieve. They are statements about the future that define the purposes of the organization: "We try to provide the best education possible." "We provide health care." "We are a group that helps women in higher education." The environment of the organization exists outside its boundaries. It is composed of other organizations and the general public. When the clients of the organization have a very limited role to play, it is easier to consider them as outside the organization. For example, we all receive mail, but we do not belong to the post office. But students, patients, or prisoners are an integral part of schools, hospitals, or prisons.

Control is exercised by the organization on each position-holder. Control is also exercised by other organizations on each other and by the general public, clients, buyers, etc.

Instruments of control extend to inputs, process, or outputs. This way of thinking is the system approach. If we consider a worker in a factory, we may say that this worker receives a salary; the salary is an *input*. We say this worker performs a number of operations; she assembles a motor part; this operation is the *process*. Lastly, we say that she assembles twenty parts per day; her production is the *output*. The organization exercises control on inputs (by changing salaries), on process (by supervising how the worker performs the task), and on output (by rewarding the worker for extra production). The same is true of other organizations. If legislators want to control higher education, they can simply control inputs. They can say, "Look here, we do not care what you do, but you cannot spend more than last year. That is our final say." They can attempt to control process: "We want to approve what courses you are teaching, how many hours per week teachers meet students, etc." They can control outputs: "We want to decide how many students graduate each year, how many degrees are awarded, and how many students are placed in jobs."

In most situations, various controls operate simultaneously.

Power and Authority

Power is the probability that A influences the behavior of B. If A does not act, B behaves differently.

Authority is the legitimate use of power. A has the right to exercise power over B.

If authority rights emerge from those who are under A, that is, if all the B's ask A to assume responsibility for certain decisions, this is legitimate authority. For example, a task group asks one member to coordinate its work because this is advantageous to the others. A gives instructions, and the B's obey these instructions because they need someone to lead them.

If authority rights derive from those who legally instruct A, these are authorized authority rights. In the prison the prisoners are B's. The B's do not give authority rights to the jailers (A's). It is the State or those who administer the prison who give these rights. The A's in this case may respond to a system of incentives. Their actions on the prisoners reflect their perception of how these actions will be evaluated by their superiors.

Power and authority originate from dependencies, and characterize the relations between individuals and groups. Intrinsic needs create power. If you need me more than I need you, if I can help you reach desirable goals but you cannot help me in the same way, you will accord me power; you will accord me the right to ask you for a favor when the occasion arises. If you find my demands excessive, you will say that I am exercising too much power over you; but if my demands are acceptable and customary, you will regard them as legitimate.

The norms of authority in social systems evolve slowly over

time. They always originate in dependencies. The serfs and peasants who live around the castle need the castle when marauders
invade the countryside. They exchange a portion of their crop
for armed protection and the refuge provided by the castle. In
time, authority rights are institutionalized. It is said that the
castle has the right to demand a portion of the peasant's crop.
If and when the dependency no longer exists, i.e., the castle is
no longer needed because peace is general throughout the kingdom, authority rights may still continue to exist: the castle still
demands a portion of the crops. The payments have become part
of social norms and customs. In time social change may take
place. The successful revolution abolishes authority rights that
emerged from dependencies which no longer exist.

Organizations create authority rights. The system of incentives
is used to organize the behavior of individuals around certain
patterns of action.

Authority rights are *created* because we have become accustomed to the notion that roles and patterns of behavior can be
invented and that individuals can be instructed about how to
behave. In a traditional society, authority rights evolve from years
of experience; peasants discover that castles help defend the land.
Over long periods of time, specialization emerges, dependencies
are established, and the nature of the authority rights is defined.
In a modern organization, there exists a precondition: the assumption that roles can be defined for the purpose of achieving the
goals of the organization. This is the fundamental advantage that
makes organizations effective.

Organizations depersonalize behavior. Positions are invented.
Each position has a role which is a set of expectations about how
an incumbent will behave in the position. The individual who
occupies the position does not act as himself or herself. The
individual acts as a member of the organization. It is possible
to invent relations between positions that have nothing to do
with the past history and lives of the individuals occupying the
positions. Again, this pattern is what is so novel about organizations and what enables them to become powerful modifiers of
behavior.

If individuals were not restricted by incentive systems, the domains of concern of individuals would not be limited by organizational boundaries. That is, the power that is *created* in organizations sharply limits and restricts the concerns of its members, even when it is clearly perceived that the well-being of the larger society is negatively affected.

Orders

Orders are directives about what to do. The policeman who directs traffic gives orders. The policeman does not actually use his authority to arrest and give traffic tickets to control traffic. He simply lifts his arms and gives signals. A shared set of expectations about what might happen if he were not obeyed leads motorists to follow his instructions. If all motorists were suddenly to decide to disregard the signals, the single policeman would not be able to use his authority to control the situation. But since a "revolt" of motorists requires a first driver who refuses to obey, the recognition that punishment may be given to the first offender deters the incipient movement. A red light does not always result in compliance when motorists believe there is absolutely no risk of being punished for not obeying it; there are drivers who will go through a red light at night when there is no traffic and no policeman in sight.

Orders are directives that emanate from the incumbent of one position and are directed to the incumbent of another position. To be effective they require that incumbents share a set of expectations about what will happen if the directives are not obeyed. This set of expectations includes notions about which orders are appropriate and which are not. If the policeman uses his power in areas that are not legally defined as his function (i.e., where he does not have the authority to act), compliant behavior may still take place if it is difficult to influence the system controlling the policeman (e.g., if he tries to collect a bribe, as is common in certain countries, you may have to pay it, even though you know that he is not authorized to do so, simply because you perceive it to be very difficult to prove the case or to approach his superior).

Orders are related to supervision. Those giving orders possess authority, and they may exercise discretionary powers to direct collective action toward a common goal. The policeman is told to expedite traffic at a busy crossroad. But he may decide which line of traffic should proceed. If the policeman acts arbitrarily and fails to fulfill his mandate (i.e., he allows only one line of cars to go through and does not explain why the other is blocked indefinitely), we expect an irate motorist to confront him and question his authority. In such a case, the underlying dependencies that sustain authority are not being met.

Rules

Rules are routinized orders. The red light is a rule. As part of your role definition as a motorist, you are told: "When you see a red light, stop and wait until it turns green or flashes yellow . . ." In organizations rules are widely used to routinize the exercise of authority. They permit incumbents of positions to multiply their influence in situations where they are not present.

Since rules are established before they are implemented, they deal with the future. They are one of the instruments that make behavior within the organization more predictable. If we know the rules, we know what to do and what not to do. Rules are used to control internal performance. They are also used to control the behavior of people outside the organization who deal repeatedly with it. There are rules for teachers in schools; there are rules for members of school boards, rules for parents, rules for suppliers of school equipment, rules for the use of facilities by community groups, etc.

A rule is a statement that describes appropriate behavior when certain conditions emerge. If a child is sick, the teacher notifies the nurse and the principal's office. The teacher does not attempt to give medical treatment. Such roles are defined before they are implemented. This means behavior in future events is predictable.

Rules are enforced by linking them with the system of incentives. There is a shared set of expectations about what may happen if the rules are disregarded. What is the probability of being caught? Can breaking the rule be explained away? If the rule emerges from felt dependencies, it will be seen as desirable, but if the rule is believed to be arbitrary, every effort will be made to subvert it. If the teacher believes it is desirable to notify the nurse and the principal's office because it saves time and defines responsibility, the rule is enforced; if the teacher thinks it is a lot of fuss for nothing, the rule may be disobeyed.

There are many sets of rules within the organization because several systems of incentives co-exist. There are formal rules established by the formal hierarchical structure. There are rules attached to the performance of professional roles. There are informal rules which emerge from relations within the structure: "In this shop we have rules you better stick to . . . we don't allow anyone to work more than needed and show too good . . . you keep your nose to your affairs and don't try to be different . . ." Informal rules are, by definition, based on dependencies; i.e., on the needs of those who invent them. For example, the informal group in the shop wants to limit the supervisors' control over the rate of work. As long as all the workers share the informal rule of not producing beyond certain agreed norms, supervisory efforts to increase production do not succeed. The advantage of working less provides the informal group with its own sources of power to assure compliance.

Rules serve several functions:

— The official function; i.e., to provide a set of impersonal role definitions that permit incumbents to act in a defined manner when certain situations arise.

— The function of providing a source of illegitimate power to those who enforce the rules. For some, the rules may apply to the maximum; for others, the rules may never be applied, although they should be.

— The function of providing legitimacy for actions which are perceived to be unsatisfactory. *Rules are a bureaucratic escape hatch.* If the organization is operating under great stress and there is much complaint about service, if incumbents are really not sure what to do, rules provide a safe role protection: "We really did not know what to do — we all knew that at some point someone would have to pay for all this mess. We stuck by the rules. What else could we do?"

Budgets

Budgets are specifications of input availabilities; they therefore control inputs. Budgets are not limited to monetary definitions. If certain resources are scarce, the budget of the organization may be defined in terms of specific resources (energy, manpower, buildings, etc.). Budgets are statements about the future inputs that the organization may expect.

In practice, budgets are usually established one year in advance, but this procedure is not a rigid limit. In some circumstances when uncertainty is high, it is advantageous to establish budgets for longer periods. Since inputs into organizations are closely related to the ability of organizations to survive, budgets tend to be the most significant means of overall internal or external control. To be sure, outputs are more relevant to the environment than inputs, and this relationship explains why considerable effort has been made in recent years to link budgetary inputs to organizational outputs. These efforts are usually called "program budgeting."

A *program budget* consists of several programs or goals which the agency is trying to achieve. "Next year we hope to achieve the following: We want to reduce car accidents in our streets by 10%. We therefore allocate x dollars for this program. We want to reduce muggings by 20% — we allocate x dollars to foot patrols. We want to eliminate drug pushing — we allocate x dollars for this." This method contrasts with a *line budget* which simply states: "Next year we intend to achieve many improvements in our police service. We will reduce car accidents in our streets, reduce muggings, fight drug pushing. For this we need 25 patrolmen, 8 police cars, 6 office workers, 1 chief, etc." The term "line budget" refers to the line items — patrolmen, cars, office workers, pencils, papers, etc. — for each of which a particular amount of money is allotted. In contrast the program budget distributes all the line items among the various programs or goals.

A *zero-base budget* is a program or line budget that has to be rejustified each year. It is called "zero base" to remind everyone concerned that every program has to be rejustified; every activity

starts at zero and will only be funded if it can justify its continued existence. Therefore, a zero-base budget is highly dependent on output measures.

Control of Inputs vs. Control of Process or Outputs

Organizations control inputs, process, and outputs. If we know a
lot about cause and effect and understand everything an organization does (for example the production of electric energy in a
thermoelectric plant) we can control inputs, process, and outputs
as precisely as we wish.

If we know very little about cause and effect we have to rely
more on the experience of professionals to define how the organization should perform its tasks. This reliance is usually the case
in universities, where the professional staff has great latitude in
deciding what is to be done. Professional controls are used to
ensure compliance and to evaluate the enterprise. Yet professional
controls are not the only ones at work. Budgetary controls assure
the environment that available resources are used as intended.
The organizational structure uses rules imposed by the hierarchy
to limit role performance for the survival of the organization (in
contrast to the survival of the professionals operating within the
organization). Output controls may be introduced to orient behavior toward certain goals that are believed to be important
either for the environment or for the organization.

Control of Outputs vs. Goals and Outcomes

Control of outputs has implications for the goals of the organization, as well as for the broad outcomes of what the organization
does in its environment.

First, let us distinguish between outputs, outcomes, and the
goals of the organization. The organization receives inputs, after
which something happens inside and outputs come out. The
outputs interact with the environment. These interactions are
the outcomes. Goals are the ends that the organization claims
to achieve. We knock on the window of the organization, and
someone opens a little window. We say, "What are you doing in

there?" and they answer, "We are improving the lot of mankind." This is what the organization calls its goals.

Ask a school board member what is the purpose of the schools, and this person will say "to educate children" or "to give the best education we can give to our children" or other such statements. Where do these words come from? They are part of the rhetoric of organizations called schools. These words serve to identify the organization, to differentiate it from other organizations. Such rhetoric may define our expectations about what it is that should be done in the organization.

Several rhetorics exist within the organization:

— The official rhetoric. This consists of the statements, written or oral, which are given to anyone and everyone. They state the official goals of the organization or other aspects of behavior within the organization.

— The official rhetoric of subgroups within the organization, such as the rhetoric of professional groups who work in the organization. The planners tell us that their purpose is to rationalize the decision-making process; they do not tell us that their purpose is to reduce uncertainty.

— The theories of the participants. For example: "Management says they are trying to improve safety measures — this is just baloney; everyone knows they are cutting costs — that's what they are after . . ." Each participant or subgroup has theories of the situation. These theories may influence individual behavior. They are the perceptions of the forces at work. At times, the theories of participants can overlap or coincide with the official rhetoric.

The official rhetoric of organizations is always intended for an audience. Its content fits the perceptions and needs of the intended audience.

For some audiences, however, the official rhetoric may have no reality; the rhetoric is not understood or believed. But other audiences understand it and find it desirable. Those who intone an official rhetoric intend it for its listeners. An official of the American military once said, "We had to destroy the village in order to save it." The notion of "salvation" is, to be sure, a notion that leads to many interpretations. This official was saying: "The goal of our organization is to contain communism. When we bomb, we are 'saving' the buildings and the inhabitants of this town from communist takeover. The inhabitants leave the town or are incapacitated. The buildings are destroyed and are of little use to the communist troops." Had we been in the field and had we interviewed the townspeople, we would have heard different views. We can imagine that a few residents might have described the activities of the American military in terms similar to those used by the American official, but most of the survivors would use a different set of statements to explain what was happening. The statement of the official was intended for a different audience located thousands of miles away.

The functions of the official rhetoric are:

— To elicit support for the organization from outsiders. In our example, the purpose is to elicit support from decision-makers in the United States, not from the townspeople.

— To elicit support from insiders of the organization. In our example, the purpose is to elicit support from anyone who may not approve of widespread bombing of civilians while attempting to evict armed infiltrators.

Therefore goals, which are ends the organization claims to pursue, are the rhetoric which describes the purposes of the organization. They are only *partial* statements about the future outputs or outcomes of the organization.

Any organization influences the external environment in which it exists. It also influences the participants and the rest of the internal environment of the organization.

A recent study suggests that organizations affect the external environment in two specific realms: outputs and outcomes (Levy, Meltsner, and Wildavsky 1974, pp. 4–8). Outputs are the goods and services produced by the organization (for example, obtaining a bachelor's degree in college). Outcomes are the way these goods and services affect the relevant clientele (for example, obtaining employment because one has a bachelor's degree).

Outputs are not limited to the official goals of the organization. A power plant produces electricity. This is the official goal of the organization. But it also produces atmospheric combustion gases, builds unsightly power lines and reservoirs, and perhaps supports political campaigns to promote nuclear power. All these indirect products are also outputs.

Outputs may be both explicit and unstated. The power plant creates jobs to which engineers, foremen, maintenance workers, etc., aspire. This output is not usually mentioned by the organization, although it is alluded to when the power company defends its locational policies: "We will, in addition, provide employment opportunities which will enhance purchasing power in the community. . . ."

The schools open at 8:30 a.m.; children are kept in the school until 2:30 p.m. Mother and father are no longer needed to supervise them. If the teachers go on strike, the children may have to be supervised at home. Supervision is an output of the schools.

Young adults in college need parental figures. At times, college officials, guidance personnel, or professors substitute for parents. This is an output.

Young adults attended Harvard, Vassar, Princeton, or other prestigious schools because such attendance provided their parents with status in their communities. The existence of a hierarchy of institutions of higher education provides an output in the relevant community.

Some outputs may be highly desirable, even if they are not mentioned as a goal of the organization. For example, one could argue that it is highly desirable to have educational institutions because they keep young people off the streets. But you do not hear of this as an official goal of high schools or colleges.

Similarly, some outputs may be highly undesirable, but no one mentions them. No polluter emphasizes pollution as an output.

This discussion of outputs is important because planning deals with official goals. Goals are the visible point of reference used by the environment to assess whether the organization is doing what it says it is doing. If the legislature asks for accountability, the legislators want to know if the schools and colleges have reached their goals. They want detailed information on goal achievement, and their authority to demand it gives them an instrument of control. If their requests are vague — if the reporting is only words — the organizations continue to produce many outputs, including some that are part of their official goals and others that are not. For example, teachers will pay attention to the special counseling needs of their students, which may have little demonstrable relation to immediate learning but which they intuitively know are important in the long run. If the instruments of control are sharpened, for example, when program or zero-base budgeting is introduced, the organization is forced to eliminate outputs which are not easily related to official goals. They will only pay attention to immediate output measures, perhaps to the detriment of the needs of students.

To be sure, such control may have both highly desirable and undesirable consequences. The point is that few people in and out of organizations pay attention to this. Members of organizations usually internalize the official rhetoric and fail to see that goals may not be the most significant task accomplished by their organizations. Making decisions based exclusively on goal achievements distorts other human dimensions of organizational life.

Incentive Systems: Control on Participants

Incentives are the rewards and punishments that motivate individuals to play their roles in organizations. Individuals pursue careers. Therefore, they are evaluated in their own organization while they pursue objectives that may go beyond the confines in which they work.

At any one time, an individual in an organization is subject to different sets of incentives. Among these are the incentives of their own organization, by peer or task groups; the incentives provided by their profession; and the incentives provided by the long-term career objectives that they pursue (e.g., the people they seek to please as they contemplate changing jobs).

Goals are part of the incentive system. Some organizations possess sufficient goals to motivate compliant volunteer behavior. Volunteers share an ideological conviction; e.g., they may work to elect a candidate or to improve hospital care, or they may proselytize for a religious cause. Such volunteers require no salaries. The success of the organization continues to motivate them as long as the goals are valued and the organization performs satisfactorily.

Outputs can also motivate participation. Some mercenaries join armies, not because they believe in a cause, but because they enjoy the excitement and danger of war.

Other components of the incentive system are:

— *coercion:* the prison or the draft uses physical or legal coercion to motivate individuals to join and play their roles.

— *money:* salaries, bonuses, prizes, etc., are most commonly used to induce participation in the organization.

— *status:* some individuals seek certain organizations because they provide prestige; e.g., social clubs, the Supreme Court, etc.

— *interest:* some individuals join organizations when they have nothing to do even if they have no economic or status dependency.

— *stability:* some individuals stay in organizations because they are accustomed to them or have an emotional investment in them, even if the original circumstances that made them join no longer prevail.

— *role path dependency:* some individuals join an organization because it is the path to another role in another organization. For example, they get elected to a city council as a first step to the U.S. Congress.

— *professional model:* some individuals are trained and internalize values about how to play their role. They join organizations in which they can play their role: e.g., doctors, lawyers, etc.

Most incentive systems in organizations are a mixture of several incentives, and individuals respond to one or more components.

From the point of view of management, the most efficient incentive system is that which requires the fewest organizational resources while producing compliance behavior. For example, identification with the goals of the organization and professional role playing is less demanding of organizational resources than trying to control behavior by manipulating salaries or other economic benefits.

Since the incentive system is a mixture of components, tampering with one or more of these components alters the entire system — either by reducing its effectiveness or by forcing management to substitute one incentive for another. Moreover, certain elements of the incentive system are linked together. Economic rewards are linked to status, and it is not always possible to alter one without altering the other. For example, it is possible to raise salaries across the board, but it is not always possible to raise the salary of only one person without altering the task or the status of the position.

Compliance

The organization requires compliance. All persons occupying positions in the organization behave according to role definitions which define permissible behavior. If the incentive system is working well, members of the organization desire to play their roles.

The range of compliance includes:

— *supportive compliance.* Individuals are devoted to the organization. They identify with and internalize its goals. They provide substantial portions of time and energy to carry out tasks associated with their position. Individuals define their own level of effort.

— *partial compliance.* A number of dependencies operate. Individuals are generally satisfied with the organization but protect privacy and identity. Within time limits individuals carry out tasks associated with the position. The organization defines the level of effort expected for role performance.

— *threshold compliance.* Individuals do not identify with the goals of the organization. One or more dependencies operate. Within the constraints of the organization, individuals carry minimum tasks associated with positions. The organization defines the level of effort; compliance is related to supervision.

— *non-compliance.* Dependencies are insufficient to ensure compliance. The tasks associated with positions are not carried out. Supervision does not function. The organization is in jeopardy.

Evaluation

Evaluation provides the link between individual performance and the application of rewards and punishments. If the worker in an organization is never evaluated, the worker is practically free to do as he or she pleases. But all organizations evaluate performance of their members at one time or another, even if the evaluation consists only in making certain that individuals are playing well-defined roles.

Since individuals pursue careers, they are, at any one time, subject to one or more evaluations: if they work in a low-level job, they may have only one significant evaluator, namely an immediate supervisor. But at middle and higher levels, the situation changes. The head of a department in a large organization wants to be appreciated by the top executive. She may consider the agency head a less important evaluator than the governor of the state. The department head is therefore controlled by several incentive systems and anticipates several significant evaluators.

Evaluation can be based on role compliance or on individual measures.

If evaluation is based on individual output measures, it is possible to tie the incentive system to specific outputs. This, of course, is the basis of many schemes in industry where workers are paid in proportion to their production. Procedures are established to reward or punish members of the organization, if and when certain output measures are achieved. These can be collective output measures (i.e., when a task group achieves certain norms of production) or individual ones (i.e., when the output of each worker can be evaluated).

To do this, the following must be possible:

— Sampling of the work of individuals and groups. In some cases, the sample may be the total output; i.e., it is possible to measure everything the worker produces. In other cases it is necessary to introduce sampling techniques (i.e., observations of performance for limited periods of time, inspection of certain dimensions of the task, etc.).

— Criteria for comparing sample results with established norms.

— Assignment of punishments and rewards which alter behavior in such ways that sampled outputs tend to approximate the desirable norms (i.e., finding the kinds of sampling techniques and the sets of punishments and rewards that actually motivate individual and group performance to approximate norms).

For a complete discussion of this topic see *Evaluation and the Exercise of Authority* (Dornbusch and Scott 1975).

Output Measures and the Incentive System

Articulation of the relationship between the system of incentives and the measures of output creates new resources of power and authority. In other words, the school principal may give instructions to his teachers. The limits of authority are established over time by the nature of the dependencies that exist between teachers and principals. As teachers become more professional, they acquire considerable discretion, and the principals' resources of power and authority are finite and established. But the introduction of output measures tied to the rewards (or punishment) of teachers alters this situation. Output measures reduce discretion by forcing behavior to fit the measures. If teachers are rewarded on the basis of class scores on certain tests, a new source of control is introduced into the existing situation.

Planning, program budgeting, and other forms of organization controls rely on output measures. These controls are effective because they are *tied to the system of incentives.* For example, in socialist economies, achievement of planned targets is the basis of awarding bonuses to workers. This procedure is also used in countries where "accountability" is practiced in public administration. Program budgets and zero-base budgets require justified achievements. Funds are provided when the organization demonstrates that it is performing as expected. Output measures are first used at the level of total production; later they are used at the group and at the individual level.

The use of output measures tied to incentives has many important consequences:

— Output measures always *fit the official rhetoric* of the organization. As we have seen, the official rhetoric does not include all outputs. It follows that if desirable outputs are not included, these will be downgraded or eliminated. If you reward commanding officers when they win battles but not when they save lives, you will tend to have more battles and more casualties.

— Output measures *distort desirable outcomes.* For example, parents and school personnel want schoolchildren to grow up into healthy, creative, adaptable individuals, but such outcomes are not amenable to measurement. Therefore, the measures used to evaluate schools have very little to do with these outcomes. Moreover, the measures may even have negative consequences on the final outcome. Teachers are rewarded on the basis of the academic achievements of their pupils, which may have nothing to do with their health, creativity, or ability to adapt.

— Output measures *distort outputs.* Output measures in a classroom may be a student's aptitude score on a reading comprehension test. The teacher is evaluated positively by the way the students perform on standardized tests. The consequences of such measurement are significant. For example, previously, teachers used to spend time introducing their students to books in addition to teaching them to read. With the new measures, the teachers are obliged to spend more time preparing their students to take the reading comprehension test and can spend less time on books. Yet, it is generally agreed that it is desirable to introduce children to literature, but the test does not measure this desirable output because there is no standardized way to measure it. When the reward system is used to manipulate behavior, whether the organization wants it or not, the patterns of teacher behavior are modified.

— Output measures *erode discretion.* An output measure is a statement that says, in effect: "Look here, whatever happens in your unit, make sure you manage to come out with these output statistics which are believed to be desirable." This statement is a rule. It limits discretion. It also says: "We do not care what the *real* problems of your client might be — just make certain the statistics come out right and that the client scores x on the test. Otherwise, you will be reprimanded."

— Output measures may *become outmoded.* Management will not introduce new output measures in an organization without some degree of compliance from those affected. An information campaign on the merits and necessity of such indicators involves outside experts specializing in testing or measurement, professionals, or other relevant participants (in schools, these may be parents, minority groups, experts from universities, etc.). A rhetoric on the use of output indicators is created. Such procedures take time; they cannot be introduced overnight. By the time an output indicator is invented, sold, and instituted, those who wanted it in the first place may no longer need it. Meanwhile, data on performance is collected, procedures of control are institutionalized, newly vested interests emerge (the people who sell tests and the experts who invent them), and the organization is locked into a new pattern of control with undesirable consequences.

Professional Control

The organized professions serve to socialize and control the behavior of their members who occupy positions in organizations.

Professions are usually defined by the following characteristics:

— *a base of knowledge, skill, or experience* which serves to differentiate the attributes of members.

— *restricted membership.* In some professions there are formal procedures of admission and certification.

— *a formal socialization process* to indoctrinate members in the skill of the profession *and* its norms of behavior. Many professions require several years of specialized training including advanced degrees.

— *a set of general rules* on professional behavior appropriate to various circumstances. These rules are usually developed from experience and reflect a consensus about how to handle problems. The rules of professions are accepted gradually by other organizations. To facilitate such acceptance, professions organize and establish relations with other organizations. In time, certain patterns of behavior are accepted as the norm. Rules are then formalized.

— *a system of incentives* of its own. The profession is able, either directly or indirectly, to provide rewards and punishments for its members as they occupy positions in other organizations: directly, by awarding prizes and other status differentiation; and indirectly, by establishing standards of peer evaluation within other organizations.

Professions form a formal secondary network that cuts across task-oriented organizations. As such, they provide a formal social invention which serves to mediate and protect the behavior of its members from certain demands of the hierarchical structure.

Since professions emerge from a base of knowledge or skill, they have considerable ability to exercise influence on the processes taking place within organizations. The principal difference between professional and output measure control is that professional control tends to rely on role performance. Professionals prefer to be evaluated by their peers, by other professionals. They prefer evaluations that weigh all aspects of their role performance. They usually reject output measure control, since such controls sharply narrow their discretion and, therefore, their ability to perform their tasks adequately.

Uncertainty and the Choice of Control Instruments

If everything is very predictable, routines can be established. Routinized behavior is easily controlled, either by output measures (e.g., in the hospital laboratory) or by rules (the nurse is instructed to take the temperature of every patient at six a.m.). In many situations, rules are sufficient to define performance, and special output measures are not necessary because the output is self-evident (the worker on the assembly line is instructed to spray paint, and output is determined by the fact that cars are painted). Quality control assures standards of performance.

If the task is highly routinized, you do not need enthusiastic or devoted workers; you need workers who simply perform the limited demands of the task. In such cases, we can expect to find incentive policies instituted to assure partial or threshold compliance. The members of the organization may not care about the organization. They work because they need a salary. They follow the routines, which remain the same every day.

If everything is uncertain, however, routines are no longer appropriate. Instead, adaptability is required. The organization must be supple, capable of adapting itself rapidly to the changing needs of its clients. The principle that has to operate is that of discretion. If good service means creativity and risk-taking, the motivation of each individual member is important because each role has to be interpreted, and only the position-holder can do this effectively. Examples of this are doctors in hospitals, researchers in laboratories, teachers in schools. In these cases, supportive compliance is necessary. Therefore, the more uncertainty there is, the more organizations must rely on professions to provide supportive compliance.

But — and here we finally reach the dilemma of modern bureaucracy — the more uncertainty emerges from fear of errors of articulation among different organizations, the more we find a call for planning, budget control, accountability, and output measures of performance.

Therefore, two opposing trends confront each other. First, a need for creative, risk-taking professional workers oriented to the needs of clients.

Second, a centralized control apparatus designed to eliminate uncertainty by reducing errors.

This paradox is the present contradiction within the bureaucratic state. It is a contradiction because the instruments of planning, coordination, and output control require centralization and routinization at a time when professional workers are still expected to be creative. Organizations are subjected to considerable curtailment of their freedom. Individuals in organizations are subjected to sharp limitations on discretion.

What does this mean?

It means that rules and routines prevail.

It means that errors are only partially eliminated so that there is still considerable uncertainty. As a result, clients, organizations, and individuals are obliged to employ defensive strategies. These defensive strategies are the games we describe in the following chapters.

* *
*

three

Games Clients Play

Games are sets of ulterior transactions, repetitive in nature, with a well-defined payoff (Berne 1972, p. 23). They are protective strategies designed to protect an individual from the failures of organizations. I use the word "game" deliberately, to stress the fact that protective strategies are not central or useful for the accomplishment of the organization's purpose. They are necessary to those who use them to protect their own narrower interests.

How do we know people are playing games? It is not as simple as it seems because behavior that may seem normal can be used for ulterior purposes. Following the rules is sometimes highly desirable. But sometimes it can be a strategy to avoid blame or to delay action. To understand games we need to have a notion of organizational health, where transactions are adequate and service satisfactory. When service is not adequate and clients have no satisfactory way to deal with the organization, they are obliged to play games.

Organizational Health

When is an organization healthy? Clark defines the healthy organization as one that allows individuals, small groups, and whole organizations "to develop and maintain themselves around tasks" (Clark 1969, p. 295). In other words, a healthy organization allows its members to develop their individual creative potential. Clark also stresses a duality between the internal and external aspects of an organization. Those who are served by the organization are as important as those who compose the organization. Therefore, a healthy organization must also provide a quality service which fits the needs of its clients.

Some might argue that any definition of organizational health should stress organizational survival. As long as the organization survives, it is healthy. This view of organizational health comes from our notion of biological health. As long as the organization is not disappearing (death of organism) or is not about to disappear (illness before death), it is healthy. It does not matter whether those who are served by the organization are satisfied. Clients are unimportant as long as their attitudes do not affect the survival of the organization.

But organizations are not biological entities. The people who compose the organization and the people in the environment are members of the human species. We can talk about their mental as well as their physical health. If we want to talk about organizational health, we want to be able to refer to them. We therefore use a definition of organizational health that is related to perceptions of the satisfaction of *needs of both clients and members of organizations.*

Some organizations are temporary in character and are destined to be abolished. There is no particular reason why we should refer to their last months as "unhealthy." Other organizations no longer meet the needs of the clients they purport to serve. Abolishing these organizations or altering their missions is "healthy" as defined here — in contrast to a definition based on sheer survival.

Our definition of organizational health is based on the satisfaction obtained by both members and clients. We can think of clients in broad terms; anyone outside the organization affected by its service. This definition means, ideally, that the organization makes no errors. We can imagine that the ideal healthy organization is one where the members do exactly what they want for their own physical and intellectual well-being, and what they do is exactly what their clients and the general public need for their own physical and intellectual well-being. No errors are made. The organization provides the right service at the right time. (We use the word "service" to refer to any goods or services.) We shall discuss organizational errors at greater length in chapter ten. But at this point, it will suffice to mention that one reason clients play games is that organizational errors are continually made. The wrong service is provided or the service is not provided when needed. The significant point is how little clients can do to influence the organization. Besides the problem of errors, most organizations also provide mediocre service. We define mediocrity in terms of what is possible: a service is mediocre when a much higher quality service could be provided.

Organizational Health and the Notion of a Just Service

If students are unhappy with school, does this mean that the school is unhealthy? If prisoners are unhappy with the prison? If welfare mothers demand better service? Clearly, the definition of health requires more precision.

The definition of organizational health cannot be based on arbitrary notions of what is good service. For example, we do not wish to classify as unhealthy an organization which *cannot* provide some particular desired service. We cannot blame the city council if it rains every day. We have to accept limitations on what kinds of services can be provided. But we can maintain some normative standards. We blame city services if storm drains are not working and the streets are flooded.

Who defines these norms?

A pattern of accepted ways of providing a service evolves over time. This pattern defines these norms. If you have many organizations competitively providing a service, in due time clients are able to select the ones they like, and they accustom themselves

to a well-defined standard of what to expect and what not to
expect. This selection takes place in any market. The definition
of just exchange between clients and organizations is the outcome of behavior tested over time in a free marketplace.

In every culture, there emerges an accepted norm about just
exchanges which is the result of the interplay between underlying
needs and the ways in which these needs are met. When needs
change, the notion of what is considered just exchange also
changes. Prices are the basis for exchanges, and, presumably, in a
pure market prices reflect availability and needs. If hens are lay-
ing few eggs, and everyone wants eggs, the price of eggs goes up.
This is a just exchange because it reflects the fact that clients
want eggs, that the organization running the poultry farm is producing fewer eggs, and that those clients having greater need for
eggs are willing to pay more to acquire them.

A healthy organization participates in just exchanges.

We say that norms of just exchanges emerge from a competitive market. What happens when the market is no longer competitive? Or when there never was one at all?

This theme is discussed in Albert Hirschman's *Exit, Voice and
Loyalty* (Hirschman 1970). Hirschman is an economist, but his
concern goes beyond the usual limitations of economists. "Exit"
in the title of the book is the act of refusing to buy a service.
The consumer who decides to buy elsewhere or not at all is exercising exit. The firm that no longer buys a raw material is exercising exit. If the market is approximating pure competition, if consumers have all the necessary information to make decisions and
can choose among alternative suppliers, they will utilize exit any
time the price or quality of one supplier does not compete with
the price or quality of another. Thus, using Hirschman's language,
we would say that norms of just exchange emerge from exchange
relations where exit takes place any time suppliers and buyers no
longer feel that they want to supply or buy under given conditions. But, as Hirschman points out, exit can only take place
when there are alternatives or when consumers can do without
service.

"Voice" in Hirschman's book is the exercise of political pressure to alter the performance of the organization. If exit does not

operate satisfactorily, voice replaces exit as the mechanism of adjustment. Consumers act through a political process or by exercising direct pressure to ensure that monopolistic agencies provide needed services.

"Loyalty" is the extent to which clients are willing to stand by the organization, the extent to which they do not exit and do not exercise their voice even when they could.

Hirschman points out that exit and voice are interrelated mechanisms. If you can exit (but others cannot), you reduce the opportunity for voice. Take education: Hirschman argues that if you have both public and private schools, if the public schools provide bad service, rich and influential parents will use exit; they will send their children to private schools, an alternative open to them. But in so doing, they greatly reduce societal ability to use voice to improve the public schools. They are, by definition, rich and influential, but they will not exercise voice since they have filled their needs. Thus, Hirschman points out, contrary to the usual economists' assumption, conditions of partial monopoly may be far worse than conditions of total monopoly, where all the clients are forced to use voice to influence the organization.

Hirschman reminds us that there are two ways for dissatisfied clients to deal with organizations. If they do not like the service, they can either take their business elsewhere (exit) or, if this is not possible, they can use the political or legal process to express their needs (voice). If a client takes her business elsewhere, the action is immediate, and the remedy is also immediate — assuming that she can find what she wants in the next store. If political or legal processes are initiated, action will be slow and remedy uncertain. The games clients play reflect the fact that there is no easy way to get the attention of the organization once exit does not operate, and exit does not operate when there are no alternatives for the available service. As we shall see in the next chapters, one of the more important games played by organizations consists of limiting services — of limiting the choices and alternatives open to clients in order to reduce uncertainty for organizations. As it becomes more difficult to exit, clients attempt to use voice. Meanwhile, they play ineffectual games.

Exit, Voice, and Professionals

In a traditional peasant economy, "pure" market conditions are more likely to exist. Everyone in the village knows everyone else's needs and abilities. Needs do not change and are patterned by well-established cultural norms. Supply and demand is overt; the list of products transacted is limited, and each buyer knows how to evaluate both needs and quality of supply. Exit operates: healthy family organizations provide quality services. In such a society, voice operates in those areas of social life where the entire community has to join together to reach decisions: voice is the basis for village government.

In a technological world, however, needs are not necessarily overt or known. Cultural norms change more rapidly, and new needs are invented. Advertising accentuates needs and presents limited information about product availability.

The complexity and long time involved in production or distribution hampers the ability of producers to respond to needs. The number of products transacted is so large that, from a practical point of view, it is impossible for consumers to know all the alternatives. The choices of consumers reflect controls imposed by suppliers or distributors: choices are made on the basis of availability and recognition. Again, elite patterns differentially affect the use of exit and voice. The wealthier and better-educated shop selectively, travel greater distances, and acquire the necessary information to make choices. The poor respond more readily to advertising or simply to the credit arrangements of the local store. In short, exit and voice do not operate as effectively. In such a society, professionals also set norms of just exchanges. What is a "good" medical service? Clearly, patients want to be cured, and patients can define (and do define) certain characteristics of desirable medical service. Another source of normative knowledge is the practice and reflections of the medical profession. What doctors or nurses think is good or bad service depends on norms that have evolved within the relevant professions on the basis of what they believe is desirable for clients and the profession. Here specialized institutions (for example the boards of professional bodies) define what is and what should be good service.

Clients are usually able to evaluate their satisfaction with the services they obtain even if they do not know how the service is performed. (One may trust one's doctor even if one knows nothing about medicine.) In some instances clients may not be able to evaluate services because they do not know how services affect them. For example, they do not know how to assess the consequences of nuclear power and are very much at the mercy of professional judgments. When the profession does not have a definition of what is desirable service and when clients cannot define for themselves what is desirable, other interests are served.

Let us examine cases where exit and voice are partially inoperative and professional judgments do not exist. For example, consider the post office. Only some clients can successfully influence decisions made within the organization, because they are more powerful than others and their voices are heard. This situation explains why the post office is perceived, quite correctly, as an unhealthy organization. It provides poor service to most clients who pay a considerable amount to use first class mail but fail to influence the organization. It provides a favored service to commercial clients who pay less for bulk mail and are a main cause for delays and errors in service. Exit is possible in a few instances. The United Parcel Service delivers up to sixty percent of parcels in some areas. Entrepreneurs have begun to compete with the post office and deliver mail in a few urban centers.

Absence of exit and voice occurs when the clientele is too apathetic or where the cost of clientele revolt is not worth the effort. Even as post office service deteriorates most clients are unable to seek alternatives. The cost of organizing consumer action is too high. The few who exit only weaken the others.

In such cases, the organization attempts to present the appearance of providing the "best" service possible. Since the organization is enjoying a situation that suits it, or suits some clients, but is not satisfying the majority of its clients, it takes pains to give the impression that clients' needs are being met. Considerable noise is made about the quality of the service, either in the form of advertising — for example, advertising by monopolies who do

not really need to advertise – or by producing many irrelevant
output measures which are used to legitimate whatever service is
provided. Therefore, an indicator of unhealthy organizations is
the appearance of unnecessary advertising by monopolies and the
production of irrelevant output measures.

. Thus when exit does not function and when voice is ineffectual, it is necessary to think of other ways of defining what is a
good service. This is a crucial problem, and we will discuss it at
greater length in chapter thirteen. But one immediate result of
the erosion of client exit and voice is the rise of mediocrity.

Mediocrity

In a complex technological society, dependency for many services
is very high: most of us are dependent on sources of food, cloth-
ing, and energy available close to or in our homes. We are highly
dependent on the maintenance of communication and transportation services; on the maintenance of emergency support services
such as health care, police protection, breakdown repairs, and
aid in disasters; on the maintenance of institutions that adjudicate conflict and those that transmit culture. In short, clients in a
modern technological world are much more dependent on services than clients in traditional societies where self-sufficiency is
higher.

The extent of organizational mediocrity is related to the clients' perception of what can be done to change the service, and
the extent to which clients remain loyal when exit and voice are
costly. Consider a garbage-collection strike in a large urban center.
It is interesting to see how many weeks or even months garbage
accumulates in the streets while the general public does not revolt. Yet we can assume that in a large urban center such as New
York, Paris, or Rome, a long garbage strike accompanied by a
sudden outbreak of a dreaded disease would result in an immediate uprising of the general public. There are obviously limits to
the clients' tolerance.

Certain failures are clearly unacceptable: If patients in a given
ward consistently die, relatives of the dead and other patients
are going to make enough noise to bring relief. If the post office

always loses the mail, there will be a public clamor. In other words, the acceptable norm is not no service but mediocre service. Service is simply allowed to deteriorate in all areas where it is hard to measure the extent of deterioration. We can find many examples of mediocrity. Arthur Stinchcombe in his recent volume *Creating Efficient Industrial Administrations* describes his own experience when he attempted to obtain a driver's license in San Felix-Puerto Ordaz in eastern Venezuela (Stinchcombe 1974, pp. 7-11). He describes with some feeling how he repeatedly went to process his application, how he was told to come back repeatedly, how he spent more than sixty days trying to complete the procedure. It was evident that he was treated arbitrarily. It was also evident that he provided amusement for the local police. "Yes, we will process your papers," the police told him, "but it is too late to start work today; come back tomorrow." "We are doing our work, you see; you would have a hard time proving we are not performing what we are supposed to do." "Come back because you have no choice but to come back if you want a license."

Organizational mediocrity is also accentuated by the use of inadequate measures of output. Output measures oblige some degree of compliance, but in most organizations where a complex service is provided, output measures deal only with a partial aspect of the entire performance. They do not capture certain aspects of the process and therefore do not control the process. Quite often, output measures are chosen within the organization, and, in many such instances, they legitimate existing mediocrity. Also, there may be opportunities to tamper with measures. The recurring comment of workers in a social agency helping people find employment was to the effect that "figures can't lie, but liars can figure" (Blau 1955, p. 45). One interviewee stated:

> They lead . . . to outright falsification. I don't say that all do that, but it happens. . . . You can't expect anything else. If you make production so important, some people will feel that they have to increase their figures by any means. . . .
> (p. 47)

Some workers distorted the quality of service and increased mediocrity: "They avoided operations that would take up time without helping them to improve their record such as interviewing clients for whom application forms had to be made out, and wasted their own and the public's time on activities intended only to raise the figures on their record" (p. 46).

Organizational ill health spreads across organizations. Members of organizations are themselves clients in relation to other organizations. As clients, they perceive poor treatment when they get it. Unless strong motivation exists in their own organization to provide good service, the tendency will be for them to treat others as they are treated: "I get the run-around when I deal with these guys so why shouldn't I give them a taste of their own medicine?"

Advertising and organizational rhetoric add insult to injury: "They not only give us the run-around, they have the nerve to boast about it."

Unless the relations between the clientele and the members of the organization are close, clients will not be able to treat the rhetoric of the organization as something to be disregarded. The client who meets a member of the organization after standing in line for half an hour will not be able to establish a prompt rapport, joking about the advertisement for "prompt and courteous service," unless such rapport is made possible by other social ties (such as a shared sentiment of antipathy to the organization). Instead, the aggression of the client will only result in further disregard of client needs by members of the organization.

Lastly, client loyalty accentuates mediocrity: "We used to do good work, but now it is no longer possible. The price of raw materials has skyrocketed, and we just cannot make these as we used to, but our clientele is crazy or stupid and still accepts this shoddy product." When the clientele is loyal, it reduces everyone's ability to define fair exchange. How can we ever know what is fair if our clients will accept anything?

Games Clients Play

Where mediocrity prevails clients do not play many games. Their relationship with organizations also tends to be of less intensity or less time-consuming than that of organization members. There are exceptions, of course — prisoners, students, ward patients, etc. — but, in most instances, the organizations where clients obtain service do not have the same importance in their personal lives as the organization where they work and spend their most productive hours. Thus relationships of clients with organizations tend to take place in sporadic encounters such as standing in line at the post office, cashing a check at the bank, buying groceries at the supermarket, applying for food stamps, etc.

In more traditional or stable societies, encounters with staff members of organizations are recurrent. The same lady used to sell stamps at the same window of the corner post office three blocks from my apartment when I was a child in Paris. It was possible to establish a personal relationship that bridged our various encounters and, in time, she came to know me and know that I collected stamps. I spent three years in the early sixties working for UNESCO and returned twelve years later to find the same butcher at the weekly open-stall market behind UNESCO, and he talked to me sadly of the death of his father which had occurred five years before. In societies with rapid rates of labor turnover, the relationships between clients and organizations are limited to the official scope of transaction. There is no bridging of relationships over time as different representatives of the organization deal with clients and move around in different positions or leave the organization. Trust has to be established anew each time a client encounters the organization, and such trust is easily eroded.

The games clients play are the result of their encounters with organizations — encounters which may be positive but are quite often unsatisfactory and frustrating. They are not important in terms of results, but they are important because they are the visible symptoms of the underlying malaise.

The principal game is "complaint." Complaint is the use of voice, in Hirschman's language, to change the service. Complaint can be done singly or in groups. The consumer movement is a complaint movement. It uses every legal and political means to pursue the objectives of clients and of the larger public.

"Acting up" is another tactic of complaint that is designed to attract attention. "Playing ignorant" is a delaying tactic for clients and a trial balloon for organizations. "Partial exit" is a

delaying tactic and an unconventional way of channeling a complaint. "Intimidation" is the beginning of the use of client power.
"Sabotage" is warfare between client and organization. The "con-
spiracy" or counter-organization is client creation of alternatives.
"Kicking someone else" is not really a game — it's more a disease
— and "escape" is the impossible game: there is no escape.

Complaint

Complaint is the most important game clients can play, and it is
played in many ways: at board meetings, through regulating agencies, through the courts, through publicity, through legislatures.
   What is a complaint?
   As the headwaiter leads you to a table in front of the kitchen
door, you complain, and the headwaiter gives you a better table
with a view. The role of client provides opportunities for negative reactions and, to that extent, complaints are taken into
account by the organization. The complaint may be part of a
ritual (as when the waiter lets you taste the wine; you complain
that the wine has turned to vinegar and ask for another bottle)
or institutionalized (a complaint box; forms for comments provided by airlines). Institutionalization is either internal to the
organization (a telephone operator in the business office refers
you to a supervisor from the same organization) or external to
the organization (the ombudsman appointed by legislatures, the
better business bureau, the possibility of writing letters about bad
service to the press or of litigation).
   Complaints are important to the organization because they
provide direct information about clients' perceptions and wants,
but the organization must protect its staff and so cannot encourage complaints beyond certain limits. Complaints are really
acceptable only as long as they either reflect a departure from
accepted standards of service (the wine *had* turned into vinegar)
or the complaint is clearly unique and non-repetitive and making
an exception will not entail a future change in the standard of
service.
   Beyond this, complaint leads to a fundamental reappraisal of
the service. The organization's ability to deal with demands for

change will vary, but the tendency of any organization is to do nothing — to wait until the clamor dies down. There are many reasons for this. One is that any complaint is a statement about a perceived error. Errors are a source of uncertainty, and the organization is afraid of errors. The message will have to be loud and clear before it is heard. Meanwhile, the easiest game inside the organization is to act as if nothing had happened: "They complained? Really? Let me see; yes, it is true; we received their letter a year ago. Let me see . . . we had an investigation; yes, we did. The investigation did not turn up anything unusual. I guess that's where it ended."

Acting Up

Clients can complain louder and louder until heard. Complaining shifts from an expected role performance to greyer areas of behavior that are more uncertain and, therefore, more noticeable. If you lodge a complaint, your complaint may be disregarded. But if you begin to act in odd and unexpected ways and strongly suggest that you have a complaint, you may receive some attention. This we call "acting up."

Exaggeration and pathetic display are the more obvious ways of attracting attention. Some clients make a remarkable amount of noise about ill treatment about which others might not say much. To succeed, exaggeration and pathetic display must be unexpected. You cannot play the same act over and over because the members of the organization will soon tire of it and disregard it. It cannot be too gradual because it will be expected. It must be played swiftly and unexpectedly. Suddenly, you are in tears before anyone could guess you would cry. But you cannot exaggerate without risking outright rejection: "He made such a scene; it was absurd. . . ." Exaggeration and pathetic display have to be just beyond the expected; they must not be a stereotype of over-exaggeration, and they must be re-invented each time because they have to appear to be spontaneous.

"It does not apply to me" is a tactic of acting up that permits one to save time and allows for a reassessment of positions. You behave as if the directive were for others — certainly, not for you — "you cannot possibly mean me," and you go ahead as if nothing were amiss. The organization has the option of disregarding your infringement of the rule. Since you have not complained about anything, you have not challenged anyone or any rule and, to save time, the organization may decide to let you deviate this one time, as if it were all in error. Or it may challenge you, in which case you now have the opportunity to act up since the scene is set; the relevant actors are present! "Are you pointing your finger at me? Say it again and louder; I want to make sure I heard you correctly. . . . Do you know who I am . . . ? etc." Your intervention is done rapidly and unexpectedly. The organization is suddenly jarred — maybe a mistake is being made; let us back away, at least momentarily.

Confusing and wasting time is another tactic of acting up. Again, it is an attempt to gain time, to set the scene. It implies "Do you really want to catch me? As you can see, I am going to be difficult." You do not complain directly, although you may complain about other matters irrelevant to the problem at hand. You speak the wrong language, although you seem to be desperately trying to understand what you are told. You fill out the forms incorrectly, although you say you hope they are correct. You tell the organization that if you are in the wrong, you will try to set things right, but you show that you are confusing everything. Your behavior is uncertain. You seem hopeless; it may be safer not to spend too much time with you, to disregard you, at least for the moment. It leads to renegotiation and settling the issue: "Look here, we will let you go this time, but, please, do not do it again," or "Okay, you can stay here. I suppose it is okay." If the organization tries to correct your behavior, you explode.

Playing Ignorant

Playing ignorant is the opposite of acting up. It is a game that is played by both clients and organizations. For the client, it is a conscious delaying tactic: "Let us close our eyes for the moment since the time to do something has not yet come." For the organization, playing ignorant is a trial balloon: "Let us see how they will react to this one — let us act as if nothing is amiss and see if they catch us. If they do we can always attend to it — meanwhile why worry?"

Playing ignorant is different from ignorance. What we do not know does not hurt. Ignorance allows clients and organizations to continue to play their respective roles even when something is amiss. Playing ignorant is the conscious decision to act as if one did not know what is amiss.

Often one party is ignorant, but the other is merely playing the game. For example, when information is available on the quality of service, access, distribution, and relative costs and benefits for different clients, client consciousness of inequities is created or intensified. Therefore, it is quite normal for organizations or for privileged clients to play ignorant, to act as if they knew nothing about prevailing inequities.

Members of organizations and privileged clients tend to assume that ignorance on the part of those who are unaware of inequities is a desirable situation. But if real needs are not satisfied, clients are not going to perceive the organization positively. Yet their ignorance is dysfunctional since their dissatisfaction is unspecific and generalized. They do not know how to react, how to remedy the situation, and, as we shall see later, can only kick someone else. Therefore, ignorance is dysfunctional since it leads to client behavior that only goes to exacerbate the problem and intensify organizational failures. Ignorance is also dysfunctional on the other side: the organization may be unaware of the extent of inequities and therefore be unable to provide any amelioration.

Partial Exit

Partial exit is the non-fulfillment of selected minor aspects of the client's role while continuing to use service so as to harass the organization and oblige consideration of complaints. Boycotting meetings where clients are supposed to be present, refusing to fill out application forms, or putting one-cent stamps on utility bills are all examples of partial exit. The client's opposition to the organization is overt, but total exit is not possible or desirable. Partial exit has two functions. First, it is a new, unconventional channel of complaint. Clients are transmitting information to the organization outside of channels, and the information is more visible because the channel of complaint is totally new. Second, the use of partial exit provides a means of organizing a clients' coalition against the organization. All along, the option exists of negotiating or even submitting to the organization, or of expanding the movement if it is initially successful.

Partial exit is therefore much more important in redefining just exchange because, from the start, it does not depend on an established complaint procedure and does not rely on existing definitions of just service for adjudication. Existing procedures that could rapidly show that the client is, in fact, receiving a just service and really has no complaint are not operative. If you refuse to see the ombudsperson, the ombudsperson will not be able to state that your complaint is nonexistent. Meanwhile, you are, in fact, complaining, and your complaint is attracting attention.

An organization confronted with partial exit seeks to move unhappy clients into total exit. But there will be situations where the organization cannot succeed without involving uncommitted clients. Closing down service for those clients who are complaining means closing services for other clients and thus expanding the number of unsatisfied clients requesting a new definition of just service. It follows that the strategy of partial exit adopted by clients will be one that forces the organization to retaliate more or less blindly, thus expanding the numbers involved in the conflict.

Partial exit is threatening to organizations because members of the organization perceive clients as operating from an advantageous position where they still benefit from the services of the organization — and limit their own personal losses — while the damage they inflict on the organization is substantial, particularly if the movement spreads. Therefore, fear that the movement might spread leads to over-reactions within the organization. Organizations will devote substantial resources to nip an incipient partial-exit movement before it spreads. One consequence is that the original grievance of clients may be forgotten and the cause of the grievance is not remedied.

Intimidation

Intimidation is the non-fulfillment of significant aspects of the client role with or without continuing to use service; its object is to demonstrate the clients' effective power. The rent strike, when organized tenants refuse to pay rent until repairs are made, and boycotts of products and services by groups opposing certain policies of the producers or distributors are examples of intimidation. Whereas partial exit is the suggestion of a movement which may occur in the future, intimidation is a client movement initiated as an expression of power. Partial exit can always revert to submission if clients decide to limit their losses. But intimidation implies commitment and persistence whatever the outcome.

The initial leadership of an intimidation movement is weak and the organization may seek to eliminate it by whatever means it possesses. These means may include physical coercion or destruction. The clients' leadership, for its part, will have a low profile — avoiding obvious identity — continually changing its composition so that the organization cannot know with whom it is dealing. This pattern continues until the movement has acquired enough strength to defend itself physically and legally from the organization. The intimidation movement, therefore, moves from a formative period when guerrilla tactics are used — the leadership is continually provoking the organization, forcing it to attend to different fronts at the same time, while keeping as low a profile as possible, sending different persons to negotiate, confusing the negotiations — to a period of maturity when meaningful negotiations can take place.

But the early transition period is obviously difficult to organize and carry out. It is similar to partial exit in the sense that the client movement has to depend on secrecy and uncertainty to challenge and threaten the organization. This transition provides enough time to expose to uncommitted clients the obvious reality of a floundering organization whose ability to resist client pressure is limited. Since the movement depends on visibility to recruit new support, it challenges the organization in areas where there is a broad sense of injustice — including areas which may be sensitive to the official leadership of the organization, such as the privileges of the organizational leadership which are not shared by the rank and file of the organization. This exposure threatens the leadership and therefore intimidation movements are easily escalated into destructive conflicts.

Sabotage

Sabotage is the covert destruction of the assets of the organization. Sabotage is often carried out when partial exit or intimidation movements have failed and some groups wish to maintain pressure. Sabotage may also be spontaneous — an act of desperation for an exasperated clientele. When sabotage takes place in large organizations, attempts are made to withdraw services from a limited number of clients or to deprive many clients for limited periods of time. Dynamiting a public utility is costly for the organization. It makes opposition to the organization visible, but it limits general clientele deprivation since circuit alternatives or rapid repairs are possible. Sabotage is often carried out in co-operation with unhappy members of the organization who can introduce the clients to weak but strategic sectors of the organization. Obviously, sabotage is best used where it benefits clients and weakens the organization — for example, introducing errors in billing or reducing the rate of billing. Except in such cases, sabotage cannot be used by client movements attempting to increase client participation in opposing the organization, since clients are, by definition, inclined to depend on the continuation of service.

Sabotage is usually non-negotiable in the sense that it is carried out by secret groups who cannot negotiate openly. It is harassment intended to provide an atmosphere in which either partial exit or intimidation can be initiated. But since its effects can be used by the organization to justify poor service or to provide scapegoats for interruptions, it is used with caution by client organizers. Thus, sabotage usually tends to be: (1) external — the work of agents of other movements external to the clientele whose purposes are much broader than those of the clientele; (2) sporadic — the work of alienated clients who take personal vengeance for alleged or real mistreatment; or (3) internal — the temporary union of client and member of the organization pursuing different yet complementary objectives.

Client Conspiracies

Client conspiracies are counter-organizations initiated by clients as alternative sources of the services provided by existing organizations. Client conspiracies are created when exit is not possible, when the resources needed to create the competing counter-organization are available, and when the necessary expertise is not monopolized by existing organizations or by the state.

This alternative is significant in service areas where the activity is easy to organize and to maintain and where continuity can be ensured by individuals involved in other tasks. For example, wholesale-buying collectives and service-swapping collectives are client-instigated to provide service at cost and to permit exchanges not otherwise possible.

Client conspiracies assume greater significance when client instigation is supported by external agencies that are not satisfied with the performance of conventional organizations. In the United States, for example, non-commercial radio and television were initially created by unsatisfied clients who were unable to reform existing organizations and who found support from private foundations or from the government when attempts at reform failed.

Clearly, client counter-organization is a powerful instrument of positive change, since it re-establishes the possibility of exit.

Kicking Someone Else

Kicking someone else involves the use of destructive acts, at random, to express dissatisfaction. It is a defensive strategy to the extent that it can be used to transmit messages about dissatisfaction. This behavior also provides an escape for pent-up frustration but is usually not constructive since random aggression tends to complicate problems instead of solving them. One can argue that the notion, "Before we can change the university, we have to change the whole society," is really a call for "kicking someone else." If exchanges are not satisfactory, and you do not see how to change anything, you want to change everything. It seems reasonable to kick anyone and everyone.

"Kicking someone else" expands the general malaise because it has nothing to do with those who are affected by the aggression. "Someone else" may be providing adequate service when, out of the blue, a group enters the person's store and destroys everything in sight. Such responses serve to increase the uncertainty of organizational environments and lead to organizational conservatism. Members of organizations realize that someone else was kicked for no good reason. And when clients do kick the organization that provides poor service, members may assume it is just part of the craziness of the times.

To be sure, "kicking someone else" cannot simply be disregarded as unfortunate or as a source of increased uncertainty. It is real behavior, and its intensity varies from breaking bottles on the beach to kidnapping or killing at random. It is behavior which is difficult to control or correct because the displacement of aggression has eliminated information about the origins of the grievance. Messages about known grievances are lost in the process, and there is, usually, an escalation of demands that goes hand in hand with the attention and fear generated by the activity.

Kicking someone else displaces the problem from the relations between organizations and clients to the entire social order. As such, it is an attack on all organizations. This attack can last for long periods of time when the relative power of the state is insufficient to suppress it and the rapid deterioration of all organizational services sends new recruits into the movement of revolt. But, interestingly, the success of the revolt — e.g., a change of government — often results in its own failure. The government may fall and be completely different, or a compromise may be reached among the various factions that are fighting, but settlement of the immediate conflict is followed by the re-establishment of organizations that continue to provide the same services with the same lack of concern for their quality. In other words, ideological conflict spreads from specific dissatisfactions into a broad, but oversimplified, vision of new power relations that does not resolve the original causes of trouble. During the early days of the French revolution when the king was at Versailles, there was more conscious discussion of inequities and privileges than during the Terror — when rapid changes in the distribution of power and access to privileges did take place; different individuals rose rapidly to power, and many heads were cut off, but the nature of power and privilege remained the same even though many roles were abolished or modified and the basis of power was different.

Escape

When nothing else is possible clients escape. The game of escape consists in doing without. But most clients cannot escape from their dependencies on the services provided by organizations, even if some can. Escape requires individual or group self-sufficiency. Individual or group self-sufficiency is possible to a very limited extent for a small percentage of the inhabitants of technologically advanced countries. Escape, or even partial escape, is not a substitute for attempting to deal with the problems of organizations. Client escape is possible and, in some cases, salutary for those who have the ability to dispense with many amenities of modern life. But it is not desirable or possible for most of the population who might have less gasoline, might possess fewer gadgets and fewer frivolities, but would still be unable to plant foods, raise chickens, or deliver a baby. It is not desirable or possible because in most technological societies, the present density of population is such that, short of widespread massacre and destruction, escape from organization is simply not feasible for all, even if it is feasible for a very few.

Escape is, therefore, only temporary, partial, or illusory. As such, it provides a substitute for kicking someone else and tempers the rate of expansion of organizational ill health. The most militant and dissatisfied clients leave the city to buy land and live in communes growing food and finding value and just exchange. Some succeed; they are fortunate but few.

Conclusion

We have briefly reviewed how organizational ill-health is influenced by the ways relations between clients and the organization develop. We have defined just service and organizational health. We have examined how exit and voice are necessary to provide a suitable definition of a just service.

When exit and voice do not operate other means are necessary to define a just service. To a limited extent, professions define just service and we suggest that it would be desirable if they could do much more. But for the moment the necessary institutions to undertake this task do not exist. As a result, mediocrity dominates. Clients are obliged to play games to protect themselves. We described these games; some appear quite ineffectual, others may merely accentuate fear or confusion in organizations.

Now we can turn to the games organizations play, games that are much more effective than those clients play.

* *
*

four

Games
Organizations
Play

How do organizations reduce the uncertainty of their environment?

Three principal strategies are used:

— Organizations reduce uncertainty by becoming indispensable to their clients. They control their clients through monopolistic practices, advertising, legitimation, artificial scarcity, or even "mortification."

— Organizations reduce uncertainty through collective action with other organizations. They agree in general terms about the future through interorganizational planning.

— Organizations reduce uncertainty by linking themselves with other organizations through organizational spread. In the private sector, organizational spread is achieved through mergers, acquisitions, control of the shares of the corporation, interlocking membership on boards, etc. In the public sector, it is achieved through personal ties, coordinating agencies, and elite corps.

Monopolistic Practices

The monopolistic game consists of controlling the availability of goods and services. Monopolistic practices do not necessarily prevail where one might think they do, and they often prevail where one might assume they do not. One might think that the military controls most of the supply of potential violence. But if one examines administrative jurisdictions, one will find that in all countries various paramilitary and police forces under different organizational jurisdictions counterbalance the possible intervention of the military in the internal affairs of the state. Control of the instruments of state violence is never left to a single organization. In contrast, one might believe that retail stores compete strongly, yet this belief disregards the extent to which many consumers have few options as to when and where they may shop.

Control of the supply of service is facilitated when the nature of the service requires multi-level integration (i.e., technological integration — telephone, public utilities, rail transportation) or when the service can only be provided by a single body (for example, the state can only be represented by a single, unitary agency; we cannot conceive of two Departments of State sending competing American ambassadors to foreign countries).

More significant opportunity for control of supply arises when competitors agree to cooperate. Such control results from three distinct processes: (1) similarity of service among competitors; (2) limits on productive capability; and (3) apathy of consumers comined with choice limitations at distribution points.

If the service or product of Company Y is similar to that of Company Z, even if they appear superficially to be slightly different, and if these companies do not attempt to provide new products and services, they are *de facto* acting as a monopoly and control the supply.

Mass production through standardization results in many advantages: lower costs, interchangeable parts, nationwide maintenance services, etc. One does not explain mass production as an organizational strategy to control supply, but control of supply is a consequence of mass production. As smaller producers are pushed out of the market and fewer large producers dominate production, product similarity guarantees control of supply:

> Beer brewing, for example, is a highly competitive industry in the United States, but almost all the breweries aim, with varying success, to produce essentially the same kind of beer. (Scitovsky 1973, p. 239)

Competitive organizations compete among themselves for a relative share of a market. But they tend to agree (spontaneously, without collusion) to define the market in a manner that reduces uncertainty.

Limits on production capability also reduce uncertainty. Once large organizations produce most of the goods and services that are consumed, a qualitative shift by a single producer does not alter, at least not in the short run, the relative ability of each organization to control its clients. Only when clients can do *without* service is control difficult. Otherwise, clients are obliged to use whatever service is available. If there are two hospitals in town, one of which provides better service than the other, once the best is full, demand must still be satisfied in the second-best. If two large producers control all the existing market, a third potential producer has to create surplus producing capacity to break into this closed market. This problem sharply limits the ability of new producers to divert shares of the market from those who already control it. Thus, the clientele remains at the mercy of two existing producers.

Control of the supply of services also takes place at distribution points. Scitovsky has argued that American consumers are passive and helpless; they fail to make the effort of choosing among products; they even seem to prefer lower-priced standard goods to higher-quality variants: "Witness the fewness and decline of specialty food stores and specially good bakeries and pastry shops" (Scitovsky 1973, p. 235).

The passivity of consumers is attributable to many factors including their vitality, their ignorance, and their economic constraints. But they are controlled because distributors stock few different brands, and it is this reality that actually determines the choices they can make. In practical terms, it does not matter to consumers how many different products exist if their choices are limited to what is available today in the only stores they can reach.

In contrast to control of supply, control of demand is related to client needs. In some realms, we can talk of biological imperatives — in others, of social imperatives. Without attempting to define how and why clients have needs (they need food, shelter, protection, and they need to look good to significant others, etc.), we are interested in the processes used by organizations to manipulate or even create a need for goods and services.

Organizations play three important games to control demand: advertising, legitimation, and artificial scarcity.

Advertising

Advertising is demand management (Galbraith 1967, p. 213). Advertising by organizations represents a very substantial level of expenditure: more than two percent of the GNP in the United States, slightly less in other Western countries, is spent on advertising. Presumably, advertising can or should sharpen competition among organizations by revealing differences among goods and services and providing consumers with better knowledge of potential choices. Organizations seem to decide to spend resources for advertising to protect or enlarge their relative share of the market. But in cases where monopolies exist (such as private or public utilities), organizations continue to advertise, suggesting, as we mentioned in the previous chapter, that advertising also serves other functions.

Advertising transmits information that creates needs where they did not exist previously. Since individuals in society have biological and social needs, advertising is used to elicit consumer response — either biological or social: "Try our new pasta; it tastes better," "A mink coat is for that discriminating person," etc.

Advertising differentiates among products and services. But such considerations hide some less obvious aspects of advertising. It is not only specific products and services that are advertised but also the idea that such products or services are desirable.

Even in those markets where advertising is used to stress peculiarities of one organization's product in contrast to those of a
competitor's product, the sum of advertising for all competing
products (say, the sum of advertising by all automobile manu-
facturers) serves to influence the total demand for automobiles.

Advertisements are produced with implicit assumptions about
the good life. Several years ago a cigarette ad on television implicitly assumed that young, beautiful persons normally smoke
in lovely country lanes with the wind blowing their impeccably
groomed hair. Needs are suggested, or even invented, by a subtle
definition of norms.

Advertising invents social norms that organizations want to
establish for their own purposes, not for their clients' purposes.
They are, therefore, an important instrument that organizations
use to control the characteristics of their clientele's demands.
The point is that clients are often at the mercy of advertisements.
If we contrast advertising with education, we immediately see the
difference: it is as if school boards were controlled only by
teachers. If we think of advertising as an educational enterprise,
and we contrast the role of education clients in school boards,
where their voice can be heard (if only faintly), with the role of
commercial clients in selecting what advertising they will see or
hear, we notice that the latter have practically no voice at all
except in exceptional cases where the advertising is sufficiently
offensive to create opposition.

It is interesting to note that the phenomenon of advertising
is not exclusive to capitalist economies. Although one might
think that centralized planning would be sufficient, advanced
socialist economies are also using advertising to manipulate demand. Whereas advertising (and even market research) was at first
considered to be inappropriate for planned socialist economies,
the sixties and seventies saw growing interest in these areas. As
Pravda stated in 1965, "Advertising is a broad, rewarding field of
work for the poet, the writer, and the artist" (quoted in Wilczynski 1970, p. 172).

To be sure, socialist advertising is supposed to be devoid of
concern for specific organizations. It is supposed to have the
interests of clients at heart:

Informative advertising enables the consumer to make a more rational choice in spending his income. Secondly, the judicious use of persuasive advertising is a tool of "consumer education" and "consumer steering," whereby, on the one hand, consumer preferences can be adapted to socially desirable planned patterns, and, on the other, unwanted stocks of goods can be easily disposed of. (Ibid.)

Legitimation

Organizations employ experts to legitimate the service they provide, especially when they are complex organizations providing services that are difficult to assess. For example, this is the practice in the military, space agencies, research institutions, etc.

Advertising may still be used, but only in a limited area that is well understood by clients. Experts are used to study the "need" for a service, and their recommendations serve to convince the general public. Often comparisons with services provided elsewhere are used to justify whatever the organization is doing. If the local school district spends twelve percent of its budget for administrative salaries, it may be justified or attacked in terms of the proportion spent in other school districts. Therefore, when most organizations are providing a mediocre service, mediocrity becomes the norm, the standard which tends to prevail even in the few organizations that were attempting to improve their service.

Military organizations often find it convenient to transmit information about developments in other countries as a basis for justifying their budget requests. When a leading Canadian Air Force officer was asked how a certain decision about an expensive item of scientific hardware had been made by his government, he answered: "There were many considerations, but in the final analysis, the argument that carried the day was that the Russians had decided to go ahead on a similar piece of equipment."

It would be exaggerating to explain all military appropriations exclusively in terms of keeping up with Soviet or American military expenses, but it is clear that this device is used.

Experts and advertising are often used simultaneously to

manipulate demand. This pattern can be seen in the art market. If I want to create a demand for an unknown artist — say, a minor nineteenth-century painter who has been forgotten — I may buy all the works of this obscure painter that I can easily find. Once I own a stock of paintings, I hire an expert to write a book about this painter. The book includes color reproductions from my collection. Once the book is published, I send one or two paintings from my collection to an international auction. I have several friends bid up the price artificially, buy the paintings, and return them to me. Now, I have "advertised" the new value of my painter. The next time I place another painting at the auction, real buyers emerge — real buyers who would not have paid the price they are now paying if the book had not been published and if I had not manipulated the demand so adroitly. I hasten to add that I have not committed this hoax! But it is done by others, and it is done in other fields also.

Artificial Scarcity

There are two aspects of artificial scarcity; first, it means that the organization produces goods and services in a quantity that is deliberately less than known demand; second, it means that the organization designs products and services that force clients to depend on them.

If the supply is kept slightly under the demand, clients are much easier to control. To use Hirschman's language again, they cannot exit. They can shop around only when there is excess capacity or when they can do without service.

In an economy where there is a deliberate national policy to underproduce consumer goods, it is easier to control clients. Advertising and other forms of demand manipulation become less necessary. Whatever is produced, whatever services are offered, will be consumed. This kind of manipulation is most effective in advanced socialist economies where ideological commitment to rapid rates of economic growth goes hand in hand with decisions to downgrade consumer consumption. Producing organizations in advanced socialist economies are far more concerned with achieving quantifiable norms of production than in achieving quality, for the obvious reason that clients have no choice but to consume what is available.

In poorer countries where there are large reservoirs of unsatisfied demand for goods and services, the notion of artificial scarcity is even more relevant. It is partially irrelevant only in newly developing capitalist countries where there are gross inequities in income distribution. These inequities result in two classes of consumers. One class has an income level as high as, or even higher than, that of their counterparts in wealthy countries; for them techniques of artificial scarcity do not apply, because they are wealthy and can substitute among goods and services (if there is not enough bread, they buy cake). But the larger population, the second class, provides a large reservoir of unsatisfied demand with no choice but to accept whatever services it can get. Therefore the poor in both socialist and capitalist countries are easily manipulated by organizations.

The other way to control clients is to create products and services that are designed to increase the clientele's dependency on the organization. For example, the organization provides a service which, adequate while it lasts, does not last as long as it might. Lamp bulbs could last longer, but are designed to burn out; small gadgets are designed so that it is less expensive to throw them away than attempt to repair them; clothes and car styles are altered, and consumers are urged to own the latest style; spare parts come in assembled sections so that several parts have to be purchased together, etc. This second technique is used in those countries where it is still difficult to keep production slightly behind demand — that is, where the level of centralization and monopolistic control is still not sufficient to place clients totally under the control of the organization.

Mortification

In a curious way, organizations need to be reassured that their clients need them. There is a constant fear that, somehow, the clientele will disappear or will shift its needs drastically. Therefore, there is need for assurance that the clientele is really committed — really needs, is truly at the mercy of, the organization.

Service is dispensed parsimoniously to test the clientele's ability to do without. Clients are forced to incur costs for access to service.

Members of the organization do not act unilaterally. Rules and procedures are invented to ensure fair play for everyone, but control of clients takes place in various ways. Goffman has described the process of mortification in total institutions such as prisons, hospitals, and concentration camps (Goffman 1961, pp. 43–48). He described mortification as an attempt by the organization to control inmates by altering their perception of self-determination. For example, in mental wards or political prisons, the staff disregards whatever the inmate says: "Often, he is considered to be of insufficient ritual status to be given even minor greetings, let alone listened to" (p. 45). Mortification is more intensive in prisons and concentration camps: "Thus, we have atrocity tales of prisoners being forced to roll in the mud, stand on their heads in the snow, work at ludicrously useless tasks, swear at themselves" (p. 44).

Mortification of clients is practiced in every organization — obviously, not always as extensively as in prisons or concentration camps — but it is practiced, because it provides reassurance. We are all familiar with the phenomenon even if we have not seen it for what it is. It includes the salesperson who makes the client wait three minutes while finishing a task of no evident urgency and the nurse who insists on registration requirements in the emergency room of the hospital.

Mortification is often justified: "It is necessary to have the children know who is in charge," or "Silence is required to protect old people," or "It is forbidden to walk on the grass to protect the public," or "These rules are for *your* protection," etc.

The use of rules and regulations to restrict service and to control clients is common. Rules provide legitimacy to acquire greater control, but rules also permit simultaneous denial of service while affirming performance of task. Suppose you cough after waiting two minutes for the salesperson? This person will say, sharply, "Please, I must finish this work." You are interrupting a role performance protected by organization rules; therefore, who are you to judge what the salesperson should do?

Unnecessary rules and other small indignities are practiced in all organizations. It is reassuring to have people wait to see you, and the longer they wait, the more important you seem to be. If clients will wait outside, in the cold, in long lines, it is comforting to know service is needed. But mortification contributes its share to the mediocrity of the service, and it fuels client revolt.

Planning Games

Interorganizational planning is a game in the sense that it serves to reduce the uncertainty surrounding organizations by reaching an agreement about what will be done in the future. Interorganizational planning embraces many independent organizations. It is usually carried out by a central planning agency and involves both government and private-sector agencies. It is prevalent in socialist economies where the private sector is practically non-existent, in many European countries such as France and Holland, in most countries of the Third World, and, to a more limited extent, in the United States, where statewide planning exists in some sectors such as transportation, water resources, health, and education. Nationwide planning has been initiated or discussed in sectors such as energy, transportation, telecommunications, military preparedness, and disarmament.

"Policy analysis" — research to help decision-makers choose among various possible courses of action — is widely used in the United States. Much policy analysis is involved in formulating a plan, but policy analysis is not the same as planning; we use the word "planning" to refer to situations in which statements are issued about intentions for the future, such as when a planning agency issues statements every six months about targets for steel production during the following five years. These targets may be changed to accommodate subsequent experience — for example, demand may have increased more quickly than was expected — and the targets for the future may be modified accordingly. But this constant stream of information about probable characteristics of future events is central to planning. If this information is believed — that is, if individuals in organizations believe the targets of the plan will be achieved — they will modify their own behavior to fit what they expect to happen.

Planning for many organizations deals with interorganizational networks (Benson 1975; Clark 1965) where authority and power are shared among many institutions, organizations, and individuals. The planning process relies more on influence and beliefs than on the use of authority:

> There were good reasons why the Planning Commission could not readily make a comprehensive plan of the kind described in the ideology of the city planning movement. Power to make fundamental decisions affecting city development . . . was widely dispersed. (Meyerson and Banfield 1955, p. 274)

Let us distinguish three types of planning: trivial, utopian, and effective or intentional.

Trivial planning provides legitimacy for decisions that have already been made. The government has already decided on a course of action; planners are called in and asked to conduct research that supports the decision; the plan is announced with great fanfare and implementation proceeds.

Utopian planning reaffirms ideological commitments but has no effect on decisions being made. For example, the government is officially committed to universal primary education, but the country is very poor, and the elite wants to expand primary education very slowly. A plan for "solving the problems" of primary education is announced with great fanfare. In the plan, there is much talk about reaching universal primary education in twenty years' time, but the plan is silent about immediate steps. The utopian plan serves to reaffirm ideological commitment and to obscure the fact that little or nothing is to be done.

Trivial and utopian planning are used to mystify clients and the general public.

Last, but more important, is effective or successful planning. John Friedmann describes effective planning as a transactive process — a dialogue between those who plan and those affected by the plans (Friedmann 1973, pp. 177–93). Effective planning is a negotiation about future collective intentions. In contrast to trivial or utopian window-dressing, effective planning reduces the uncertainty of the future because the organizations affected by the plan know that a dialogue has taken place, and they therefore know and believe in the intentions described in the plan. Belief and trust are central to effective planning because collective action by many organizations cannot be integrated beforehand unless there is common agreement about characteristics of future events. Such belief is obviously limited to specific domains and events. There are aspects of the future which always remain unknown, and effective planning never eliminates all uncertainty.

How is a common belief achieved? Belief is achieved by using three sources of influence and power. The successful planner for many organizations uses (1) a shared belief in knowledge — i.e., people believe in the ability to predict selected events or to predict the consequences of policy options; (2) knowledge that there is an agreement among a coalition of supporters; and (3) whatever controls planners can exercise on budgets. These three sources of influence provide a shared belief that the plan will be implemented. I have discussed these points in *The Politics of Expertise* (Benveniste 1972).

Once there is widespread belief that the plan will be implemented, once the intentions of a plan are perceived to be statements about the future, all the relevant organizations (i.e., those that, in one way or another, implement the plan) reorient their own actions to fit the plan. This is the multiplier effect in effective planning. It is based on a shared image of the future which is sufficiently convincing that different organizations with different purposes come and align themselves with it.

The multiplier effect (which is explained at greater length in *The Politics of Expertise,* chapter two) results from the subjective probabilities that individuals in organizations associate with the plan. If you really believe that the targets for steel production included in the plan will be reached, and you produce spare parts for steel furnaces, you are going to plan your own production in light of the expected demand for spare parts which is implied by the targets for steel production in the plan. Thus, a plan generates an effect similar to a self-fulfilling prophecy.

The Game of Not Really Caring About Clients or Beneficiaries

Suppose you are a planner and you want to convince relevant implementers that the steel production targets of your plan have a very high probability of being achieved. But you have a limited amount of time and resources to elaborate the plan. You have to consider the costs of your own planning exercise, and within these constraints, you are going to attempt to establish targets that are credible. You are going to do a fair amount of research and policy analysis to determine the characteristics of the probable demand for steel products. Systematic market research will provide information about the probable needs of consumers. Policy analysis will provide insights into the consequences of various programs to expand consumer demand. Out of this work, various scenarios about future targets will be prepared.

The second stage will consist of negotiating an agreement about future production and the consequent policies (financing arrangements, subsidies to certain industries, agreements on wage limitations, etc.) needed to reach a selected scenario for desirable steel outputs. This negotiation is central to persuading individuals and organizations that the plan can be implemented.

It is the implementers — the organizations that control financing, labor, raw materials, equipment, etc. — who matter at this stage. They, in turn, are concerned about their clientele, but do not necessarily need the agreement of clients to negotiate the plan. Other beneficiaries are also irrelevant.

Some participation is possible in planning, and some participation is essential for plan implementation. But participation is dictated by the logic of the planning process and is limited to that minimum coalition of supporters sufficient to bring about the notion that the plan has a high probability of implementation. In any planning situation, participation involves those implementers who are organized and can exercise power. These political actors are relevant to the planner. All others will be disregarded, not because planners are against participation, but because they do not have the time to handle any complex process of interest aggregation. The operating problem of any planner is not the illusion of participatory planning, but to have enough time (a strict minimum level of effort) to organize a supportive coalition that will permit the plan to be carried out.

Therefore, planning is an elitist activity. Participation exists in appearance but not in fact. If clients are mystified by utopian or trivial planning, they are frustrated by effective, successful planning. Plans are elaborated for them; their needs are discussed; they are studied; they are observed. But they do not participate in planning except when they are well organized.

The Game of Not Caring about Legislators

Planning also affects the political process. It shifts influence from legislative bodies to the executive, because it is the executive that hires and controls the planners. The plan is often presented to the legislature as a *fait accompli,* and legislative participation in planning is after the fact unless the legislative branch takes energetic steps to upgrade its own research and planning capability. This shift of power reduces the influence of the elected representatives and increases that of the corporate bodies that are close to implementation. This process pervades every social, economic, diplomatic, and military sector where planning has emerged in recent decades.

We should not be surprised by these developments. Since planning emerges from a need for central regulation, it encourages centralization. Centralization requires organization and linkage to implementation. It is the organized corporate bodies that control implementation who will benefit from such shifts.

Elected bodies are bypassed because it is difficult for a large elected body representing many different interests to participate as a whole in the elaboration of the plan. One possible alternative would be for political parties to undertake planning on their own. This is called partisan planning.

> . . . The suspicions of Congress are not unfounded. Once you accept the political dimension of planning, the solutions proposed are simply too aseptic and unreal. It is all well and good to urge Congress as a body or committees of Congress to use systems analysis as if they were helping all

congressmen. This has nothing to do with the partisan nature of the enterprise. Congress is rightly suspicious of letting in the enemy. Increasing the staffs of committees would only reduce the influence of elected members. Data banks and computerized information can increase the research capability of the Library of Congress, and individual congressmen can avail themselves of these services, but this will not improve the planning capability of Congress sufficiently. Eminently political bodies can only use expertise if expertise is partisan. This has to be recognized from the start.

This does not mean that various expert capabilities in Congress would necessarily improve the efficiency of budgeting or planning or result in a better budget. It would allow congressional partisans a more dominant role in negotiations. If advocacy planning can help the poor in their dealings with the experts, partisan legislative planning can help another weakened minority in its dealings with the executive and the private sector. Of course, any budget reveals the nature of existing influence groups, but a link is missing from that argument. Some influence groups have acquired excessive power because they control the experts. Elected representatives do not always pursue the strategies they want to pursue because they do not know the alternatives. Partisan legislative planning would remedy excesses and distortions. It would not replace politics with rationality; it would use a rational language to allow politics to take place again.

Both the left and the right have been suspicious of experts. The result is visible: legislatures have lost ground. If the left and some on the right do not wish to give up to an emerging corporate state, they have to learn to use experts and, in so doing, re-establish their intended role. (Benveniste 1972, pp. 204–5)

To be sure, legislatures do exercise some influence in a planning process. They can modify budgets and alter some aspects of any plan. But these are delaying tactics. At most, Congress can thwart the planning effort of the executive by withholding its approval; otherwise it can only delay decisions and eventually be bypassed. For example, most of the important SALT decisions on nuclear disarmament, which involved much planning, were taken without reference to Congress (Newhouse 1973, p. 32).

The Game of Increasing Everyone's Frustration

Oddly enough, planning increases social tension by sharpening conflict about the future. On one hand, planning serves to reduce social tension by making the future seem less uncertain. But on the other, it increases tension by providing detailed facts about what is to be done.

As long as the future is unplanned, much uncertainty prevails, but no one is believed to be responsible. The social order may be in disarray, but the forces at work appear mysterious. It is the "market" or the "economic conditions" or even the "depression" that is causing uncertainty. Governments are blamed, but most governments seem to have similar problems. The moment planning is introduced and planners specify what the future may look like, human intervention is perceived, and — more importantly — human preferences are expressed. When uncertainty prevails, the future is, so to speak, secret. Secrecy permits all contenders to hope. They may not hope very much, but — at least — they have aspirations.

In the bureaucracy, secrecy allows different schools of thought to coexist because the situation is vague and undecided. Then planners intervene and announce that activities X will be increased by ten percent while activities Y will be reduced by ten percent. The conflict between the department in charge of X and that in charge of Y explodes. Why ten percent more for them and not for us? Who made this recommendation? Why? In an unplanned situation, these two departments might have coexisted for a long time, hardly aware that their activities were being cut or increased. But the plan is public; the fact that everyone knows the Y's are "getting it" creates a new threat. The plan removes secrecy and exposes explicit value judgments about activities.

When economic growth is the motor of planning, this dilemma is less significant. The bureaucracy can easily handle a situation in which everyone is getting more. When planning is not protected by economic growth, it accentuates future conflicts and extends the period during which battle takes place. The bureaucracy fights the current battles and those of coming years — not only the inevitable ones but imaginary battles that later events may make irrelevant.

Organizational Spread: The Conglomerates

Organizational spread is the merging of independent organizations into larger organizations to provide better protection in an uncertain environment.

Organizational spread permits organizations to reduce uncertainty by controlling other organizations. Such control ultimately facilitates control of clients. Spread is not necessarily the same phenomenon as organizational growth. The purpose of organizational spread is to create large bastions of organizational strength which can resist environmental threats.

In the private sector, spread is well understood. Mergers of organizations, acquisitions, interlocking boards of directors, contracts and agreements provide linkages that protect the linked organizations. Growth is part of this process, and the international dimension of the phenomenon is well documented in the current literature on multinational corporations (Barret and Muller 1974; Brooke and Remmero 1970; Dunning 1972; Eells 1972; Gonzales and Negandhi 1967; Kindleberger 1970; Rolfe and Damm 1970; Sethi and Holton 1974; Turner 1971; Vernon 1972).

In the public sector, the process is similar. Growth of the bureaucracy is the most evident symptom, but not the only one. To a very large extent, coordination and linkage of government bureaucracy provides a mechanism of joint defense against the environment.

Statistics reveal some aspects of organizational spread. For example, the percentage of total corporate assets controlled by the largest corporations in the United States and in Western Europe has grown steadily. Thus, in the decade ending in 1969, the share of total United States corporation assets held by eighty-seven corporations with assets of $1 billion or more had increased from 26 to 46 percent (Bannock 1973, p. 41).

Spread cannot be explained solely as an attempt to reduce uncertainty. It is also related to such factors as profits. The share of total profits of the eighty-seven corporations just mentioned rose at the end of the decade to half of all profits. Corporate spread is also related to other forms of uncertainty manipulation (it facilitates planning, permits the organization to become indispensable, etc.). It also justifies higher salaries for top management (where average salaries are related to size of organization). Corporate spread also relates to productivity and economies of scale.

From a societal point of view, the only relevant justification for organizational spread is increased productivity resulting from economies of scale. Since profits seem to increase with greater size, it is easy to assume that productivity increases result from organizational spread. But analysis of cause and effect is not easily undertaken since the empirical data reflects the effects of economies of scale as well as other factors. Large private organizations can mobilize private financial resources more effectively and, possibly, more efficiently. They can integrate certain functions, such as market research and production distribution. They can advertise more efficiently. But on the other side of the ledger, there are many hidden inefficiencies. There are higher administrative costs. There are longer decision lead-times and inherent rigidities since very large organizations provide more opportunities for routinization of decision patterns and diffusion of risk-taking. These costs are important but not necessarily the most important. We will discuss in greater detail in the next chapter costs that may be totally hidden, i.e., the games individuals in large organizations play.

For any service, we can project a desirable organizational size which is determined by economies of scale. This desirable size is related to technological considerations (the nature of the processes the organization undertakes; the relative cost efficiency of electrical equipment) as well as to the peculiarities of the spatial distribution of raw materials, energy resources, labor supply, and consumer demand.

If we tentatively agree, disregarding for the moment externalities such as ecological issues, that economies of scale are the only societal justification for organizational spread, we can conclude that most current organizational spread does not have an economic justification. As a leading economist points out, there may be distinct apparent economies of scale in any centralized organization, but there is also a need for responsibility and responsiveness to the general public (Arrow 1974, p. 79).

Schumpeter, writing in the late forties, already feared and predicted the organizational giant:

> We have seen that the function of entrepreneurs is to reform or revolutionize the pattern of production. . . . Technological progress is increasingly becoming the business of teams of trained specialists who turn out what is required and make it work in predictable ways. . . . Economic progress tends to become depersonalized and automatized. Bureau and committee work tend to replace individual action. . . . Since capitalist enterprise, by its very achievements, tends to automatize progress, we conclude that it tends to make itself superfluous — to break to pieces under the pressure of its own success. The perfectly bureaucratized giant industrial unit not only ousts the small and medium firm and "expropriates" its owners, but in the end it also ousts the entrepreneur and expropriates the bourgeoisie as a class which, in the process, stands to lose not only its income but also, what is infinitely more important, its function. The true pacemakers of socialism were not the intellectuals or agitators who preached it but the Vanderbilts, Carnegies and Rockefellers. (Schumpeter 1947, pp. 132–34)

Organizational spread in the private sector is well documented; spread in public administration is harder to document. To be sure, it is easy to document the growth of government bureaucracy. But it is not the growth of individual units of government or of the total number of units that interests us most. It is the growth of *articulating units,* such as coordinating committees, task forces, commissions, and regulating agencies, which serve for the public administration the same function that mergers and acquisitions serve in the private sector.

The Department of State cannot readily absorb the Department of Defense on the grounds that increased efficiency would result. Opportunities for organizational spread are constrained. Organizational spread does take place when periodic administrative reforms call for consolidation and rationalization of services. But the phenomenon of organizational spread in public administration is different from that in the private sector. In the public sector it is based on expansion rather than acquisition. Beyond size, there exist a multitude of linkages and ties that permit uncertainty to be reduced. For example, educational selection provides personal ties for top civil servants.

Elite educational institutions such as Oxford and Cambridge in England, the École des Sciences Politiques until 1944 and the École Nationale d'Administration in post–World War II France, legal training in selected universities in Germany, engineering in the Soviet Union, provide both a "democratic" system of selection and, once constituted, an elite class with personal contacts within one generation (Wilkinson 1969). A network of personal relations is established with norms of reciprocity and friendship which guarantee that graduates will keep in touch and help each other.

Top managers in civil services usually reach their positions between the ages of 43 and 52. In the United States, 22 percent reach top management positions between 40 and 49 years of age and 46 percent between 50 and 59. Data from England and West Germany seem to show a slightly younger trend. Patterns in the Soviet Union and France are similar to that of the United States (Armstrong 1973, p. 240). Since induction into the civil service takes place when civil servants are in their twenties, the strategic age seems to be around 35 when recognition and visibility are going to be most important for subsequent advancement. Educational ties will be most significant during the decade following graduation when personal relations are still maintained.

In all countries, a more important device of integration is provided by the circulation of middle- and top-level officers in various agencies and ministries. For example, dozens of officers are exchanged each year between the Department of State, the Department of Defense, and the Central Intelligence Agency. These liaisons provide both formal and informal channels of communication.

Special elite corps within the civil service also serve to integrate the public bureaucracy. The best example is the French "Grands Corps" such as the Inspection des Finances, the Conseil d'État, the Cour des Comptes, or the Corps des Mines (Suleiman 1974, pp. 241–81). These agencies have specific functions but also constitute a supre-organizational group as their members pursue assignments in other parts of the administration. Elite corps do not play an important role in the United States (for example, the Army Corps of Engineers, which is the American equivalent of the Corps des Mines, plays a minor role overall, although it can be very influential in its domain of responsibility). The equivalent function tends to be performed by other institutions, particularly by the think-tanks such as RAND, Battelle Memorial Institute, and the Stanford Research Institute, and to a more limited extent by foundations and universities.

The think-tanks undertake contract research on important policy issues for many different organizations, both public and private. Their staffs circulate in these organizations constantly, and their research places them in contact with many others. They provide an important linkage among organizations.

Universities and foundations also provide career locations for individuals who serve in government for limited periods of time and who remain in touch with a small but important group of integrators.

Other informal ties are also important. As men and women gravitate toward positions of importance they attract a retinue of individuals who pursue careers with them. Individuals who have proved effective assistants in previous assignments are called again to join successful employers in their new functions. Thus younger elites move from assignments in state capitals to Washington — from one agency to another until they acquire a name in their own right. Such personal identification tends to acquire a political identification since individuals occupying top positions necessarily belong to a political party, and their careers are ultimately linked to political affiliation.

One consequence of these processes is to make the public administration far more conscious of political reality than would otherwise be the case. Elite members of public organizations are not only members of organizations but also members of political and friendship affiliations that transcend their commitment to single agencies. As we would expect, this is not only an American phenomenon but is also prevalent in other nations (Putnam 1973).

Formal linkages are also provided by a multitude of groups that coordinate interorganizational activity. Regulating agencies, interagency coordinating committees, interagency task forces, Presidential Task Forces, Governors' or White House Conferences, local, state, or national commissions, etc., serve the function of placing members of organizations in contact with others in the public administration and with the private sector. One ironic consequence of this process greatly reduces the effectiveness of coordination within the administration. Since effective coordination should encourage conflict resolution, one would expect that emphasis on coordination would, in fact, resolve problems. But coordination is a type of organizational spread. Its function is not to resolve conflicts about clients' needs but to resolve conflicts about organizational jurisdictions. Therefore, grass-roots problems are frequently seen as irrelevant. From the point of view of clients and of activists in the organization, coordinating committees are often strangulating committees — that is, committees that make it extremely difficult to accomplish anything.

To summarize: the function of organizational spread in both the private and public sectors consists in reducing uncertainty. Organizational spread has two dimensions: (1) to reduce the uncertainty created by clients, to eliminate as much as possible their ability to exit or use voice; (2) to eliminate the threats posed by competing organizations. In practice, organizational spread means that the system is overcontrolled and overcoordinated. We will see in the next chapter how these games also serve to protect the careers of members of organizations.

* *
*

five

The Serious Game
of Survival
inside Bureaucracy

To understand the games played within bureaucracy, it is necessary to understand individual career motivations. Individual career paths determine some of the strategies that bureaucrats use to protect themselves. In some cases individuals are attempting to climb a status ladder; in other cases they seek to stay where they are. They are satisfied with their current situations. Without agreeing with the Peter Principle, which states that individuals in organizations climb the ladder until they occupy a position they are unable to perform and, therefore, move no further (Peter 1970), it is correct to say that, for one reason or another, many position-holders are where they want to be or have no illusion that they can do better elsewhere. They have reached the top of their salary scale and there is no incentive for them to take any risk. But these individuals also need to protect their positions and so they too play games.

In this chapter, we describe how individual needs for protection result in several games. We discuss output measures, and such rules as bureaucratic insurance, risk avoidance, excessive coordination, documented histories, and doing nothing.

Organizational Careers

Members of organizations occupy successive positions in one or more organizations over time. The succession of positions one occupies forms an organizational career (Glazer 1968).

Closed sector careers take place either in a single organization or in other organizations that are similar. Knowledge and experience with the organization or the sector is of first importance. Transfers from organizations in other fields of endeavor in different sectors occur only in rare instances. Once an individual initiates a career in such sectors as cinema, education, the military, banking, etc., the experience is most valued in the same area. A person may go from sales to production to assistant director for R & D to general manager. Moreover, in many such closed sectors, career paths are strongly determined by the status of the initial appointment location. If one is first appointed as an assistant professor in an unknown junior college, the probability of ever being appointed in a large university is low; but if one is first appointed at Columbia, there is a higher probability that one may end as a full professor at Harvard.

Open sector careers are skill-oriented. It is not the sector that matters (i.e., banking, education, etc.), but the kind of work performed. If one is a specialist in control system design or in public relations, the specialization may take one to different kinds of organizations as one acquires renown in the skill or profession: "This person is very good; she worked with the teachers' unions — got them in order and then went to . . ."

The level one occupies within an organization is related to the nature of the skill: "She is a top-notch personnel manager — has a background in government service but worked several years with a private utility . . ." Certain skills permit upward mobility within organizations: "He started as a production troubleshooter for an electric firm, later became a negotiator in international sales and, ultimately, became their lobbyist in Washington, D.C. . . ."

Location-dominated careers are controlled by desirable locations. It is not the sector or skill that matters. The relevant progression is from less desirable to more desirable locations: "When I got out of school, I could not find a job. Finally, I started teaching in a small town in a rural area. . . . Four years later, we moved to Boston, but we did not like it there. . . . We came west to California, and I run a bookstore. . . ."

"Career movement for the Chicago teacher is, in essence, movement from one school to another, some schools being more and others less satisfactory places to work" (Becker 1952, p. 383).

Evaluations and Evaluators

Each person in the organization plays the incumbent role according to his or her perception of the way the performance will be judged by significant evaluators. Those seeking advancement desire positive evaluations. Those who want to stay where they are seek to avoid negative evaluations.

Significant evaluators may be located within the same or in another or several other organizations; they can be a single person or they may be a multitude of persons who, in one way or another, are perceived to be important to one's career.

This point is particularly important because much of our current thinking treats organizations as units of analysis. We assume that behavior within organizations is explained in terms of the structure or the reward system of individual organizations. In fact, organizations operate in a larger environment, and that environment may be more important than the organization in explaining individual behavior.

Individual perceptions of evaluations may be vague and indefinite. To be sure, individuals who are pursuing closed-sector career paths often possess precise knowledge about how their performances are evaluated and by whom. But in some large organizations and at the higher levels of responsibility, individuals often do not have a clear perception of their evaluators. This lack of clarity occurs in large government bureaucracies, especially when the general environment is perceived to be threatening, but when the exact source of trouble or potential trouble is vague. Such ill-defined evaluators create fear. "You never know who might be watching — who might send an anonymous report." As one worker reported, the supervisor "can push a button on this special console. Just to see if I'm pleasant enough . . . [or] if I make a personal call. Ma Bell is listening. And you don't know. That's why it's smart to do the right thing most of the time. Keep your nose clean" (in Terkel 1974, p. 69).

In many organizations, there are no criteria of evaluation because there is no exact knowledge about how the role should be played. For example, this is true of teaching where it is not possible to know what makes a good teacher. In such organizations, pseudo-evaluations are often used; in education, it is possible to invent criteria of competency, but these are often considered meaningless by teachers. This imprecision tends to exacerbate the uncertainty of evaluations since no one really knows what criteria are used in making decisions.

These fears are shared both by those who strive upward and those without ambition. In fact, fear may be more serious for the latter type. If individuals remain in the same position or the same line of work for many years, they may become obsolete for most other tasks. Such people recognize how vulnerable they are if their organization or department is embroiled in any difficulty and if, as a result, they fall into disgrace. If these people are middle-aged and have acquired responsibilities, they are doubly vulnerable. Even with strong unions or civil service protection, the fear prevails because everyone has heard, or seen at first hand, cases of individuals who were destroyed by events beyond their control. As a business consultant reports:

> Fear is always prevalent in the corporate structure. Even if you're a top man, even if you're hard, even if you do your job — by the slight flick of a finger, your boss can fire you. There's always the insecurity. You bungle a job. You're fearful of losing a big customer. You're fearful so many things will appear on your record, stand against you. You're always fearful of the big mistake. (In Terkel 1974, p. 531)

Closed-Sector Career Paths

At the beginning of a career, closed-sector career path evaluations take place within subunits of the organization. As one starts a career, the relevant evaluator is the immediate hierarchical supervisor. As one's chances improve, and after a few promotions, the alternatives for future mobility become more restricted while the number of significant evaluators increases. To be promoted from sales manager to vice president for operations in Company X means that six or eight division heads have to agree not to oppose the appointment; the board, the president, and two other vice presidents have to agree to it. The significant evaluators include not only the person who has to make the final decision but all those whose opposition to the promotion might jeopardize it. The more important the position is in terms of the number of individuals affected by it, the larger the number of significant evaluators. Therefore, the more one advances in a closed career path, the more difficult it becomes to make the next progression upward and the more one becomes cautious and avoids risk.

In closed-sector career paths, the possibility of mobility from one organization to another decreases the longer one is identified with a single organization. Individuals who have served four to six years in one organization and who are still young may be able to move to another organization, but these opportunities tend to become scarcer the higher they move and the longer they stay within one organization. Therefore, such individuals are increasingly concerned about their lack of mobility and their excessive dependence on their position.

One result of this concern is that at the middle level, there is a tendency to maintain friendly relations with members of different organizations in the same sector. Contrary to expectation, there is considerable supportive behavior between members of competing organizations simply because one's competitors are also one's potential employers.

Since the rhetoric prevailing in all organizations is oriented toward innovation, risk-taking, and getting results, the cautious game is one that appears to innovate and appears to take risks, but really focuses on preserving the status quo. Perhaps a few errors are permitted, but not many. The strategy consists of looking good and conforming:

> A New York management expert says that he would never promote into a top-level job a man who is not making mistakes — and big ones at that. "Otherwise, he is sure to be mediocre." (Proxy 1969, p. 65)

In politics, as in surgery, a big mistake can be fatal. But in a fast moving, modern corporation, mistakes are inevitable. It's the number and frequency that makes differences on balance sheets. (Horn 1964, p. 88)

Can a business maverick survive in today's modern corporate structure? In a large company, the answer is yes but only at the relatively low levels of the management structure. The minute the business maverick reaches middle or top management, his jealous associates cut him down as a trouble-making non-conformist. (Lund 1973, p. 109)

1. You decide what is is you want to find out from this meeting and what you want to impart during it.
2. You decide what it is you want to press hard for.
3. You know the impression you want to create.
4. You know the particular problem you want to get solved.
5. You try to anticipate what most of the others in the meeting will do and say and how they will react. (Edgett 1972, pp. 199–200)

These statements suggest that in closed-sector paths, the growth of one's organization is the stimulator of one's career progression. This process is particularly clear in new organizations, in which being at the right place at the right time can lead to greatly expanded role responsibility as the organization expands. Thus, the incentive for organizational spread and domination is also related to its resulting impact on the careers of middle and top echelon personnel.

Open-Sector Career Paths

Open-sector career path evaluations are recognized as taking place both in one's organization and in other organizations. To the extent that outside evaluations are important, they include both the individual's performance and the performance of the organization. While in closed-sector career development one is not too concerned with the way one's organization is perceived, such perceptions are important in open-sector career assessment.

The principal strategy consists of "being seen," of finding a way to do things that capture the imagination and attract attention to one's name. Open-sector career paths mean that individuals are less concerned with overall task performance and more with the way their organization — more specifically, *some aspect* of their organization — is perceived by significant outside evaluators. Inside evaluators, and clients, are of little relevance as long as outside evaluators think that "something interesting is going on."

Individuals in open-sector career paths do not disregard inside evaluations. It is not as easy to move from one organization to another if one is forced to move. Successful pursuit from the outside frequently depends on one's ability to wait. Therefore, inside evaluations must at least be positive. For this reason, individuals in this situation tend to be as conservative and cautious as their colleagues pursuing closed-sector career paths, *except* in a single narrow topic area where they pursue the limelight.

If accountability is the fashion, they will support accountability and seek to make accountability "the thing." If community participation is fashionable, they will attempt to be known as people who know how to make community participation work. If these individuals are talented, they will invent new approaches; they will be real innovators. If they are mediocre, they will only *seem* to invent.

The advantage of appearing to invent is that little change occurs. Such inertia has a double benefit. For some outsiders, you appear to be an innovator, and this is an advantage. For those in the know, however, you are really conservative, but you know how to appear to be innovative, and this duplicity may be a second advantage. Therefore, this mediocre approach tends to prevail. A copy chief reports:

> There is a kind of cool paradox in advertising. There's a pressure toward the safe, tried and true that has worked in the past. But there's a tremendous need in the agency business for the fresh and the new, to differentiate this one agency from another. Writers are constantly torn between these two goals: selling the product and selling themselves. (In Terkel 1974, p. 117)

Open-sector career paths mean one is more concerned with how one is perceived by people in the organizations one wants to move toward than with one's immediate co-workers and clients. A city manager in a small town, aspiring to move to a larger town, pursues policies and earns a reputation for handling those aspects of small-town problems that are more akin to the problems of the larger towns where he hopes to be in five years' time. He is grooming for his next assignment. He wants his work in his present assignment to look good to those who will hire him later. He does not really care about his present clientele. If the clientele belongs to one class (the poor) and the significant evaluators to another (upper middle class), we can expect him to be more attentive to the class to which the evaluators belong.

Open-sector paths also mean that one is more concerned with public relations than with task performance: even if the clientele is aware that the service is terrible, that the morale of the staff is collapsing, that the place is in disrepair, the public relations of the organization will continue imperturbably as if nothing were amiss. The rosy messages sent out are intended for people other than the clientele, for people who are unlikely to find out what is actually happening.

Location-Dominated Career Paths

Individuals pursuing a location-dominated career path reject the traditional definitions of success and focus on location or other characteristics of employment. They are less concerned with status and prestige and more with the quality of life in different locations, including the characteristics of the job itself. Yet status and quality of life tend to converge. The more desirable locations gradually attract the best talent because everyone wishes to move there, so that these locations tend, ultimately, to have the higher-status schools or hospitals, or whatever.

Location-dominated career paths have been labeled "touristry" (Pape 1964). Members of organizations move from city to city or from country to country to experience different life styles and pleasures. "Moving around" is the desirable pattern. Status is not an important consideration, although even such nomadic patterns tend to select desirable locations where opportunities exist for enjoying whatever it is that can be enjoyed: "'Living is Fun in Southern California!' and 'X Hospital means the center of things and the best of everything for you! . . . more satisfaction in work and at play than you ever dreamed possible'" (advertisements quoted in Pape 1964, p. 390).

People in these career paths avoid commitment to the organization since they intend to depart. They do not wish to become indispensable since there might be pressure to retain them. They might even receive a raise! So they perform their work adequately; they do not want to be pushed out; they want to leave in good order with recommendations and a positive record, but they try to keep a low profile so that there will not be a scene when they suddenly announce that they are leaving for a job in Tokyo or a trip around the world. They use friends who have already moved or who know someone who can advise them about possible openings. In some cases, job negotiations take place before moving; or one moves first, lives with friends, and finds employment once there.

These members of organizations do not innovate and do not take risks. They are pleasant and friendly. They come and go.

Output Measures as Evaluation Insurance

Output measures serve as evaluation insurance. When evaluators and criteria of evaluation are unknown, output measures are used to demonstrate performance. But different output measures can be used by different evaluators, thus causing confusion for those being evaluated. For example, legislative bodies wanting to control an agency may focus on one kind of performance evaluation while members of the agency may focus on another, thus placing the management of the agency in a conflict between the legislature and the professionals. Such conflicts are common in universities where funding agencies may be concerned with such measures as teacher-student contact hours and output of Ph.D.'s per year while the faculty evaluates itself on the basis of the quality and volume of its publications.

Nevertheless, while there may be some dispute about what output measures are relevant and should be used, there is a natural tendency for members of organizations to prefer output measures because they remove some uncertainty from evaluations. If it is not clear who is doing the evaluating or what criteria are used, there will be a preference for output measures that can be easily applied to one's own performance. These measures will be one's own outputs or, if one holds a middle-level position, the outputs of one's unit in the organization. This standard greatly limits discretion for cooperation with other parts of the organization and leads to the well-documented practice of non-cooperative bureaucratic empires having little, if any, relation to other parts of their organization.

It also leads to a narrowing of responsibility. Individuals are more concerned with the consequences of their acts during the period when they believe they are evaluated than with longer-term consequences which will not show up in the output measures. In many organizations, cost-cutting is a visible output easily attributable to the unit achieving it. Increasing productivity can be achieved by reducing costs per unit, and increases in productivity are a central concern of all modern organizations.

If there are no known ways to change a process or if change cannot be implemented because internal conditions are not amenable to change, it will not be possible to reduce costs through an increase in productivity. Therefore, one might be evaluated unfavorably even though one had no good way to act differently. A normal strategy in such cases would attempt to reduce costs without altering productivity. This alternative means reducing the quality of the goods or services produced.

The game of using cost reductions to protect one's career leads to mediocre service, particularly when the organization controls supply and clients have no alternative suppliers and so cannot exit. Organizations often produce mediocre products and services, not because clients really prefer mediocrity, but simply because individuals within the organization need to protect themselves, can only look good if they can reduce costs, and therefore reduce costs at the expense of the service as long as consumers do not balk. This practice is evident in universities in times of budget restrictions when cost savings are applied at the expense of the long-term development of the university (such as radical cuts in library budgets resulting in the erosion of acquisitions and even destruction or loss of collections for lack of adequate staff), or at the expense of the immediate productivity of the faculty (a well-known professor at an eastern university who was asked to review this book chose to decline because his secretarial help had been completely eliminated and making comments on the telephone was too difficult).

Rules as Evaluation Insurance

When output measures are unavailable or when it is not known how a different course of action might lead to different measures, members of organizations use the rules of the organization to justify and protect their behavior.

Suppose we have a department head in a large bureaucracy — a ministry in Ruritania. This person has no idea about how things are going to work out in the coming three years; there is conflict among the clients of her department; the politics are unclear; great energy is spent by eight different factions attempting to push the department in different directions. The top administration of the ministry is unpredictable; most of the directors and the minister have just been appointed. It is not clear how the president thinks, if he thinks at all, or how the department head perceives her evaluators or their criteria for evaluation.

Obviously, there are no guidelines to follow, and whatever this individual does will result in unknown outcomes. The individual does not have a clear basis for choice. It is not possible to relate actions to desirable evaluation results. What is left? When outcomes cannot be predicted, rules are used as protection: "When in doubt, be sure to be clear; follow the rules."

The more the environment is uncertain and the more it is difficult to predict outcomes, the more there is need for process rules to protect individual role performances, and the more rules will be established for this purpose. In addition, the more that rules are used to protect individual behavior, the more need for documented evidence; that is, the more bureaucrats produce forms, reports, accounts, and other written (or taped) documents. These are the defensive histories used to legitimate actions. In other words, when the environment is uncertain and the organization needs to be flexible, the members of the organization pursue defensive strategies that have exactly opposite consequences. They establish a barricade of rules which rigidifies performance and guarantees that service will be that much poorer than otherwise.

The Game of Risk Avoidance

Taking risks results in positive evaluation *only* if the outcome is successful — that is, if the risk solves the problem at hand. Any innovation that fails implies bad judgment by the innovator, who is implicitly criticizing what was done previously.

Even if the outcome is successful, evaluators may react negatively. Any innovation that succeeds implies that the innovator exercised bad judgment by pushing herself too much; the innovator also exercised bad judgment in threatening others less successful than herself.

Not taking risks implies that the non-innovator feels that past procedures were correct, that past evaluations were reasonable. The non-innovator presents no threat to anyone. It is safe to evaluate such a person positively. Not taking risks means that the service continues to be mediocre, as it has been in the past, but at least it is predictable. No innovation also means that there is no need to keep trying to innovate, because there is no better way to provide service.

For these reasons, risks are taken only when past procedures are clearly inapplicable. For example, when the organization is in crisis, introducing innovations is not perceived as criticism of the old ways, especially when continuing in the old ways is perceived as too risky.

Risks are taken only when the situation has clearly changed and it is apparent that risks must be taken. But most individuals in organizations are not ready even for these risks. As far as possible, therefore, they attempt to avoid recognizing this condition. By contrast, however, the rhetoric of organizations emphasizes risk-taking. Therefore, there is a tendency for individuals in organizations to *appear* to be taking risks and to invent false risks.

In government, high-level appointments are made for political reasons and are usually of short duration. One is appointed Secretary or Assistant Secretary for an unknown term and is dismissed at discretion. High-level government appointees want and need to "make a difference" either because it is possible to make a difference (this is exercise of personal power and is most satisfying to the ego), or because their high ambitions in open career paths require them to be highly visible. In these situations, risk-taking is part of the reward system and is an accepted way of life. Since dismissal or forced resignation is always possible, there is little time to act. Risks have to be taken immediately; there is a great hurry to bring about changes and innovations. It is no surprise that large government bureaucracies are continually being reorganized or announcing major new programs.

In contrast, the majority of individuals in the organization are part of the permanent hierarchy. They pursue closed career paths within the civil service and respond to a perceived reward system that deters risk-taking. It makes no sense for low- or middle-level bureaucrats to stick their necks out. Their aim is to remain quiet, to follow instructions, to stick to the rules.

This dichotomy is the basis for conflict. Individuals on the lower levels of the organization clearly perceive these differences. But they have to seek support outside the organization if they are to resist their hierarchical supervisors. To accomplish this goal, the public administration often reveals its conflict outside the organization where other arbitrators are available. Allies are sought in the permanent staffs of other departments or in the legislative bodies charged with the overall control of each agency. When allies are unavailable, the bureaucrats turn to the general public and leak stories to the press. Sooner or later, the ambitious masters realize the power of their minions, and the major reforms become small changes which may not be any reform at all.

Sending Risks Upstairs

Low- or middle-level bureaucrats prefer to send risky decisions upstairs. The top echelon — in government or private service — wants power, is anxious to intervene where it can be seen, and invites the upward flow of decisions. The top echelon may require the lower levels to channel all controversial decisions upward, particularly if it mistrusts its troops. But the top echelon receives more messages and is forced to deal with more issues than it can possibly handle. It therefore cannot spend as much time as it should on those decisions that are best taken at the top. The top echelon panics and decides to avoid risks. Big reforms become small adjustments, which may not be any change at all.

Inventing False Risks

Lower and middle levels respond positively to any suggestions from above that *appear* to be major innovations but do not alter any fundamental aspect of the way things are done. Since upper echelons are anxious to seek the limelight, since the easiest innovations they can introduce — that is, the innovations that the lower and middle levels will readily endorse — are those that are mostly appearance and little reality, it follows that most administrative reforms follow particular fads which provide legitimacy without affecting procedures.

When there is a change in the administration and a new government takes control, many of the new approaches of the previous administration are quickly forgotten; the new administration returns to normal before embarking on another set of innovations. The rapidity of these swings is well documented. For example, a study of the 1965 reform of the administrative unit of the Department of State showed that as soon as the Undersecretary of State for Administration resigned, his reforms were abolished:

> Hence, within nine months of Crockett's departure, every experimental program in the former Office of Management Planning had been eliminated, eviscerated or totally redirected. MOP (Management by Objectives and Programs) had been mopped. (Warwick 1975, p. 55)

Excessive Coordination

As we saw in the last chapter, one function of coordination is to facilitate organizational spread. Another function is to protect members of organizations by providing a formal *sharing* of the responsibility for any decision. Coordination also has the advantage of creating the appearance that the house is in good order, that duplication is avoided and redundancy eliminated. But attempts at coordination do not alter the fact that most large organizations are composed of many independent empires that do not allow effective coordination to take place. Therefore much apparent coordination is not concerned with the rationalization of service but with providing protection for the members of organizations. We call it excessive coordination.

Excessive coordination is achieved through three processes: (1) lateral coordination via clearances; (2) lateral coordination via intra- or inter-committee work; and (3) hierarchical coordination. Two of these processes (committee work and hierarchical coordination) also serve other functions, such as providing visibility and mobility for middle-level staff (open career) and providing opportunities for defensive coalitions against top echelons and for hierarchical visibility (closed career).

Coordination procedures are rules that provide (2) documentation and (1) evidence of shared responsibility. If and when risks are taken, they are not taken by a single position-holder but by a long series of endorsers who agree to a decision and sign a document. This document becomes part of the evidence that is used to legitimate errors.

The more uncertain the environment, the more need there is for risk-sharing. This situation, in turn, reduces the extent of discretion and simultaneously creates a need for an increase in coordination procedures. But coordination takes time. Therefore, the more uncertain the environment, the more the organization is sluggish and slow to respond.

The Warwick study of the Department of State highlights the high costs of coordination, the long lead times involved, the inability to respond to rapid changes, the opportunity for conflicts, and clogging up of channels of communication, and even the high costs of message transmission. It points out that in 1967, State handled about 45,000 cables a day, leased 100 overseas teletype lines, dealt with 300 international telephone calls a day, and processed about 20 million pieces of mail a year (Warwick 1975, p. 117). The pressure to centralize coordination means that the top echelons are overburdened both by the need to know (centers of responsibility are displaced upward) and by the need to be sure that they cannot be criticized because of an apparent failure in coordination (the cost of the ideology of coordination).

> The combination of a heavy message volume, a high degree of centralization, and tight security procedures . . . sets the stage for the elongation of hierarchy and the proliferation of rules. . . . The result is a massive clogging at the upper levels. (Warwick 1975, p. 123)

Interestingly, the ideology of coordination is never questioned. It is argued that government agencies must be coordinated because they cannot pursue contradictory policies and that foreign governments cannot deal with the U.S. government if it makes contradictory statements. But these assertions do not take into account the costs of coordination. Governments can deal with ambiguous or contradictory policy statements just as well as any other organization, as was the case during the Cuban missile crisis when the Soviet leader, Khrushchev, sent several contradictory statements and President Kennedy chose to ignore some and act on those that suited U.S. objectives.

We find therefore that when the environment is highly uncertain, organizations invent complex means of sharing responsibility among many members to reduce the possibility that any single individual might be blamed for errors.

Documented Histories

Documented histories, as the name implies, are written or otherwise preserved documents that serve to protect individuals. Rules generate forms that confirm performance. Thus, individuals can document that they follow the rules; coordination clearance procedures provide documented histories. Coordinating committees write reports and memos providing proof of past individual behavior.

Documented histories are circulated to improve their defensive usefulness: "How can you blame us now? You knew all along what we were doing; your office was kept informed of every decision; we sent your office copies of all our internal memoranda and of our correspondence." Copies of documents are sent out "for information" or "for initial clearance." Instructions are requested in writing. "We would appreciate if your office would confirm these instructions in writing."

Documented histories are the assets of a bureaucracy in fear. Files are jealously kept up to date. Even when conversations are not confirmed in writing, it is common practice to immediately dictate a memorandum for the file which can be used later as proof of one's original understanding. Most senior officials use a secretary to transcribe telephone conversations in shorthand, and the practice of taping conversations received much publicity during the administration of President Nixon.

A well-documented history can be used as both a defensive and an offensive weapon when difficulties arise. Therefore, all parties attempt to build histories that justify their actions. Since documented histories are used to share risks, bureaucrats resist becoming implicated in the documented histories of other departments or individuals. Officials who receive copies of decisions made elsewhere which they are supposed to clear or even concur in, defend themselves by suggesting changes, asking for additional information, or sending different points of view. One purpose is to show that the concurring unit never really approved the move. Another is to discourage others from involving one's unit in risk-taking.

Coordination meetings illustrate these processes. If several departments have to agree before a decision is taken, the originating unit seeks endorsements in order to share the risks with "others." But the "others" seek to avoid responsibility. They lengthen the decision-making process and avoid participating in the discussions in order to protect themselves from future involvement. They insist on the most minute documentation from the originating unit to justify their own participation. "We asked them to document their arguments, which they did, and we were reasonably satisfied that we could proceed."

These bureaucratic processes easily become intolerable, and for this reason informal exchanges emerge: "I'll gladly give you a clearance for this, but give me a clearance for that." As a result, mutual trust emerges gradually. If and when trouble arises, elegant performances are appreciated. People who stand on their own feet and are not unreasonable in placing blame elsewhere acquire a reputation for "playing the game fairly." They become trusted members of the organization and acquire the ability to transact business. Trust is built gradually over the length of bureaucratic careers, and it is central to bureaucratic survival.

But trust is easily lost. When personal careers are at stake — when the issues are highly controversial — it is difficult for any one to be sure that others will behave elegantly. The card castle collapses as everyone attempts to protect his own interests. Accusations fly into the open; the scandal is leaked outside the organization, and trust evaporates. The organization is in crisis.

Doing Nothing

Many persons in large organizations pursue a simple strategy: do nothing. Doing nothing is relatively safe because it is noncontroversial.

Doing nothing is not as easy as it sounds, because organizational roles have discretion; there are decisions to make; decisions are opportunities for controversy, and controversy can lead to negative evaluations. Moreover, the ideology of the organization calls for active innovations.

Doing nothing, while appearing to act, is accomplished as follows:

— By greatly complicating the sequences of clearances, reviews, and reporting, so that considerable energy is spent by anyone attempting to do something within the organization. Careful procedures are established to guarantee that every attention is paid to make the new venture succeed. Proposals for new efforts are scrutinized indefinitely until their timeliness is past.

— By starting small pilot projects that dissipate the energy of the innovators without committing anyone. Once the pilot project is completed, other pilot projects are initiated.

— By encouraging competitive proposals for innovations from different portions of the organization and letting the innovators spend their energies competing against each other.

— By introducing outside experts who are asked to assist in

redesigning projects. The internal innovators enter into competition with the outside group. They spend their energies against each other.

— By initiating a major review of existing activities and a massive reorganization. During the period of internal insecurity, when reorganization is under way, all new programs are postponed.

* *
*

six

Corruption

Corruption has both legal and organizational definitions. In this chapter we discuss varieties of corruption, its so-called positive functions, and its impact on planning, on output measures, on centralization, and on equity.

Corruption takes place in every organization, yet little is written about it. Obviously, documentation is difficult to obtain except when corruption is revealed in newspapers, autobiographies, or courtrooms. Most current texts in the sociology of organizations do not mention the word. One has to turn to historical studies of reforms in public administration — for example, the creation of the Federal Civil Service Commission through the passage and approval of the Pendleton Bill in 1883 — to remind oneself that bureaucratic corruption was also a concern of theorists and reformers (Foulke 1919, Lee 1960); or to the literature on government, particularly that about city government and agencies, where corruption is discussed extensively (Appleby 1952; Banfield and Wilson 1963; Gardiner and Olson 1974; Heidenheimer 1970; Sherman 1974; Zink 1930); or to the literature on organized crime (Gardiner 1970; Kefauver 1951; Landesco

1968; President's Commission on Law Enforcement and Administration of Justice 1967; Tyler 1962); or to the literature on corruption in the bureaucracies of developing countries (Bayley 1966; Braibanti 1962; McMullan 1961; Nye 1967; Scott 1969, 1972; Wraith and Simkin 1963); or, lastly, to the somewhat scarce sociological literature on corrupt power (Brasz 1963).

Some Definitions of Corruption

Discretionary corruption is any act which, while appearing to be legal, is nevertheless not generally accepted practice among members of the organization. For example, doing a favor for a friend who is a client without appearing to do it; giving a new appointment to a white rather than a black on the false grounds that the white person appears to be better qualified. No rule is overtly broken, and therefore risk is reduced. This kind of corruption is hard to correct because it is difficult, if not impossible, to document that it is taking place.

Illegal corruption, as the name implies, is any act that violates the language or intent of the law, regulation, or rule. There is an implicit risk in the performance of the act. This kind of corruption may be effective, but it is also more amenable to control. It requires secrecy for its performance.

Mercenary corruption is any corrupt act for personal gain. It involves bribery. It is the misuse of power and authority for gains which need not be only monetary (Bayley 1966, p. 720; Brasz 1963, pp. 111–12). Mercenary corruption can be either discretionary or illegal; for example, hiring a paramour on one's staff or accepting a cash payment in return for a government contract.

Ideological corruption is any discretionary or illegal act pursued for fomenting the goals of a group. The Watergate episode under the Nixon administration was carried out by individuals who placed their ideological commitment to their President above the law.

Changing norms of corruption reflects the idea that what is considered corrupt now may not always have been so. Today, public officials are not supposed to use their positions for private advantage. In the seventeenth century, however, it was common in France for the Crown to sell public offices which could be used as one would use any other property.

"In the know" refers to those who know how corruption is practiced: knowing when and how bribery is expected and is to be paid. Usually mercenary corruption is the least publicized; that is, those in the know tend to be those who have to transact business, but the rest of the public is kept in the dark. Ideological corruption is usually known and is discussed freely in the organization: "Of course, X was not promoted; they think he is too leftish, and they do not like his ideas."

So-called "Positive Functions" of Corruption

Corruption generates sectors of efficient service within inefficient organizations; it therefore serves as a "model" for other individuals in the organizations. When some members of an organization can be bribed, they deliver the services by cutting red tape; they are more effective than other sectors of the organization.

Corruption indicates a real need and commitment on the part of clients who bribe. These clients really want the services since they are willing to pay extra for them. The corrupt individual may argue that this need should be recognized in one way or another.

Corruption is a way to make sick bureaucracies work. It is a return to the free play of market mechanisms. It provides the necessary incentives for risk-taking. It transforms dull bureaucrats into new Schumpeterian enterpreneurs.

Corruption humanizes the bureaucracy. It permits individual treatment and attention. Rules and regulations do not think; people think and act. Corruption liberates the bureaucracy from rules and regulations.

Corruption provides strong informal links between members of organizations and some of their clients. As such, it is an additional system of control that keeps organizations and clients relating to each other.

Corruption reduces conflict in the political system. Since one can buy one's way, one does not have to use the political system or generate conflict to achieve one's aims. Given the fact that those who are wealthy and powerful prefer to let the laws stand as they are, it is easier simply to sidestep an inconvenient law. Otherwise, the powerful might seek to change the laws, possibly generating conflict and threatening existing social institutions.

Corruption and Planning

Large-scale corruption in government means that any plan, any agreement about the future, is subject to constant alteration since bribery always takes place. Moreover, it is not the actual act of bribery that matters but the potential of bribery. As we saw in previous chapters, the success of a planning exercise that is not trivial or utopian depends on shared beliefs about the future. It is this trust about the course of action agreed upon by the implementers that leads others to climb on the bandwagon and permits the multiplier effect to operate. If it is well known that the implementers can be bribed, many planning exercises will fail. At best they become utopian, at worst trivial; they provide legitimation for corrupt acts.

Belief in the prevalence of corruption in government is widespread. It has grown in the United States to the point where 34.5 percent of the population in 1973 thought that a lot of people running the government were a little crooked (against 23.4 percent in 1958); 43.1 percent thought not many were crooked, but only 18.2 percent were willing to state that hardly any were crooked (Katz et al. 1975, p. 148).

Social systems that succeed in planning tend to be those that have made extensive efforts to wipe out corruption in public service. This is the case in the Soviet Union, China, and other socialist countries.

One might argue that corruption should not be a real problem for planning. After all, the existence of a well-disciplined, corrupt underground organization that is known to exist could be used by planners to create a strong belief that the plan will be implemented once this secret organization has let it be known that the plan fits its own interests and is supporting it.

In fact, there are many interests and many secret mercenary or ideological organizations, and there are many divergent groups "in the know." Interest aggregation among these groups is rarely possible, not to mention that most planners might find such an effort undesirable.

While planning is not helped by corruption, planning contributes to it. Suppose, for example, that planners let it be known beforehand that they intend to downgrade highway construction in favor of railroads. Such a policy would affect competing contractors and other interested parties. If those who want highways bribe planners, the policy can be re-examined — at least until the bribes are received from railroad interests, and the plan is finally published.

Planning economic development investments provides another opportunity for corruption. It is more difficult to collect bribes on routine payments such as salaries of civil servants who "buy" their appointments than it is to collect a percentage of a single large contract. Development expenditures for infrastructure investments are more vulnerable to corrupt practices than routine recurrent expenditures which tend to be controlled over time.

To maximize corrupt profit-making in infrastructure investments, it is preferable to collect bribes and not complete projects. Thus, this kind of maximization of corruption leads to "white elephants" that are never completed. The planners announce a white elephant project, bids are sent out, bribes are collected, the project is initiated, and when the contractor has earned the bribe, the project is abandoned. Another common practice is to initiate many more projects than can be handled. For example, a city administration often initiates more street-paving projects than it can finance. Bribes are collected. Later, the street will be torn up for months, users will complain, and other projects that are not subject to bribery will be cut back.

We find, therefore, that effective planning is eroded by corruption, while trivial or utopian planning contributes to it.

Corruption and Output Measures

"My school director just told me that if I want to keep my job, I better make sure our scores [on a standardized national test of school achievements] look good."

Corruption of output measures is common. For example, when grant monies are related to the needs of low achievers in public schools, it may be preferable to show that remedial programs are having some success, but are not having too much success, since continued funding is predicated on a need, and success means the end of funding. When standardized tests are used, agencies (schools, hospitals, etc.) seek to score slightly lower or higher than the median. If one scores very high, one is implicitly providing "too good" a service, and it is difficult to request budget increases based on need to improve quality of service. If one scores very low, the service is bad, and it is debatable whether the program is having any effect. But since it is difficult to know exactly how one will be scoring in relation to others when tests are first administered, the original tests tend not to be manipulated. Once experience is acquired, manipulation is initiated and scores tend toward the median, thus reducing the standard deviation of the distribution of scores. It follows from this that it is possible to develop a rough indication of the extent to which manipulations of scores take place.

Corruption of output measures distorts the information that such measures could provide. Once it is clear that evaluations can be corrupted, doubt about their policy implications arises.

The clients who take tests — for example, the children being tested on reading ability — perceive weakness in the procedures and also come to suspect corruption: "How can one tell if we know since one can guess an answer even if one does not know?" Obviously, test designs take into account the probability that guessing occurs, and in the aggregate, this effect is not significant. But clients do not understand the subtleties of statistics, and the result is that fear of corruption raises doubts about the usefulness of this kind of endeavor: "Why do they give these tests and never tell us what we did wrong?"

Corruption and Centralization

The "in the know" group is an organization within the organization. When several "in the know" groups exist, they compete secretly against each other.

The reason centralization reduces corruption in the periphery is that the center cannot afford to relinquish its control of the periphery to secondary secret societies. If too much corruption is allowed, the representatives of the center will be unable to exercise control, and the local secret societies will become the effective centers of power. The creation of European public civil services and the abolition of the Crown's practice of selling appointments were brought about by this need.

As long as a public office could be bought and exploited as an investment, those buying such appointments were free to raise funds in accordance with the privileges of the office. Public civil service based on meritocracy radically changed the situation. The center defined the scope of discretion and socialized an elite corps to behave according to well-established norms. Thus the center could be sure that its officers would behave as instructed and would not yield to corruption. Control shifted from the periphery to the center.

Corruption may lead to centralization. Since corruption in many instances is a human reaction that results from face-to-face relations, centralization shields individuals from their personal reactions: "I only wish I could help you, but the main office won't let me . . ." Therefore, the clamor for reducing corruption has an unforeseen consequence; it leads to a centralized hierarchy which reduces corruption in the periphery and transfers it to the center.

Second, centralized corruption benefits from economies of scale. Whereas in the periphery it takes considerable effort for a small-time chiseler to collect a percentage of public-employee paychecks, at the center a discreet phone call can channel a large contract in a desirable direction.

Third, large-scale corruption at the center by secret societies means that these societies are not going to allow competing secret societies to exist on the periphery. The more efficient secret societies at the center absorb their competitors on the periphery to ensure coordination of action when bribes on large-scale projects involve both central and local interests.

Lastly, independent secret societies on the periphery need protection from the central interventions of the government. This is particularly true when the center has authority to investigate the performance of independent units of government on the periphery. For example, this pattern is manifested in the regime of *tutelle* in France, where certain central agencies examine the budgets and accounts of elected or appointed bodies responsible for the communes (the equivalent of the American county). Therefore, corruption leads to centralization and vice versa.

Corruption and Efforts to Abolish It

Start with some corruption. Institute rules to control and eliminate it. These rules then become a source of new corruption: "It used to cost about $1,000, but now we also have to pay the inspector from the Ministry. It means $2,000 each time he comes."

Corruption is eliminated when the controllers charged to eliminate it cannot be corrupted. This situation only happens when a sufficient ideological and/or professional commitment exists. The center can eliminate corruption on the periphery. Then it can be eliminated at the center by using two sources of power: (1) an elite at the center whose career paths cannot afford to be tainted in any way; and (2) the demands of the periphery for a cleanup at the center.

The key to the elimination of corruption is the existence of elite corps who are not amenable to manipulation. These elite corps must have status and rewards, and must occupy positions that are well protected: members must not be vulnerable to attacks from those they are supposed to supervise.

In the United States at present this function is poorly met. The sources of remedy are various, dispersed, and relatively inefficient. Consumer movements, the legislative and judicial branches, and the news media combine to create a force for corruption reform. The judicial branch and to a lesser extent the legislative branch and the news media are composed of members at the center whose career paths are relatively more immune than those of civil servants within the administration. Consumer movements are the overt demands of the periphery for reform. But these institutions seem insufficient to the needs of the times.

Corruption and Equity

If everyone knows about corrupt practices and has equal access
to them, and if everyone practices them, these corrupt practices
are equitable and, in time, will no longer seem to be corrupt.
Bribing becomes tipping. But until then, corruption is not practiced by everyone, and therefore is not equitable. There are those
"in the know" and those not in the know. More important, there
are those who are keenly aware that differentiated service is available, but who cannot afford the extra fees involved.

A shared notion of equity is central to the maintenance of
organizational life. Perceptions of unfairness, unjust favoritism,
and unjust differentiation are fundamental sources of organizational alienation. These perceptions arise directly from perceived
differences between the normative ideology of the organization
and actual practices. The more actual practices depart from a
normative ideology, the more individuals may disrespect the
organization. For those "in the know," the organization ideology
is pure sham, and anyone who believes it is naive or immature:
"Sure, these guys talk as if they believe it, but either you know
better or you're lost here." Those who are not part of the secret
society either know nothing about it — but are bound to notice
inexplicable irregularities — or, more likely, suspect something
unusual is going on. Their suspicions may be realistic: "For those
who can pay, it is always possible to arrange things"; or they may
be out of touch with reality: "The entire department is controlled
by Jews and Communists." The net effect is to alienate members
of the organization.

Such alienation leads to radicalism. As long as equity issues are
amenable to political give-and-take in a system that responds to
emergent values, social changes are possible. But corruption is, by
definition, secret and not amenable to open negotiations. The
alternative is confrontation: "If 'they' break the laws, 'we' can
break them also." The mercenary secret society generates the
ideological secret society. Conflict emerges, and the organization
is further weakened.

As the situation becomes intolerable, norms of behavior within
the organization deteriorate further: "If everyone is doing it, I

might as well." The level of uncertainty rises. Service is inadequate; salaries are not paid; contracts are given away; morale is down; fear mounts as everyone suspects that sooner or later matters will come to a head. As the scandal becomes public knowledge, the clamor for reform mounts. Those who have milked the organization are first to call for an end to practices they originally encouraged. Scapegoats are found and placed in the limelight. Minor reforms are instituted. The secret society lies low and awaits better times.

* *
*

part two

Current Remedies

seven

Organization Development and Participation

Organization development, or OD for short, and participation, or organizational democracy, are recent responses to the crisis encountered by organizations.

OD is concerned with the well-being of people inside the organization. The OD movement has a strong commitment to systematic, rational thinking designed to adapt work situations to human dimensions. It is also committed to designing organizations that are flexible and easily adaptable to changing needs of clients.

Participation is the attempt to limit hierarchical barriers within organizations and to open decision-making to all interested parties. The organizational participation movement is committed to giving a greater management voice (1) to workers and other members of organizations and (2) to clients and the community at large.

Organization Development (OD)

In 1960, Douglas McGregor published *The Human Side of Enterprise*, a book that reflects postwar thinking about organizations

(McGregor 1960). Using somewhat mysterious categories — he called his new approach "Theory Y" and conventional wisdom "Theory X" — McGregor presented a human view of the organization.

Theory X, McGregor argued, evolved from a set of assumptions about human nature which were misleading and, therefore, ineffective. These assumptions were:

— that human beings, on the average, dislike work;

— that they have to be coerced to work;

— that they prefer to be directed; they wish to avoid responsibility; they have little ambition and want security above all (pp. 33–34).

Once you make these assumptions, McGregor said, you inevitably invent means of control that take them into account. Therefore, Theory X means that individuals are coerced by an organizational control system based on individual rewards and punishments. The carrot and the stick are used to align individual performance with organizational purposes.

In contrast, Theory Y is based on different assumptions:

— Human beings really like and need to work to express themselves. Therefore, their best response does not result from fear; they will exercise self-direction and self-control if they are personally committed.

— They will be personally committed if they receive ego satisfaction and can pursue self-actualization *at the same time* that they pursue organizational goals. In other words, they receive personal satisfaction if they have internalized the organizational goals.

— They like responsibility; they can exercise high degrees of imagination, creativity — in short, there is an excess human capability which is not used if individuals are not committed to the task (pp. 47–48).

Once Theory Y is understood, it is possible to transform the entire organization, to make it more flexible, more adaptable, more creative, and more quality-conscious. In short, it is possible to create organizations that are adaptable to an uncertain environment. McGregor's book typifies the ideas of the OD movement.

Feedback

A central idea of OD is feedback. Feedback involves providing information to participants about the way they act and about the way they are perceived by others so that they can learn, adapt, and modify their behavior. Feedback takes place in meetings of two or more individuals who have the opportunity of learning how others perceive them.

The concept of group feedback originates in the work of Jacob L. Moreno, the inventor of psychodrama and role-playing. Starting in 1919 in Vienna and coming in 1925 to the United States, psychodrama and the spontaneity theater use groups and action for therapeutic purposes (Moreno 1964, pp. 1–20). Moreno would have the patient interact with actors who represent significant absent persons as well as the therapist. The idea was to have the patient re-enact, spontaneously, past events that continued to cause anxiety. Feedback takes place during this creative re-enactment, and the patient perceives what is causing anxiety.

The possibility of using feedback to train members of organizations was discovered somewhat accidentally by Kurt Lewin. Lewin and co-workers held a summer workshop in human relations in 1946, at which the staff observed and recorded a group of participants. After the observations, the staff would discuss the raw data at a meeting unattended by the participants. One day, the participants asked to listen to the discussion. At first, Lewin and the staff were reluctant, then agreed. The participants who joined reacted with interest. The striking experience for them, and for everyone, was a heightened level of self-awareness. Thus, the first T groups — or sensitivity training, or laboratory training — were born. Feedback was discovered to be a powerful learning experience (McGill 1974, p. 99).

In the late forties and fifties, considerable research on the dynamics of small groups was undertaken by psychologists and sociologists (Cartwright and Zander 1960; Hare, Borgatta, and Bales 1965). This work and its potential applications in organizations led to the creation of the National Training Laboratory (NTL) in Bethel, Maine, and to the widespread use of "laboratory" training for middle- and upper-level personnel in business and government organizations.

At first, training was provided on an individual basis. Typically, an organization would send five or ten managers to a series of week-long training activities where they would discover, through the eyes of others, their own managerial styles. They would see how their behavior was dysfunctional in their relations with co-workers. They would thus acquire "interpersonal skills." T groups and sensitivity training were, and still are, widely used to train middle and senior personnel in organizations. Hundreds of centers appeared with programs running from only two and one half days to as long as three or four weeks, meeting six to eight hours each day (Klaw 1961; Siroka 1971).

Organizations were not the only users of these new training activities. In the sixties and early seventies, the T group, sensitivity training, and encounter group movement flourished. Its uses spread to areas involving family, marriage, sex, race relations, child-rearing, old age adaptation, and adult living communes. Its techniques became more sophisticated; attack therapy, psychodrama, marathons, nude encounters, nonverbal exercises emerged. But its concern remained making individuals better able to work in groups while achieving self-awareness and development.

It became clear that the effect of such training in organizations was limited: several managers spend a short time in a training course in a pleasant site away from the office; upon return to the organization, however, they find the same old problems. Their own self-awareness has improved, but they face colleagues who have not participated in training. They may be enthusiastic at first, but they are rapidly absorbed into the existing situation. They soon return to the old style of doing things. The lesson is that a few managers is not enough. It is necessary to train the entire organization instead of selected individuals: OD was born.

Organization-wide Interventions

There exists a burgeoning literature on OD. Most of this literature was published in the sixties and early seventies (Argyris 1970; Beckhard 1969; Bennis 1969; Blake and Mouton 1964;

Burke 1972; Franklin 1973; French and Bell 1973; Golembiewski 1972; Lippitt 1969; Schmuck et al. 1972; Trist et al. 1963).

What is OD?

First, it is the use of feedback learning to improve the entire organization — or to change important segments of an organization.

Second, it is an attempt to intervene through change agents. The change agents sometimes include members of the organization but, in practice, they are outside experts who work with members of the organization. The experts are usually hired by management, but they may be hired by other parties (say, by labor unions). If the effort is sustained, an OD unit may be established within the organization. Most OD practitioners emphasize the need for management support.

Third, OD interventions are concerned with (1) beliefs, attitudes, and values of individuals or groups; (2) to a lesser extent, with organizational structure — particularly the reward system; and (3) at lower levels, with the relationship of technology to work (e.g., how the technological process can be altered to reduce the alienation of blue-collar workers).

Fourth, OD interventions are oriented to specific needs. The OD intervention originates by letting people in the organization express their concerns. Therefore, OD interventions are as varied as the problems that emerge from individuals in each organization. Since the movement inherits the traditions of group therapy, it seeks to break down mystification and artificiality and encourages individuals to reveal their deeper concerns. The extent to which this is achieved depends, of course, on the strength of the controls that motivate individual behavior. Since OD intervention does not eliminate these controls, there are limits to the possibility of demystification.

Fifth, OD interventions use actual work situations and perceived task needs to resolve conflicts. Once barriers of communication are eliminated, conflicting opinions emerge. A basic assumption of the OD movement is that individuals will resolve conflicts in terms of the real needs of the work situation, as long as no one is hurt in the process. Since OD cannot eliminate conflicts of interest, that is another limit to its success.

Team Building

Team building is used in many OD interventions. How does the change agent select teams to be trained? The formal hierarchical structure is often used since departments or other sub-units of organizations have tasks to accomplish that require coordination of effort — i.e., teamwork. But the hierarchical structure hides other teams that may be more important to the organization. To reveal these teams the change agent analyzes the functions performed. For example, though we may be interested in improving student attendance in a school district, there may not be a "department of attendance" or even a "committee on student attendance." Instead there are a number of relevant individuals who are involved with the problem. Identifying the problem leads to identifying the function. This, in turn, leads to identifying the team. Once the team is identified, it can be trained to improve the members' ability to work together. Membership on teams may cut across the formal organization and across hierarchical levels.

Most of team-building is centered on improving interpersonal skills by establishing mutual trust. How is mutual trust achieved? There are many intervention techniques, but the underlying principles are always the same:

(1) increasing individual sensitivity to the position of others;
(2) attempting to identify barriers to cooperation, and
(3) removing these barriers.

Whether the team is trained in an intensive one-week off-site situation; whether the change agent initiates a long-term series of interventions; whether individuals are lectured at or participate in "fishbowl" arrangements where they are watched — and can watch others — or undertake a systematic review of their tasks, roles, assets, and techniques of decision-making, the main goal is to increase trust and to use trust to expand capability.

In a previous chapter, we discussed how individuals respond to uncertainty by pursuing cautious strategies, avoiding risk, sticking to rules, seeking excessive coordination, and building documented histories. Trust allows individuals to act with others, to take risks. Thus, team-building deals with fundamental symptoms of organizational ills.

Team Linking

OD interventions are also concerned with the relations between teams. Here, change agents use the concept of the "linking pin," which was developed by Rensis Likert (Likert 1967, pp. 156–88). The linking pin idea originates from the assumption that individuals identify with their task groups, particularly if they are rewarded for performance in these task groups. Likert points out that conventional thinking in organization theory says that an individual should have only one superior and should be given orders only by this single person (Likert, p. 159). If one accepts this assumption, the structure of organizations looks like a hierarchical tree. Each position-holder heads a well-defined unit and reports to a single supervisor who, in turn — with others — reports to a single supervisor, and so on, up the hierarchy.

This conventional structure leads to autonomous units which, as we saw in the preceding chapters, jealously pursue their own objectives.

The way out, says Likert, is an overlapping group structure. Individuals are assigned to work groups, but some individuals are assigned to more than one work group, and thus belong to linking groups. Their dual membership (i.e., they may have more than one superior to whom they are reporting) provides a mechanism of integration:

> The individual . . . who is the subordinate under two superiors, can exert upward influence via group decision making processes in both work groups. As a consequence, when one superior . . . and the work group reporting to him approach decisions which are incompatible or in conflict with the point of view held or decisions being arrived at by the other superior . . . and his work group, the individual who is in both work groups is obligated to bring such information to the attention of both work groups. (pp. 160–61)

Likert argues that conflict will have a better chance of resolution because members of the work groups are likely to be members of other linking groups so that, even if a superior tries to disregard such information, there is a common need among all members of linking groups to resolve conflicts: they are concerned about their evaluations. If one is evaluated by two supervisors, one does not wish to be responsible for conflict between them.

The linking-pin structure completes the structure of the formal hierarchy. Integration at the top (when several department heads report to a single individual) is reinforced through organic integration at other levels (through overlapping membership of linking groups).

The OD approach to linking teams uses the same training techniques used for team-building to improve the interpersonal skills of significant groups within the organization. The selection of significant groups depends on the perceived needs.

At one extreme, there are interventions designed to involve the entire organization. One such intervention, called the "confrontation meeting" (Beckhard 1967), is used to involve all levels of an organization to obtain a rapid reading of organizational health and to set action plans for improving it. Other interventions use survey questionnaires and involve all levels of the organization in collecting and analyzing the data.

Partial interventions focus on certain key groups (i.e., individuals in linking roles) or on complementary groups (groups that have to help each other to succeed; for example, a group in marketing and one in advertising dealing with the same product).

Complementary-group interventions usually involve all members of at least two groups. The techniques are similar to those used in team-building except that the procedures take into account the fact that these groups are different and have stereotyped assumptions about each other. Techniques have been developed for groups whose relations are strained (Blake et al. 1965; Fordyce and Weil 1971).

An intervention called the "organization mirror" is often used to process feedback information to a target group from members of many other groups about how they are perceived and understood. The "organizational mirror" provides information to one group (or even a single individual) regarding perceptions in many other parts of the organization. Where the team-linking approach involves all the members of two — or possibly three — groups, the "mirror" involves all the members of the target group and selected representatives of most or all other organizational groups.

Not much work has been done to improve linkage outside the organization, although these techniques can be applied to clients or sponsors. Cost is an obvious deterrent. Most organizations cannot afford to train their clients or their sponsors. But feedback information from the environment can be brought systematically into the organization. The technique of the "organization mirror" can be used externally, using semi-structured interviews or questionnaires (Kirkhart and White 1974).

OD and Uncertainty

OD is concerned with uncertainty — but as a response, not as an attempt to control it. The idea is to design organizations that are flexible, pliable, and capable of responding to rapid change.

The focus of OD interventions is the internal organization, not the environment. When OD uses the word planning, it is referring to the systematization of change within organizations, to the application of social-science knowledge to organizational problems (Bennis et al. 1969).

One reason is that OD emerges from an intellectual tradition with a concern for what is human, organic, emergent, and possible. As such, it views uncertainty as a profound experience. When the movement addresses itself to the problems of alienation in industry, it is concerned with the dysfunctions caused by routinization. Job enlargement attempts to make the tasks of individual workers more varied, thus increasing workers' discretion and responsibility (Friedlander and Brown 1974, pp. 322–23; Steward 1967). At those levels of the organization, it is not only excessive uncertainty that matters but also excessive certainty. Job enrichment goes further and attempts to restructure the technical process — usually, a series of vertically connected tasks into teamwork — to increase the sense of work identification, accomplishment, and responsibility of workers (Burke and Hornstein 1972; Maher 1971). While the results of these interventions may not be clear as yet (Alderfer 1967; Lawler et al. 1973; Paul et al. 1969), the concerns are evident.

Even when OD attacks problems at middle and higher levels,

it still stresses diversity and adaptability. It is, to use OD language, "situational emergent":

> There is a more strictly "here and now" concern with organizational functioning, a belief in the efficacy of working with what *is*, rather than what should be, taking people and situations as they are. (Kirkhart and White 1974, p. 134)

There is an element of romanticism in OD — a hope that, somehow, very different approaches can coexist in the organization, that if we can understand the special ways of individuals, if we can put ourselves in their shoes, conflicts will be resolved.

One obvious limitation of OD is that it has little impact on reducing external uncertainty. In contrast to interorganizational planning, which can reduce external uncertainty, OD is an attempt to make organizations more responsive to change.

OD is concerned with organizational health and with the symptoms of bureaucratic illness, in sharp contrast to the accountability movement which we will discuss in the next chapter. But OD pays too little attention to interorganizational planning and, for that matter, the planning movement pays too little attention to OD. Yet OD and planning are complementary.

One reason for this neglect is the lack of theoretical knowledge about the nature of organizational environment. One stream of current research identifies the characteristics of organizational environments (is the organization part of a larger organization? what influence do suppliers and consumers have? is the organization accountable to any groups? etc.) and the characteristics of the internal structure (routinized or not, degree of centralization, degree of role specialization, autonomy, size, etc.) (Aiken and Hage 1968; Dill 1958; Mindlin and Aldrich 1975; Simpson and Gulley 1962). But there is still considerable debate about the findings (Child 1972; Donaldson et al. 1975; Pugh et al. 1968). It is not yet clear what normative statements can be made about the relations between internal and external environments.

Another stream of research springs from the traditions of political science and conceptualizes complex social systems as aggregates of organizations that form "interorganizational fields" (Turk 1969, 1970; Warren 1967). But its concerns remain, for the moment at least, centered on macro phenomena instead of on smaller units of analysis such as individuals and role categories (Turk 1970, p. 1). This research emphasizes prediction of certain kinds of activities: for example, does knowledge of the organizational characteristics of cities help us predict the level of interorganizational activity in the war on poverty? Again, this research does not, as yet, provide normative statements useful for organizational intervention.

The other reason for the lack of integration, which is far more important, is that OD deals with organizations and not with societies. It does not concern itself with the overall relationships among organizations — even though these relationships are the major causes of organizational uncertainty.

A second weakness of the OD movement is its inability to deal with organizational power, particularly organizational punishments. To use our language, we say that OD cannot address itself to issues of internal uncertainty. Interventions, team-building, and other techniques do not alter the fact that risk-taking is penalized when it fails. OD helps to remove masks and tries to orient members of organizations toward mutual help. But the games individuals play in the organization do not emerge by chance. They are protective devices against internal threats. If an organization discovers serious problems and many employees must be fired, what use is OD, and what happens to trust?

OD is concerned with democratization of the organization and with participation, but it cannot go beyond pious concern. The scope of OD interventions is limited by the position of its practitioners as external agents of change usually hired by management: OD does not threaten management because management can always fire the OD practitioner. We can say that OD eliminates false fears or false uncertainty, but it does not alter the relative power of those who are in conflict or of those who are insecure in the organization.

A third, but temporary, weakness of OD is the lack of attention given to client needs and client uncertainties. Part of the reason for this neglect is that a normal first priority of management is with the organization and not with clients. OD interventions have rarely helped clients in their relations with the organization, yet there is no particular reason why OD techniques cannot be used to expand the perceptions and abilities of clients. Work in this area will probably become more common in the future.

Participation

Participation, as the name implies, is the sharing of power in organizations. The participation movement is closely related to OD, at least in the United States. It is also heavily influenced by recent developments in other countries where, as a result of strong trade-union interventions, legislation is being passed to increase the participation of workers in management. This is particularly true in Western Europe, including Germany — where worker participation on corporate boards already is a fact.

From a conceptual point of view, participation is not limited to worker participation in management. Participation is the exercise of "voice" in the affairs of the organization. The participation movement is concerned with all relevant actors: workers, other employees, clients, and the general public. For example, we find participation efforts to give a larger voice to the community in the management of social institutions — as was the case in New York City in 1969 when a school decentralization law gave new, if limited, powers to community representatives on local school boards (Fantini and Gittell 1973; Gittell et al. 1973; Zimet 1973).

We have efforts oriented to the members of organizations: for example, there is the Scanlon plan, conceived in the forties, which consists of workers participating in management, particularly in managing the production process and in sharing in the productivity gains of the organization through wage bonuses (Scanlon 1948). The classical American case study on participation is that of the Weldon Company, a pajama manufacturer which was acquired by a competitor, the Harwood Company. Weldon was run by a traditional management and was losing money. Harwood had a long history of "participative" or "consultative" management and was making money. In 1963, Weldon was reorganized to allow participation, and the success story is well reported (Marrow et al. 1967; Seashore and Bowers 1970).

There is a large literature on motivation and participation

which has received considerable input from OD writers (Argyris 1964; Blauner 1964; Blum 1953; Blumberg 1969; Emery and Thorsrud 1969; Lesieur 1958; Sutermeister 1963; Vanek 1971; Vroom 1960, 1964). There are also documented cases on participation (for reviews, see Blumberg 1969, pp. 70–122; Katz and Kahn 1966, pp. 368–89). Developments outside the United States are covered in various studies (Bienen 1974; Covarrubias and Vanek 1975; Duffy 1975; Furstenberg 1969; Hunnius et al. 1973; Wachtel 1973; Zimbalist 1975).

This literature clearly points to important changes brought about by expanded participation in organizations — as long as participation is genuine, and power is widely shared.

In terms of worker satisfaction and morale, the conclusion seems positive. Most of the research on participation points one way:

> There is hardly a study in the entire literature which fails to demonstrate that satisfaction in work is enhanced or that other generally acknowledged beneficial consequences accrue from a genuine increase in workers' decision-making power. Such consistency of finding, I submit, is rare in social research. (Blumberg 1969, p. 123)

But it is still not clear whether participation per se improves the morale of those participating or whether the improvement is the result of the pioneering status of the organizations that are studied; perhaps what is observed is the satisfaction of being part of pioneering organizations. A question that remains to be answered is whether morale stays high when participation becomes a routine.

Regarding efficiency, the data are less conclusive. First, it is not as easy to attribute efficiency results to participation. In the Federal Republic of Germany, where legislation places workers on the boards of companies (from one-third to one-half workers on boards, other members appointed by shareholders), the conclusion seems to be that worker directors do not damage enterprise efficiency and may even make a positive contribution to it (Duffy 1975, p. 105). Beyond that, it is difficult to generalize from a multitude of different cases where the word participation is used to describe many different levels of intervention, going from trivial pseudoparticipation to real sharing of decision-making and responsibility.

The literature on participation also tends to be committed to the cause. For some writers, participation and industrial democracy are values that transcend other issues. Other writers are overly concerned with its potential impact on efficiency.

From the point of view of this book — we are interested in the impact of participation on uncertainty — several positive and negative considerations must be stressed.

First, it is clear that participation has important beneficial results when it provides an institutional framework for resolving internal or external conflicts. To the extent that "voice" operates again, participation improves organizational health. Second, participation demystifies the organization. It provides formal linkages between different parts of the organization that might not otherwise have been linked. More important, it alters the power structure of the organization and for this reason can have far-reaching consequences on perceptions of uncertainty.

On the other side of the ledger, participation as presently conceived has drawbacks. The first, but not necessarily the most relevant, is that participation is costly in terms of the time and effort devoted to the sharing of power. It can also be costly in terms of the quality of decisions made. (Can a better-trained small group take better decisions affecting the welfare of a larger group? The answer is yes if the small group has access to the necessary information and if it formulates the problem in terms of the aspirations of the larger group.) It can be costly in terms of lead times and response capability (if one has to consult fifty persons, it takes longer than if one makes decisions unilaterally).

Second, participation does not necessarily reduce conflict. In fact, participation may well provide a forum and a legal basis for destructive attacks on the organization. To be sure, this may be necessary and, in that sense, community participation on policy boards helps the public at large in its dealings with the organization. But as long as members of organizations are threatened by external interventions, as long as there are no guarantees to protect them, the extension of external conflict into internal affairs raises the level of uncertainty.

Third, much participation is pseudoparticipation, which can exacerbate alienation. Even when management espouses an ideology of participation, this ideology tends to be oriented upward and not downward, i.e., the middle-level managers are all in favor of participating in top-level decisions but do not see much need for having their subordinates give them advice except to the extent they already trust them (Miles 1964, 1965; Miles and Ritchie 1970; Strauss 1966). On the other hand, pseudoparticipation can have a utility of its own since it provides communications, thereby removing some of the mystification of organizations without some of the costs of real participation. Writing about a large-scale effort of pseudoparticipation in planning the future of education institutions in England, one author points out:

> They lunched as a group. . . . Ties formed in these ways were reinforced by informal social contacts. . . . Friendships formed, small groups met for lunch or a beer, invitations were extended to inter-institutional parties. Even when more frequent contact brought no increase in personal affect, it created a mutual confidence that springs from a sharing of experience. One college member summed the matter up: "In the course of these endless meetings, we have become allies rather than rivals." (Nias 1972, p. 176)

Fourth, and most important, participation means the creation of smaller units of decision-making. The greater the extent of participation, the more decisions have to be made in a decentralized manner. This means that participation can only succeed if decentralization is possible. It also means that legislation that obliges participation in organizations has the effect of displacing decision-making to the level where participation takes place. If workers participate in the governing boards of organizations, decisions that affect workers tend to take place where they exercise power. This means, for example, that wage negotiations tend to take place at the level of the organization instead of industry-wide. A contrary trend, however, is that high levels of uncertainty are encouraging organizational spread, which is a centralizing tendency. On one hand, participation and responsibility-sharing stimulate decentralized units; but on the other, high levels of uncertainty stimulate centralization.

To summarize, we are saying that participation, the sharing of power and responsibility, is essential for organizational health. But if participation is to succeed, it is necessary to deal with the issue of decentralization, namely, that decentralization means more errors of articulation; this, in turn, means greater uncertainty and fear of punishment. It also means that errors of articulation need to be corrected. As long as decentralization is not feasible, we can assume that much participation will be rhetoric: at best, pseudoparticipation, and at worst recriminations and accusations, blaming others for whatever happens.

* *
*

eight

Accountability

Accountability is a general term used to describe how organizations demonstrate that they are fulfilling their mission. As such, it is both a symptom of the problems of organizations and a potential remedy if used properly.

Accountability, as used commonly, refers to three kinds of interventions:

— First, it refers to the verification of the use of organizational resources. Accountability demonstrates that monies are used for the purpose for which they were appropriated. All organizations are subject to accounting controls designed to limit errors or corruption.

— Second, it refers to selecting targets, programming, implementation, and evaluating desired outputs. Accountability is an overt internal process whereby an organization plans, budgets, schedules, implements, and evaluates its own activities.

— Third, it refers to external evaluations of organizational outputs. Accountability is an external intervention designed to find out if the organization is doing what it is supposed to do.

Evaluation research conducted by outside experts is used for this purpose. When we use the word "accountability" in this chapter, we refer to the third definition: we are interested in external interventions based on evaluation research.

Accountability is a symptom of the illness of organizations because it is a defensive/offensive weapon used either to protect the organization — "Here is the evaluation report on our welfare program. It shows that by and large we are doing a very creditable job indeed" — or to attack the organization — "That evaluation report was devastating. It showed they were terribly overextended. They had to cut back on many programs, and this gave us a chance to move in and start our own."

It is a remedy when evaluation research provides new knowledge on how to do things better. But as we shall see, in the context of excessive uncertainty, evaluation research tends to exacerbate internal fears, and learning does not take place.

Evaluation research serves different functions:

— First, it serves a legitimation function: "We continued our programs with pregnant mothers because last year the evaluations were very positive — not that we think this is the best way to help pregnant mothers, but that's all the State is willing to fund."

— Second, it serves a defense function: "I can assure you that the greatest care is being taken to avoid waste. We are undertaking three simultaneous evaluations of these programs."

— Third, it serves a delaying function: "We will postpone decision until these evaluations are in. . . . I know how concerned you are, but this task is being undertaken by a talented team from the university, and we should not attempt to decide before they make their recommendation. . . ."

— Fourth, it serves as a trial balloon: "We tried it during the training program . . . it worked! . . . Their evaluation suggested a new way to think about it . . . it was well received, we went ahead." "The evaluation also suggested firing ten percent of the staff. There was such an outcry that we knew we would not go ahead with that plan."

— Fifth, it serves as an offensive weapon: "We have the evaluation. It has definite implications for our continued support of your group's activities. I'm afraid you are going to have to change the way . . ."

— Sixth, it serves to provide employment to intellectuals: "I am going into evaluation — because that's the new exciting field in education."

— Seventh, it serves to reduce uncertainty: "This evaluation cleared the air — the level of effort has to be increased, but now we know how to do the job."

— Eighth, it serves to increase uncertainty: "I do not see how they expect to evaluate us. They want to see proxy measures of student achievement, but no one knows what these will measure, if anything. . . ."

The Evaluation Research Movement

Evaluation is a common social process and a normal activity in organizations. What differentiates this new movement is:

— Evaluation is undertaken by outside experts, trained in a scientific method, usually a team hired for the specific purpose of evaluating a specific program.

— These experts are not usually hired in response to a felt need in the organization being evaluated. For example, a school system may be obliged to have an evaluation of a program funded by the federal government. The school board hires the experts in response to a requirement imposed by another agency (the Congress in passing the legislation or the federal agency administering the funds).

— As a rule, the evaluators are not members of the organization being evaluated. Although they may attempt to become integrated into the organization, there will always be much suspicion because they influence the eventual continuation of the programs being evaluated.

The evaluation movement is a phenomenon of the nineteen-fifties and sixties. To be sure, outside evaluators have been used in public and private organizations for centuries, but the systematic use of experts trained in the social sciences started in the thirties (Glueck 1936) and expanded rapidly in the post–World War II period. First there were the foreign aid programs. Then the federal government and private foundations initiated large-scale social programs in the sixties. External evaluations emerged from the need to fund organizations and to control recipient organizations. This need was accentuated by great physical distances (such as when a funding organization in the United States sponsored a development project in a developing country) and the relative administrative independence of the recipient organizations. Evaluation research became common practice in foreign aid, particularly in the programs of private foundations and of multilateral organizations. The practice was adapted to the programs of the "War on Poverty" of the nineteen-sixties. Since then, external evaluation is being used increasingly in large public administrations to control diverse professional bureaucracies.

Physical and administrative distance makes it difficult for the funding organizations or for top administrators to know exactly what the operating recipients are doing. Control cannot be exercised informally in the routine course of administration. Administrative independence (particularly of foreign governments or of state governments vis-à-vis the federal government) means that only outsiders can be used without threatening the apparent autonomy of those being evaluated.

Foreign aid involves donors, usually in wealthy countries, and recipients, usually in poor countries. Contrary to popular belief, the donor organizations are highly dependent on the performance of recipients for the success and continuation of their own activities. For example, a scandal or a white-elephant project in a recipient country is bound to reflect badly on the donor agencies and therefore pose a threat to the survival of the donor organization. At the beginning of aid programs, to ensure quality control for the use of donor resources and to permit better use of technical assistance, donors moved away from providing blank budget support to foreign governments to channeling aid in the form of specific development projects. Donors could then point to specific activities — say, the development of a river basin, transportation, energy, or the building of technical schools — to demonstrate that the foreign aid was well spent. At that time, existing techniques of project appraisal and evaluation were reassessed (for example, the techniques used in water control projects or in electric development) and a new literature on methods of project appraisal and evaluation emerged (Hirschman 1967; International

Bank for Reconstruction and Development 1960, p. 23; Reutlinger 1970; Roemer and Stern 1975; Tinbergen 1958; United Nations 1958, pp. 193–242).

At the beginning, appraisal was more important than evaluation since donors and recipients well understood the probable consequences of the projects undertaken. These were conventional river development, hydro- or thermoelectric plants, rail and air transportation, and other infrastructure investments. Donors needed assurance that the projects could be carried through to completion, and appraisal consisted in making sure that the necessary capability for implementation was present.

As donors and recipients moved into more complex fields such as nutrition, education, health, rural development, and small industries, the need for evaluation increased as the knowledge of probable impacts diminished.

The principal intellectual contributions to evaluation analysis came from engineering and economics, where cost-benefit analysis has a long tradition in facilitating the selection of investment projects, particularly in water, conservation, and energy. To this were added techniques of project management and implementation suited to conditions in other cultures, and techniques of overall economic planning.

Evaluation, therefore, meant more than implementation; it involved social scientists who were interested in measuring the impact of interventions on the social milieu being altered (Hayes 1959; Holmberg 1958). Hayes' early study of evaluation described the evaluation process as consisting of four steps: (1) describing the project and specifying its goals; (2) deciding what data to use to measure results; (3) collecting the data before, during, and after; and (4) analyzing and interpreting findings, and reviewing with interested groups.

During the sixties, the growth of social programs sponsored by private foundations and government agencies, particularly in the "War on Poverty," led to the expansion of formal evaluation efforts. The needs of U.S. federal agencies funding social action programs were similar to the needs of international donors. Were programs implemented? Did they work? Were federal funds being used wisely?

Title I of the Elementary and Secondary Education Act of 1965 provides federal funds for school purposes for disadvantaged students. It requires formal evaluations at several levels: each project submitted by a local community includes a built-in evaluation; state Title I coordinators and state superintendents are required to take responsibility for evaluation. Overall evaluations of the broad impact of Title I programs were initiated by the Office of Education; an internal Office of Education staff paper issued at that time illustrates the demand for evaluation and the need for experts in this field:

> The Congress quite understandably has placed considerable stress upon evaluation of programs supported by Title I. This is not simply a report in the sense of how many children were served and where the concentrations of dollars occurred. This is a request to be advised how well the programs worked and what programs seemed to produce the most benefit. It is part of a growing mood of public accountability for expenditure of public funds. There are somewhat less than 25,000 operating school districts in the United States. Twelve of the largest school systems employ a majority of the 200 persons identified as having research and evaluation responsibilities in schools. We have learned that probably no more than 50 persons per year were trained for research and evaluation work in public school systems. (Committee on Education and Labor 1967, p. 436)

Evaluation of federal programs coincided with the use of program planning and budget systems (PPBS). As John Gardner, who was Secretary of Health, Education, and Welfare, commented at the time:

> First let me say that I believe that one of the areas I have found most in need of further development in our Department generally, and I would say in the Government generally, the Executive Branch, is the capacity for effective planning and then evaluation of what you are doing.
>
> Today, most of our knowledge of the effectiveness of our programs comes from the impressions of people administering the programs. I would not for a moment downgrade the validity of these impressions but in the modern world we

have more systematic and more effective methods of evaluation, which we can put into operation if we wish to. (Committee on Education and Labor 1967, p. 422)

The responsibility for planning and evaluation was centered in newly created offices with that name, and instructions required that an evaluation component be built into all programs. It was apparent that evaluation would be linked directly to annual budgeting.

The peak of the PPBS phase ran from 1965 to 1970. During those years, accountability meant that each department in the bureaucracy was expected to enumerate the specific objectives it was pursuing; it was expected to demonstrate that it had selected the best way to accomplish the task and that evaluations of results were used as feedback to improve programs. PPBS and evaluation were therefore perceived as a new way to control the bureaucracy. Evaluations could readily be translated into language that meant continuation or termination of funding, since the evaluations were tied to budgeting.

Interestingly, in many agencies PPBS did not survive, but evaluation did. There are many reasons why PPBS failed to be a practical way of controlling some of the bureaucracy. Most important, the PPBS format did not accommodate the way decisions are made in agencies whose goals are complex and not easily measured. Department heads in these bureaucracies go through a complex, messy process of trying to put together a budget that satisfies the demands of all those who have a stake in it. Once this was done, the department heads would invite a so-called PPBS expert and write up the budget to look convincing and efficient. In this form, the budget would be sent for approval. At the other end, legislatures and other bodies would read between the lines to find out what was happening. PPBS made control more difficult. Once bureaucracies had learned how to use the PPBS language, once they had hired their own analysts to confront other analysts in the central office, PPBS was no longer useful; it served no particular function and its costs could not be justified.

But the utility of evaluation continued. Where PPBS encouraged bureaucratic maneuvering, evaluation was more difficult to co-opt. Evaluation experts came from traditions of scientific research. It was easy to translate any budget into terms of "pseudo-goals–objectives–targets" and to pretend to be rational and precise. It is harder to obfuscate the results of evaluation:

> There are no formal differences between "basic" and "applied" research or between "research as such" and "evaluation research." Research designs, statistical techniques, or data collection methods are the same whether applied to the study of the most basic principles of human behavior or to the most prosaic of social action programs. Whatever differences there are between pure research and evaluation research reside primarily, if not exclusively, in the social and political relations of the research processes involved. (Rossi 1969, p. 17)

The literature grew rapidly (Bernstein and Freeman 1975; Caro 1971; Guttentag and Struening 1975; Miller 1965; Popham 1974; Rossi 1967, 1969; Scriven 1969; Suchman 1967). New courses in evaluation research were instituted in the relevant professional schools of universities.

The methodologies of evaluation rely on the notion of cost vs. benefit. The central problem, of course, is to define what are relevant costs and what are relevant benefits.

Goals and Output Measures

Some evaluators ask what the official goals are, and proceed to measure outputs and the immediate consequences of these outputs in order to find out if these goals are being accomplished. Other evaluators argue that the official goals are less important than the informal goals that emerge during the development of programs. Still other evaluators believe that goals should be disregarded; they prefer to concentrate on consequences, whatever these may be.

If the evaluators are independent, they will argue that it is the consequences that matter. If the evaluators are paid by an organization that is striving to make sure that a set of objectives is met by another organization, they will focus on these objectives and pay close attention to output measures.

This contrast reveals the conceptual difficulties faced by evaluators. Whose goals are being evaluated? Whose values prevail in the evaluation? Who defines what is significant and what is not? Who defines costs and benefits? Is the evaluator an advocate of the client or of the public at large? Will the evaluator define the problem the way those who hire him define it or the way those who are evaluated do? How do these choices affect the careers of evaluators?

Although evaluators recognize that inputs, process, and outputs can each be the subject of evaluation, the evaluation movement generally focuses on outputs. Since experts are hired for short assignments, it is possible to gather more significant data about outputs than about process or input variables. More important, evaluators are on safer ground when they focus on output variables. The staff of the organization being evaluated is expert in the process — and if the evaluators attempt to evaluate inputs and process, they move into unfamiliar territory where their expertise may be challenged by those they evaluate. Outputs are safer: "I do not know how you are doing it, but you have a very high drop-out rate in this school," or "You have a high mortality rate in the delivery room."

To be sure, definitions of good performance are still subject to expert knowledge, but the goals of the program provide benchmarks against which the evaluator can make uncontestable statements: "They are only accomplishing twenty percent of the target they intended." Comparisons with other organizations also provide benchmarks: "Their scores are under the median for the state." This may be a meaningless statement, but it still leaves the evaluator on safe ground: "We do not know why this is so — but it is a fact." The evaluatee is on the defensive and has to argue that the median is not a relevant benchmark.

The evaluator is on safer ground still when the evaluation focuses on external consequences of programs. What is the long-term impact of certain agency interventions on the affected population? The staff which is being evaluated may be unable to defend itself: "How come thirty percent of your graduates find no employment two years after graduation?"

Outside vs. Internal Evaluation

Internal evaluation is an instrument of organization defense against the environment, whereas external evaluation is an instrument of control by one or more organizations over others. Internal evaluation may be seen as a defense against external evaluation: "Let us evaluate ourselves to demonstrate that we are doing what we should be doing — and quick, before they attempt to evaluate us."

Internal evaluation provides knowledge to improve service — just as external evaluation does. But in the case of internal evaluation, the decision to use this knowledge rests only with the organization, whereas in the case of external evaluation it rests elsewhere. For this reason, internal evaluation is part of the OD movement while external evaluation is not. Internal evaluation may raise uncertainty within the organization, but it may also reduce it; accountability always raises uncertainty within the organization being evaluated.

Accountability in Perspective

The evaluation research movement arose as a consequence of the growing complexity of the exchanges between organizations in areas where no markets operate and where political processes are inadequate. For example, there are insufficient channels of control between the beneficiaries of foreign aid programs, the legislatures in donor countries which appropriate funds, and all of the operating agencies involved — or there are insufficient channels of control between the Congress, the federal agencies, and the beneficiaries of federal programs.

Four layers of organizations are usually involved in large-scale social programs. First, there are the legislatures (Congress, state legislature) that provide the necessary appropriations. Second, there are the central executive agencies that have overall responsibility for the programs (e.g., AID or the Department of Health,

Education, and Welfare). Third, there are intermediary agencies at the state level (the State Department of Health) or in the foreign country (the ministry of education). Lastly, there are the actual operating organizations undertaking the funded programs: schools, hospitals, etc.

Distrust exists at all levels of the relationships between these four layers of organizations because individuals in organizations transmitting resources to other organizations correctly perceive that what is to the advantage of someone down the line may be an expensive cost to someone up the line. The organization operating the program in the field may be concerned with the needs of certain minority clients or it may be concerned with defending the status quo and protecting the interests of an elite that controls it. But these local interests do not reflect the actual distribution of influence at the center and do not fit the intent of the legislature that voted the funds. These conflicts are threatening for the members of the organizations. In addition, the fear of corruption complicates the situation.

The agencies providing the funding have to look good; the individuals in these agencies who promote programs are seeking the limelight. They can ill afford to have their programs fail, and if problems emerge they want to be the first to know about them.

Moreover, all the agencies involved want to avoid risk, and generally try to place the blame on the operating field organization. This happens especially when the promoters of the programs are at the center, far from the operators, and when high expectations were created when the programs were first promoted. As programs fail, there is growing dissatisfaction and blame is delicately passed from top to bottom.

From that perspective, external evaluation serves several purposes:

— It emphasizes the risk-taking ability of the promoters, particularly in the organizations that promoted the programs at the center: "You see we are well aware how complex these problems are. . . . We are quite willing to try everything we can think of, but we are not going to waste any resources. . . . If the programs do not work, they will be brought to an end."

— It provides documented histories to justify sharing blame

with the operating organizations or placing it entirely on them.

— It provides an outside staff that can keep the promoters informed of what is happening and provide lead time for defensive maneuvers.

— It provides legitimacy for ending or continuing programs; that is, it provides legitimacy for ending the attack on old problems so that funds can be transferred and an attack on new ones can be initiated.

Relations between Funding Agency, Evaluators, Implementers, and Clients

Let us discuss the relations between the funding agency (the organization which hires the evaluators), the implementers (the staff of the organization being evaluated), the evaluators, and the clients. Who needs whom?

The funding agency needs the evaluators. When it cannot use its own staff, it must hire them.

The evaluators need to be hired. If they come from universities, they may not need contracts except to the extent that they pay well. But think tanks and private consultants are dependent on them.

The implementers do not want the evaluators. They would prefer an inside evaluation. They perceive the evaluators as an additional threat. They are highly dependent on the outcome of the evaluation.

The evaluators do not need the implementers. If the implementers do not cooperate, the evaluators can exercise sanctions. The evaluators are not attempting to create a new program that requires cooperation. Evaluators either support the status quo (yes, what you are doing is good, do more) or support it partially (these things you are doing are good, these are not) or eliminate it (this program is costly and has no apparent consequences — abolish it). They do not invent programs.

The clients want better service, either the existing program or something else. Since the evaluators do not concern themselves with the something else, it is not always clear whether clients benefit from the evaluation.

Let us contrast accountability with OD and with planning:

In an OD intervention, someone, usually management, hires experts. But the experts cannot operate without the support of the implementers. The experts are highly dependent on the staff of the organization for the success of their intervention. They need to comprehend the reality of the organization being changed. The success of the OD intervener is tied directly to the success of the OD program. Both interveners and staff are involved in a creative attempt. The dependence of the OD intervener on the staff limits the extent to which the OD intervention can be dominated by management — or the intervener.

In a planning exercise for several organizations (such as a national planning exercise or a statewide effort involving many autonomous units), the planners do not operate in a vacuum. The success of their careers as planners depends on their ability to formulate plans that are implemented. They are hired by someone, but again, they are highly dependent on the cooperation of implementing agencies. A successful planner cannot disregard what is going on inside the organizations whose cooperation is needed to carry out the plan, and this dependence limits the power of those who hire planners over the performance of their role.

What about accountability?

What does success mean in a career in evaluation? It means to be hired to undertake more evaluations. Who needs to be pleased? The agency that hires the evaluator. What does this agency want? The agency wants to look good. How does an agency look good? By starting new programs that are imaginative. How does evaluation help? Two ways: either you end old programs — thus releasing monies for new activities — or you expand activities that can be expanded. You do not let satisfactory activities go on without change. Change is needed for the sake of change.

What about implementers? What power, if any, can they exercise on the evaluators? They can pit their expertise against the expertise of the evaluators, but in many situations that is not enough.

What about the clients? They are not going to influence the process unless they are organized and can influence political power. They are no more or less important to accountability than to planning or to OD.

Effects of Accountability on Organizations

External evaluations increase levels of uncertainty, particularly at medium and higher levels. Since external evaluations result in public documents, it is difficult to predict what effect they may have on significant evaluators who are important to one's career: "Oh! you were involved in that program that failed?"

External evaluations erode whatever risk-taking propensity might exist inside the organization. Most programs being evaluated are new and required considerable investment on the part of those who participate in their implementation. External evaluators are likely to be perceived as insensitive to the difficulties involved, and if the evaluation is negative, it will be considered unjust, biased, or erroneous — thus increasing internal alienation.

External evaluations erode professional self-image. External evaluations involve a meta-profession that can assess other professions. When evaluation is done in social services where professional identity is weak, external evaluations tend to weaken the profession further.

External evaluations are perceived as wasted resources. External evaluations consume program time and effort. The staff of the program will perceive such effort as an additional obstacle and diversion of resources.

External evaluations tend to homogenize the quality of services across organizations. One of the worst consequences of the use of modal benchmarks is that they result in conscious attempts by all service organizations to reduce differences among them. When evaluators use output measures to assess performance and make statements like "How come your school scores ten percent below the state norm?" it encourages all schools to attempt to score about the same. Such statements criticize the existence of a normal distribution of scores and force all organizations to look like all other organizations. This homogenization reduces risk-taking and increases conformity. Some might argue that it forces the poor performers to upgrade their performance toward the higher levels achieved elsewhere. But it also erodes risk-taking among high performers. Those who score high are fearful of scoring less high the next time around, so they become cautious; those who score low are fearful of the consequences of the low scores, and in a climate of fear they may be unable to improve and find it more convenient to tamper with or falsify measurements. Evaluators are committed to the search for knowledge, to finding better ways of doing things. But when careers or employment are at stake, the desire to learn is lost.

To what extent do evaluation and uncertainty remedy undesirable bureaucratic patterns, and to what extent does the treatment become part of the problem? It is highly probable and plausible that the entire evaluation movement is having more negative than positive consequences. It is also highly probable and plausible that we are witnessing a vicious cycle: the more uncertain the environment is, the more the bureaucracy performs poorly, the more unhappy the clientele is, the more demands there are for accountability and evaluations, the more the environment becomes more uncertain, and the vicious cycle is repeated.

How can evaluation be used properly? By separating learning from organizational attempts at control. Evaluation is an important remedy. But it has to be used in a context that does not threaten the jobs and careers of those who are evaluated.

* *
*

nine

The Myth of Decentralization

Decentralization *and* centralization are phenomena that take place every day. The current literature on the twin subjects of decentralization and centralization discusses the forces that bring about one or the other of these tendencies. This discussion reveals the growing importance of centralization as a bureaucratic reality and the growing rhetoric of decentralization as reaction to this reality (Baum 1961; Derthick 1974; Goodman 1971; International Union of Local Authorities 1971; Maas 1959; Niskanen 1971; Porter and Olsen 1976; Rein 1972; Savitch and Adler 1974; Stenberg 1972; Zimet 1973).

Organizations are continually altering administrative arrangements either to centralize or decentralize — that is, they go through both processes and often alternate between reorganizations that centralize and reorganizations that decentralize. But the main tendency is toward centralization. The concern for decentralization is only a concern — a reaction to the need for centralization and its consequences.

This trend toward centralization has already been noted in previous chapters. Now we bring together previous arguments and discuss three main forces for centralization: externalities, articulation, and internal benefits.

Externalities

"Externalities" refers to the effects of the decisions of individuals or single organizations on a larger collective.

Though single individuals or organizations (we call them units) may make rational choices as far as their own affairs are concerned, these choices may not be rational for the larger collective. Externalities are remedied through centralization:

— because the units do not have the relevant information to make decisions. Take, for example, the problem of matching the output of the schools to future employment possibilities. If the problem is treated by individual schools, each school decision reflects the school's preference and capability. But such preferences may be unrelated to what the aggregate future labor market will look like. The school is an impractical level on which to make this decision because the individual school does not know how the total labor market is changing and what other schools are doing. The sum of all independent decisions cannot be anywhere near the quality of decisions that would be possible if one took a central overview of the present output of all the schools and matched it with an overall review of immediate employment possibilities.

— because the rational acts of units have repercussions that cause undue damage to other units. This tendency is the basis for government regulation and control. As technology becomes more sophisticated, the possibilities of damaging one's neighbors increase. If an upstream factory discharges polluted residues into a river serving other communities, intervention is necessary. A central regulating agency protects units composing a technological system.

— because collective action is necessary to improve the well-being of all units, and there is no incentive for units to act singly in the collective interest unless they are assured all other units will act simultaneously. This is the problem of the "commons." The commons are the facilities that are used jointly by the collectivity, such as common lands, air, water, etc. (Dorf 1974, pp. 139–55). I have a car. If I spend $250, I can reduce the amount of air pollutants my car produces. But my own rational calculus leads me to do nothing because I will hardly benefit if my car is the only one that emits fewer air pollutants. Only when everyone else is obliged to modify his or her motor, will my benefit materialize. As technology becomes more sophisticated, the need for collective action increases, and this means more centralization.

Articulation

Articulation is the process of relating the actions of units to those of other units. Centralization is necessary when:

— the costs of articulating decisions of many interdependent units are too high if each unit attempts to bargain with all other units. A central articulating unit decides more rapidly, effectively, and at less cost. For example, imagine a railroad network where each train engineer attempts to negotiate with other train engineers concerning what time each of them will use the rail lines.

— duplication of service is wasteful. For example, until the late nineteen-forties, Mexico City was served by two independent telephone companies; as a result, subscribers of the Ericson Company could not reach subscribers of the Mexicana Company. To reach all subscribers, it was necessary to subscribe to two services. The merger of the two services reduced duplication and improved effectiveness.

— conflict between units whose work is interdependent must be adjudicated. For example, the consolidation of independent city services under one administration or the trend toward consolidation of area-wide administrations where the use of natural resources has to be coordinated and restraints have to be enforced.

Internal Benefits

Internal benefits are the advantages or desired consequences of centralization:

— Economies of scale result from centralization. If you centralize purchasing in a large school system, you may benefit from savings in bulk orders, savings in storage and delivery, and savings in administrative costs. With the development of new technologies, the possibilities of new economies of scale through centralization are enhanced.

— The center attracts the best talent. In all situations, there is a scarcity of managerial talent. The best talent gravitates to the more challenging position — i.e., to the center. It follows, therefore, that in theory at least *the center tends to be more capable* and better able to take decisions.

— Centralization provides an institutional basis for equalizing services across units. This is the *equity* argument. In the United States, education services are provided by independent units of government which have unequal access to financial resources. By contrast, in countries where education is centralized, financial inequities in level of expenditures are diminished or non-existent. Therefore, as equity issues become important, the tendency toward centralization is accentuated.

— Centralization permits *control*. Since control implies social power, we can assume that as long as there is a desire to exercise social power, there is a desire to centralize. In other words, all other things being equal, we expect that the appetite and pleasures arising from the human exercise of social power lead to a constant tendency toward centralization.

— Technological advances, together with the dramatic development of data handling capability through computers, widen domains of control. For example, an American ambassador in the nineteenth century was far more independent and exercised far more judgment than his modern counterpart who operates at the end of a telecommunication network linking the embassy directly with Washington. The center of decision-making tends to shift from the periphery (the embassy abroad) to the center (the Department of State, the White House, etc.).

— Elimination of local corruption. Centralization *shifts corruption from the periphery to the center*. One argument for centralizing police services into a national force is to eliminate local influence and corruption. Since the center is usually more "visible" — that is, less able to hide actions, more open to public scrutiny — the argument can be made that, all other things being equal, centralization tends to cause an overall reduction of corruption.

— Centralization permits *standardization and simplification* of administrative norms. As the legal basis of administration is made simpler, it becomes possible to understand what each administrative unit is doing. Such knowledge facilitates interventions from the public or their representatives. In countries such as Italy where there is still considerable administrative overlapping, it is more difficult for the public or for elected government officials to influence the course of action. Centralization and standardization of appointments, evaluation procedures, and pay scales permit greater administrative responsiveness to public demands.

Decentralization

The literature on the theory of decentralization distinguishes between political and administrative decentralization (Altshuler 1970; Fesler 1968; Hart 1972; Porter and Olsen 1976; Schmandt 1972).

Political decentralization is the transfer of existing powers to *another* organization closer to the periphery — for example, the transfer of powers exercised by a national government to provincial or local governments:

> Proposals for decentralization embodied in revenue sharing schemes call for "political decentralization." Authority is exercised by territorially based units with general powers. Much discretion is left with the receiving unit. States, provinces, counties and municipal corporations are examples. Proposals for general and special revenue sharing suggest the transfer of resources and power to these governments. (Porter and Olsen 1976, p. 73)

Administrative decentralization is the transfer of existing powers to lower hierarchical levels within the same organization — for example, the shifting of discretion to decision-makers who are closer to operating conditions within the same organizations.

This distinction is important because the concept of decentralization has to be understood in the context of control and discretion. Decisions can be made at lower levels and still be controlled at the top through rules and regulations. Such rules limit discretion even if there is an appearance of decentralization. Therefore, discretion is implied in our definition of decentralization. Similarly, an apparently centralized system may contain areas of considerable discretion where local unit directors assume responsibility for actions and have considerable authority of their own.

It is convenient to define decentralization as the extent to which interdependent units select their own objectives as well as the means to reach them. A completely decentralized system is one composed of many independent, yet interdependent, units — each of which is free to select its own objectives and the means to reach these objectives. Each of these units may then negotiate with others to reach an agreement about what to do.

In contrast, a centralized system is one composed of many units where the choice of objectives and of the means to reach them are delegated to a central body which instructs each unit about how to proceed.

Therefore, centralization and decentralization form a continuum. Some decisions are taken at the center; some decisions are taken at the periphery. The trend is toward centralization: as we just saw, modernization means that many more decisions are made at the center. But the more that important decisions are taken "elsewhere," the more there is a sense of powerlessness and even of uncertainty, and the more there is a call for decentralization and participation.

Limits on Centralization and Decentralization

It is useful to distinguish between centralization of decision-making and centralization of production or services. Centralization of decision-making is of greater interest to us because it deals with issues of control, morale, professionalization, and the taking of responsibility for decisions. Centralization of production or services is less relevant because it is dictated by logistic or economic factors. For example, should an organization centralize warehousing or decentralize such facilities? This introduces an operations research problem which can be handled adequately by a conventional optimization analysis. But the centralization or decentralization of decisions (e.g., what should be decided by the ambassador in the field and what should be referred to Washington?) is a problem that does not lend itself well to conventional optimization techniques.

Centralization or decentralization of decision-making is constrained by:

— the extent to which the decisions of the periphery can be routinized, which depends on the extent to which the environment is predictable. If the problems faced at the periphery are not predictable, decisions must either be made on the spot or must be referred to the center. The corollary is, how much does the periphery want, and how far can it afford, to substitute local judgment for routine decisions that can be made economically at the center?

— the extent and quality of communications between the periphery and the center. Can meaningful messages be transmitted to the center? If the messages sent by the periphery do not provide an adequate basis for the center's decision — that is, if the center cannot interpret the messages — there is no basis for centralization.

— whether decisions can wait. What is the relative cost of waiting for the center to decide versus the cost of acting at the periphery?

— whether the center can handle the flow of decisions. If the center is overloaded with decision requests, it either does not act — which is a way of deciding — or it acts without having enough time for problem-solving. In both cases, overloading reduces the quality of decisions. The corollary to this is the distribution of the load on the periphery. Does the periphery get overloaded from time to time, and would backing from the center improve effectiveness?

— the additional costs of centralized administration versus the direct benefits attributable to centralized decisions. Cost-benefit analysis eliminates marginal decisions or actions where differences between periphery and center are not important and not worth direct costs such as transportation, communication, and administrative costs at the center.

— the extent to which centralization lowers other performance indicators (spill-over effects). What is the impact on professional norms, decision-making ability, sense of responsibility, etc.?

The decision to centralize or decentralize decision-making is amenable to a rational calculus if one considers variables such as lead time, costs of communications, load factors and other quantifiable data (Kochen and Deutsch 1969; Levy and Truman 1971). But it is less amenable to rationalization when one attempts to consider broader implications that are not measurable, such as the impact of decision centralization on professionalization, propensity to take risks, tendency to play by the rules, and, most important, responsiveness to client needs. As Levy and Truman point out in their criticism of Kochen and Deutsch, the development of a rational theory of decentralization is useful for economic producing units, but is not yet applicable to government organizations (p. 179).

Unfortunately, in the absence of a theory of decentralization, one is left with a trend towards centralization.

The Process of Centralization

Centralization and government intervention in previously uncontrolled areas are always seen as a loss of prestige or power by those who were formerly independent (e.g., small businessmen, independent firms prior to merger, independent units of government prior to reorganization, etc.) (Jacoby 1973, p. 174). Centralization is not only a condition, but is also a process. The process of centralization has other consequences:

— The rules of the game affecting career promotion are altered. Centralization is *perceived as a threat because it alters evaluation procedures.* Moreover, one may not know how the new arrangements will work, whether it will be possible to use the altered situation to one's advantage and, in any case, whether the reduction of discretion which is implicit in any centralization move means a reduction of degrees of freedom in one's career plans. Therefore, in the short run — if not in the long run — centralization tends to accentuate fear within the organization even when it reduces external uncertainty.

— Considerable time is lost in the process of centralization. While this is not usually documented or discussed in the literature, centralization processes always involve large reorganizations that take considerable time out of the working days of middle and senior officials. Considerable time is lost because individuals in the organization perceive, quite correctly, that any reorganization is a time of uncertainty when one's position is in doubt. It is important to float upward and not be shunted to a dead end. Reorganizations are evaluations in the sense that they are used to eliminate individuals who have become expendable, unnecessary, or even undesirable. Reorganizations for the purpose of centralization are particularly useful in this respect because they entail bringing together various smaller organizations with duplicated services. Before reorganization, you had three vice presidents for financial planning; after reorganization, you will have only one. The opportunity for getting rid of people is high and the politics of these reorganizations more intense — to the detriment of one's role performance and, therefore, to the detriment of one's career plans. To be sure, some win; but the losers are more numerous.

— The process of centralization creates a history of conflicts which are perceived, correctly or incorrectly, as threats to one's long-term career. Inevitably, as factions within organizations advocate or oppose mergers, integrations, or consolidations, unavoidable conflicts occur which cautious bureaucrats would never have entered into if so much had not been at stake. The process of centralization is a crisis situation within the bureaucracy, and it often leads otherwise cautious but fearful members of the organization to act in panic. Even when the conflicts are settled, the uncertainty generated by the battles remains. One remains unsure about how one performed, who evaluated whom, and what jealousies were fostered.

— The removal of discretion creates a strong sense of "we" versus "they." Decisions that were once taken in the field are now discussed, reviewed, approved, processed, or evaluated elsewhere. When judgments differ, group conflicts are exacerbated.

— The creation of new hierarchies facilitates "passing the buck": "Why should we worry about this problem; let the main office try to handle it; it's their baby now." It facilitates transferring the blame: "We sure would like to help you, but we still do not have the papers back from the main office." It facilitates inertia and apathy: "I see no point in trying to push them on this; they never care about these issues." It facilitates complacency and erosion of standards: "Send it as is; they won't know the difference out there." It facilitates falsification of information: "Make sure to mention it in the weekly report; that's what they want to hear." It facilitates secrecy: "What they don't know won't hurt them." It facilitates building walls around the small empires within the organization: "I do not trust purchasing to play ball on this one; they are always trying to do us in." It facilitates loss of personal importance and job satisfaction: "Sure we used to do this, and it took us five days to get an answer. Now, with the computer, you have your answer in five minutes, but we just punch keys now; there's no more fun to it." It facilitates self-pity: "Those guys won't let us work; look at these stupid forms I have to fill out."

— Loss of discretion discredits the service in the eyes of the clientele. There is little discussion of this in the literature, but we should not underestimate the impact of centralization on the way clients play their own roles. Clients (whether they be patients, welfare cases, students, or whatever) are quick to perceive that officials and professionals on the periphery are unable to make decisions and are controlled from above. Where leadership or organization exists, clients attempt to co-opt it in order to confront the center jointly. Otherwise, clients simply disregard the local authorities as irrelevant to their problems and needs; they bypass or pay little attention to them. This pattern further exacerbates the sense of futility of the profession; it leads to conflict between the profession and clients, which ultimately results in client alienation. Sabotage of the service organization is initiated, and in some cases — such as schools — this alienation may lead to violence.

— At the center, problems are stereotyped in similar patterns. This leads to throwing the ball back to the periphery: "Tell them we cannot process their request because they did not fill out the forms properly." Transferring the blame: "Of course we failed, but it's not our fault; we have to fire some of these guys. We inherited a lot of dead wood; incompetence is all over the place." Apathy, inertia: "There's no point trying to do it right; those guys cannot do a job properly." Complacency, erosion of standards: "Why try to kill yourself on the job? There's no way to push the bureaucracy around. Forget it. . . ." Falsification of information: "Disregard their report; they probably do not know how to count down there." Secrecy: "I see no point in telling them; they would not know what to do with it." Loss of self-importance: "We have to do everything here; there's no time to consider large policy issues; we have to do everyone else's job." Self-pity: "The President wants us to move forward, but there's no way for us to act if we cannot fire these old dodos."

The Myth of Decentralization

When we speak of decentralization, we refer to a process that follows centralization. What is not yet centralized does not need to be decentralized. When the consequences of centralization are too costly, attempts at decentralization follow. But if centralization emerged because of a need for coordination and integration to reduce environmental uncertainty, decentralization will not alter this reality. Only if centralization came about for other reasons, or if the environmental uncertainty has been removed, will decentralization work. But this situation is the rare case.

What are the consequences of decentralization when it is attempted without concern for solving the threat of environmental uncertainty?

— One purpose of decentralization is to permit participation in decision-making. But this is not going to happen if the conditions for participation are not present. As the center appears to move responsibility back to the periphery, there is a brief enthusiastic period. But since the center keeps controls, participation is more apparent than real. To deal with uncertainty, the center uses new controls such as performance evaluation and management by objectives. These controls acquire the importance that was once held by other controls. The result is that those who were invited to participate perceive participation as a sham.

— If considerable authority is transferred, the question becomes, can the periphery handle the problems and take the blame if the attempted solutions fail? If the periphery is faced with a very uncertain environment — which means fear of punishment for mistakes — participation is going to be perceived as a way to be blamed for events that are out of one's control. Contrary to expectation, no one is going to want to participate: "The cards are stacked; it's like a shooting gallery. Those who are foolish enough to attend these meetings will be blamed for the consequences."

— To the extent that individuals at the periphery have different opinions about what to do or how to do it, delegation of authority creates greater conflict. Such disagreement means that participation in decision-making — while desirable from many points of view — turns out to be excessively time-consuming, particularly at the beginning. It follows that whatever solutions are adopted also require the managing of hurt feelings. When decisions were made elsewhere, blame could always be associated with distant decision-makers: "They do not know what they are doing." It is more painful to discover conflicts in one's own back yard and to have to live with them. In situations of high uncertainty, decentralization means that members of the organization cannot avoid these confrontations; therefore the level of intragroup conflict will tend to be higher.

— If the periphery is unable to cope with decentralization, it will make every effort to create a system of rules or regulations that protect it and provide legitimacy for placing the blame elsewhere. If the center suggests that programs should be evaluated, the periphery will interpret the suggestion as a hard and fast requirement and spend considerable effort in formal evaluations. If the center suggests planning procedures, the periphery will go a long way in establishing detailed, top-heavy procedures which provide legitimation for decisions. Since these procedures are unnecessary, they are resented, and conflict will erupt at the periphery as some members of the organization continue to advocate these protective approaches while others challenge their utility.

Thus, the cycle is completed. After an appropriate period of gestation, the decentralization moves are brought to an end. The pendulum swings again, and the centralization reorganization is initiated.

* *
*

ten

Errors and the Ombudsman

Organizations make errors that affect their clients and the public. To what extent is redress possible? In this chapter we distinguish four types of errors and we examine how clients obtain redress through both informal and formal institutions such as the ombudsman.

An organizational error consists of providing the wrong service (or product) or not providing a needed service (or product). Errors in the delivery of services or products fall into four broad categories: marginal, commons, articulation, and control. Marginal errors are "normal" errors; commons errors arise from the fact that organizations do not pursue the well-being of the entire society; articulation errors arise from the complexity of the system; and control errors are the consequences of the efforts of organizations to protect themselves. Marginal and commons errors are subject to some regulation — and therefore to partial redress. Articulation errors are not subject to regulation or redress. Control errors are subject to redress only when they are illegal.

In a complex technological society, organizations make errors with important consequences, affecting the organizations, their

169

members, their clients, or the public at large. But the fear of errors — because of its consequences for organizations and for their members — leads to uncertainty, which leads to the pathologies we describe. Therefore, we address ourselves to this issue: how can the effects of organizational errors on (1) organizations, (2) members of organizations, (3) clients, and (4) the public at large be corrected without unfairly penalizing anyone?

Marginal Errors

Mistakes are made at the margin of normal operations. For example, we predict that the post office will lose a percentage of the mail it handles. Similarly, we predict that a percentage of the products of a company will be defective. We also predict that "normal" errors will be made in most institutions.

Marginal errors can be caused by uncontrollable events, the consequence of a normally accepted level of quality control, or the result of a failure or deliberate breaking of the rules or laws of the organization.

Hospitals do not normally schedule wrong operations, but occasionally errors creep through all the safety arrangements, and the rare event of a wrong operation takes place.

Marginal errors are remedied in accordance with established procedures — for example, it is possible to return damaged products and have them replaced, it is possible to complain about service, or it is possible to seek redress through formalized arrangements in the organization or through the courts if the damage is serious and legal fault can be demonstrated.

Most organizations providing services or involved in manufacturing processes recognize an accepted level of quality control, and marginal errors are allowed, depending on the nature of the service or product. The standard of what is acceptable quality control changes over time. For example, most airlines today consider as desirable a lower percentage of lost baggage than they did a decade ago. In contrast, most public utilities and their clientele seem to accept a higher frequency of interruptions of service.

Any service can be designed on a 100 percent error-free basis, subject to uncontrollable events. The choice of the acceptable level of quality control depends on: (1) the significance of the service or product to the client, (2) the existence of government standards and controls limiting organizational discretion, and (3) the relative cost to the organization of improving quality control.

Acceptable levels of marginal errors evolve over time and become the basis for the relations between clients and organizations. In the normal course of transactions one comes to expect certain patterns — and these are accepted and understood. When there are deviations from the pattern — i.e., when a client is subjected to too many errors, or when these seem not random but deliberate — complaints are initiated.

Commons Errors

Commons errors derive their name from the commons — that is, from what is public and belongs to everyone. Commons errors happen when organizations affect public well-being or harm public property even when acting rationally. For example, if organizations can make a profit while polluting the atmosphere, organizations will make a profit and pollute. These errors are different from marginal errors because they are consequences of organizational actions that are deliberate and rational: they benefit the organization, they may even benefit its clients, but they harm a larger public. Since technology is a cause of many of these errors, they become important in modern society.

Commons errors are a basis for government regulation. Laws and regulations provide the basis for redress. The political process is responsive to citizen needs when the affected population is large. Interestingly, the political process is less responsive to the effects of redress on organizations. There are no institutions that automatically help organizations when these are asked to redress commons errors and face complex and expensive readjustments. Partly for this reason, organizations normally resist such attempts and the relationship between regulating agencies and affected organizations is adversary in nature.

Articulation Errors

Articulation errors result from the absence of coordination or mutual adjustment between needs and availability — the supply does not fit the demand. Articulation errors are much more threatening to organizations than marginal errors. A marginal error involves providing the wrong service or not providing a needed service in a *small* percentage of cases, as the result of uncontrollable events, part of an "acceptable" level of quality control, or as a result of some deliberate act within the organization. In contrast, an articulation error is providing the wrong service or not providing a needed service in a *large* percentage of cases, as the result of changes in the demand for service.

For example, a firm produces widgets, and for years, there is a growing demand for widgets. This organization is doing well; it grows each year, etc. Suddenly, the demand for widgets evaporates. Something happened in the environment which made widgets unnecessary, and, for one reason or another, the organization did not foresee this change. Articulation errors are a main cause of organizational uncertainty.

In most situations there are no remedies for articulation errors. These errors are not subject to laws or regulations. Redress through the courts is not available. If articulation errors affect many clients and if the damage is serious, redress through the political process may be possible. Legislatures sometimes provide relief to corporations near bankruptcy when sufficient political pressure is exercised. But the impact of articulation errors on clients is usually without remedy, and in most organizations — public and private — it is the cause of the games described in this book.

Control Errors

Control errors are the consequence of articulation errors. In response to an uncertain environment, organizations use defense mechanisms to control their clients.

Control errors arise when organizations control and, therefore, decide on the nature (or absence) of service on the basis of their own needs and not those of their clients. In other words, a control error takes place any time an organization (or an individual or group within the organization) has enough power to impose its definition of what is (or is not) desirable service — independently of client demands. To the extent that power is exercised illegally, control errors are amenable to redress, but in most cases control errors are legal.

For example, a corporation that produces missiles secretly pays leading foreign government officials a percentage of the contract these officials make possible. Such corruption is a means of controlling clients. This is probably a control error since the organization is using illegal power to sell its product to the client. (It would not be a control error if the client wanted the product and the kickback was the equivalent of a price reduction.) Redress is possible if legal action is initiated and the illegal act is demonstrated.

Here is a different example: A primary school teacher, very talented but also very influential in her school, always gets the "better" pupils assigned to her class and avoids teaching the "harder" pupils who come from lower social class backgrounds. The private interests of this teacher go against the needs of those pupils. She manages to control the situation without appearing to break any rule or regulation. Redress is much more difficult. A company forces clients to buy a spare-parts package that includes spare parts they do not need. No law is broken. Presumably the client is not obliged to buy spare parts. Clients might argue the case in terms of the use of scarce resources but at present there does not exist an easy way to get redress.

Client Redress

Client redress from errors is provided (1) by the organizations that made the errors or (2) by designated external bodies.

Organizations provide redress by attending to informal complaints or by establishing formal complaint procedures such as appointing an executive or internal ombudsman or an internal administrative review board.

External bodies are used when the organization cannot properly handle its own errors. Examples of this are: citizen police review boards; the classical ombudsman as originally conceived in Sweden; specialized administrative courts charged to ensure that certain regulatory government agencies do perform their functions in accordance with the law; the legal courts where the general public can take its grievances against organizations.

The principal basis for the redress of client grievances is the law. Has a rule or a law been broken? Has an illegal act been performed? To a more limited extent redress is provided for the performance of professional services that fall below customary standards. Lastly, redress is sometimes provided because sufficient political pressure is exercised.

A client may not like a product, or a client may not like the way a bureaucrat sneered when he or she applied for welfare payments. Redress is not based on individual likes or dislikes but on rules. Likes and dislikes are exercised in the selection of service. When the client buys a product, it is a matter of choice. If the client finds that the product is defective, redress is possible. If the client buys the product and does not like it, however, it is not a proper area for redress (we disregard the fact that some stores are willing to exchange unsatisfactory gifts). If an applicant for welfare payments can prove that a sex-based or ethnic slur has been made, the client may obtain redress; but if the client complains of having to wait for long hours or that the staff looks dull, the complaint will not be attended to.

There is not much research on complaining in bureaucracy, but what research there is shows that most clients do not believe that it is possible to obtain redress for maladministration. This attitude varies with education and socio-economic level, and also with the existence of formal channels for processing complaints (Friedmann 1974). But the public seems to be aware of the relative power of organizations and clients.

The mounting criticisms of bureaucracy have resulted in a proliferation of formal institutions for handling clients' complaints. The most famous is the ombudsman. Others include review boards, administrative boards, and courts.

The principal differences between these institutions are the extent to which they are directly controlled by organizations or independent of them, the extent to which they can receive complaints and can initiate investigations of their own, the extent to which they have access to all relevant information and documents, and finally the extent to which they are able to prosecute cases and make decisions that are binding on the organizations affected.

There has been a proliferation of new interventions by the courts in the affairs of organizations — for example, as a result of legislation on affirmative action — and a rapid growth of new administrative quasi-judicial bodies charged with ensuring that adjudication of grievances meets the requirements of the law. As a result, the courts have gradually had to expand their concerns — not only with the grievances of specific parties, but also as a surrogate political process to allow a fair representation of a wide range of clients who are, in one way or another, hurt by organizations (Stewart 1975, p. 1670).

The courts have always been hampered in their dealings with organizations, first by the sheer difficulty of handling the volume of decisions made by administrations, and second by the lack of precise definition of the limits of discretionary rights. The question is: to what extent can the court substitute its judgment for the judgment of professionals the inside the administration? Even in countries like France where specialized administrative courts are widely used to control the public administration and where the courts are staffed with persons who are professionally trained in public administration, there are limits to the extent to which they can depart from the letter of the law and enter into a discussion of what is desirable practice. The highest French administrative court, the Conseil d'État, achieves this in part because of its prestige (Wildavsky 1975, p. 96), and also because the staff of the Conseil d'État is trained in administration and often serves in the administration (a topic we will return to in the next chapter). (For studies on the Conseil d'État see Brewster 1963; Freedeman 1961; Jacquemart 1957; Kessler 1968; Rendel 1970; Waline 1957.)

Since the courts cannot readily review administrative decisions, other institutions are needed — and these fall into two broad classes: formal channels of appeal within organizations and formal channels outside. The ombudsman is well known because the institution is designed to serve the general public. But other administrative courts also exist — for example, the Court of Claims, which was established in 1855 to deal with customs, and the multitude of internal review boards that exist in most state and federal administrations. In the following pages we discuss the ombudsman because this administrative instrument highlights the problem that interests us — namely that not all organizational errors are amenable to redress.

The Ombudsman

The Swedish parliament by a constitutional act of 1809 appointed an Ombudsman to receive complaints from the public about bureaucratic errors. The Swedish ombudsman is elected by parliament, has a small staff, earns the same as a Supreme Court judge, and is now charged with supervising the observance of the laws and statutes on the part of the courts and public servants. The Swedish ombudsman handles about three thousand complaints a year. He also has access to all government documents including secret files. Government agencies are obliged to relinquish any information requested. The Swedish ombudsman can act as a prosecutor, although in most instances the remedies recommended are adopted and there is no need for prosecution.

In 1919 Finland established a Parliamentary Commissioner patterned on the Swedish model. Denmark followed suit in 1953, Norway and New Zealand in 1962. In the United Kingdom a Parliamentary Commissioner for Administration was established in 1967. He is appointed by the Crown upon advice of Parliament. He investigates citizens' complaints submitted through a member of Parliament. France also has a similar parliamentary ombudsman. Several other nations, several American states, a number of Canadian provinces, and many cities and counties have established an ombudsman. Many organizations have also done so. (Anderson 1968; Gelhorn 1966; Rowat 1968; Stacey 1971; Weeks 1973; Wyner 1973.)

The classical model — i.e., the Swedish model — differs in several respects from the usual American application. The Swedish ombudsman is elected by Parliament for a four-year term and can only be removed by Parliament. He can inspect jails, government agencies, courts, and military camps. He can review the procedures used in criminal and civil proceedings. He receives complaints but can also investigate on his own. He can prosecute. It is a very powerful office, at least on paper.

In contrast, recent American adaptations are usually appointed by an executive; that is, they are appointed by a governor, a mayor, the president of a university or college. There are exceptions such as Nebraska and Hawaii where the ombudsman is appointed by the legislature. But in general, they work for the executive — and this is why this model is called the executive ombudsman (Wyner 1973).

The executive ombudsman is not only a facilitator for client complaints, but also an agent of the center who helps control the performance of the periphery. The mayor pays attention to the reports of the ombudsman because they indicate potential trouble spots. The executive ombudsman is an agent of centralized control whose function is dissipating excessive friction between clients and the bureaucracy. It is interesting to note that offices of executive ombudsman can be easily established and just as easily abolished. They are directly under the control of the organizations they serve. While they are supposed to protect the interests of clients and to expedite settlement of their problems with the bureaucracy, executive ombudsmen cannot go beyond the limits imposed by their organizations or, more exactly, by the chief executive, and these limits are going to be — in most instances — narrow limits.

But on the other side of the coin is that the executive ombudsman is far less threatening to the organizations he serves than his classical counterpart in Sweden. He is very much like an internal evaluator and can, within the narrow domains where he operates, get the organizations to respond rapidly and flexibly to complaints of clients. This is evidenced by the heavy case loads carried by these offices. The Mayor's Office of Inquiry and Information in Chicago reportedly handles 55,000 cases a year and the case load in Boston's Little City Hall runs as high as 42,000 cases a year (Wyner 1973, p. 12). On the other hand it also appears that while many complaints and inquiries are received and handled, executive ombudsmen rarely pursue a case to its final resolution. "Their follow-up procedures often leave something to be desired" (p. 13). Obviously the members of any organization know how to protect themselves from their clients. When blatant marginal errors have been made or rules have clearly been broken, clients may get remedy through the ombudsman. But other errors are harder to demonstrate and possibly more threatening. The executive ombudsman may bring them to the attention of a department head or of the chief executive for whom he works, but remedy may be very slow or simply denied through inaction.

There are also other contrasts between the original Swedish model and the executive ombudsman. For example, the latter has access to internal documents, but must usually demonstrate a need to see them. The Swedish ombudsman need not demonstrate a need. The executive ombudsman usually cannot initiate inquiries on his own (which means that the person who complains must reveal his or her identity, with the attending risk that the organization being accused of misdeeds might retaliate). The Swedish ombudsman, however, may initiate inspections on his own. This procedure facilitates the flow of confidential information about misdeeds — he can be tipped off about what is going on by insiders or outsiders and has the right to find out what is happening. Lastly, and quite importantly, the Swedish ombudsman has a bite. He can prosecute if he believes that the organization is not providing relief. Even if he prosecutes rarely, the threat of action is always present. In contrast, the executive ombudsman is, at best, advisory to the head of the organization. He can recommend remedy — and if he is wise he will tend to recommend the remedies he knows the organization is willing and able to provide. He can always be fired. Even when the Swedish model has been introduced, as in Hawaii where the Ombudsman Act of 1967 creates an ombudsman appointed for six years by a majority vote of the state legislature, the ombudsman has no authority to prosecute. He only refers evidence of misdeeds to the appropriate authority. It is only when blatant misdeeds come to his attention that the executive ombudsman can be effective in eliminating corruption. In such situations the ombudsman can be more powerful than those who hire him because he can expose them.

It is interesting to note how the ombudsman idea became an instrument of organizational defense in the United States — whereas accountability and evaluation became instruments of organizational control over other organizations. There are many similarities between accountability and the ombudsman. Both are designed to ensure that the organization performs. But whereas in the United States *external* evaluations are widely used to protect organizations against errors made in other organizations, the use of the *external* ombudsman is rare. One can only conclude that protection of organizations and of those who work in them is more important than protection of clients or the general public.

The Ombudsman and Errors

The ombudsman and other complaint-processing agencies provide limited redress for clients affected by marginal and commons errors. They are able to act when evidence can be provided that the organization is not performing according to well-defined customs, rules, regulations, or laws. They have no relevance to planning errors. They intervene in control errors only when the control attempts of the organization are illegal.

But the ombudsman does not provide any relief to the organization — and here we have the kernel of the problem. The concept of the ombudsman is an attempt to make bureaucracy responsive to the needs of clients: to limit excessive illegal, marginal, commons, or control errors. One could argue that the concept of the ombudsman is incomplete. If there are ombudsmen for clients, there should be ombudsmen for organizations. It is not fruitful to decry bureaucracy. The current anti-bureaucratic movement does not resolve uncertainty; it only exacerbates it. These constant attacks accentuate fear and result in more organizational control and control errors.

An interesting question about the future of organizations is their course of evolution. If the institutions we have invented to date are less than suited to our times, can we expand existing institutions, and invent new institutions, to permit organizations to function in a changed context? What does this mean? It means that we want to invent institutions which would alter conditions so that organizations would:

— make no control errors. Organizations would be oriented to the needs of clients and the larger public. The needs of organizations would be secondary to the needs of clients and the larger public.

— minimize commons and articulation errors. The consequences of these errors would be corrected as soon as possible. Institutions charged with providing relief to clients and organizations would be established.

— establish acceptable levels of marginal errors in cooperation with their clients.

* *

*

part three

Models and Ideas about the Future

eleven

Three Ideas
about the Future
of Bureaucracy

Three ideas about bureaucracy will receive much more attention in coming years. These ideas are related to ways of reducing excessive uncertainty so as to limit the extent to which fear becomes dysfunctional in organizations.

First, we can reduce uncertainty in organizations by creating a centrally planned social system where ideological conformity is assured by a single-party system, and articulation errors are eliminated ahead of time.

Second, we can reduce uncertainty in organizations by eliminating complexity. This means adopting a much simpler technology, reducing the standard of living to austere levels, and achieving small self-sufficient units of production and consumption.

Third, we can reduce uncertainty in organizations by creating institutions that correct or at least provide partial remedies for the consequences of articulation errors.

Bureaucracy will change gradually. Small incremental steps will be taken to adapt this human invention to new needs and circumstances. We cannot predict how bureaucracy will change in coming decades. But we can be certain that these three ideas will be increasingly in the forefront of our concerns.

Centralized Planning

This approach assumes that centralized planning can be used effectively to reduce articulation errors and that the elimination of such errors leads to the elimination of control errors. Since the Soviet Union provides an ongoing demonstration of the possibility and limitations of centralized planning, we can discuss the Soviet experience for a better understanding of the strength and pitfalls of this approach.

Elimination of Complexity

This approach rejects current Western values of economic growth and assumes that it is possible to create new attitudes towards production and consumption. If people are willing to live simpler lives, or at least more gentle lives, simpler technologies can be employed. As complexity is stabilized, the rate of change decreases, the fear of errors of articulation should decrease, and it should follow that control errors would be gradually eliminated. Several authors have written about this subject and we can discuss these works to comprehend the utility and fragility of this approach.

Correcting the Consequences of Errors

This approach assumes that variety and change are desirable. The scheme does not attempt to eliminate uncertainty. The issue is not errors per se, but the *consequences* of errors. New institutions have to be designed to remedy the consequences of articulation and commons errors.

Organizations do not act; it is individuals occupying positions within organizations who make decisions that lead to articulation and ultimately to control errors. Therefore, corrective measures must first address themselves to the needs of individuals inside organizations. Uncertainty impinges on individual *careers;* therefore it is necessary to create new institutions that protect the careers of individuals against unforeseen or undesirable errors that affect their organizations and consequently affect their careers. This involves more than assuring people that they can always be employed. It means assuring people that they can count on significant work throughout their careers.

But it is not sufficient to protect individuals inside organizations. If we are too benign, what assurance will we have that the needs of clients and of the public at large will be met? We must therefore simultaneously consider ways of making the voice of clients and the public effective. The scheme must provide new institutions designed to correct for the errors that clients and the public encounter.

Lastly it is necessary to attend to the needs of organizations *qua* organizations. There will be many instances when the needs of those who work within organizations and the needs of clients can be most effectively satisfied by helping organizations cope with the consequences of unforeseen errors. This problem will also require specialized institutions.

Since we start with the assumption that variety is desirable, we are going to foment decentralization, which means duplication and overlap. Redundancy in administration is not necessarily bad; it permits error suppression, increases reliability, provides flexibility, and provides parallel channels for creative acts (Landau 1969). But duplication, overlap, and decentralization mean more errors of articulation which, in turn, will require new institutions to correct the consequences of these errors.

There is also the issue of the public interest versus the interests of individuals in organizations, of organizations, or of clients. This is the problem of the commons, the management of the collective assets of society. The scheme requires efficient and effective means of passing professional judgment regarding the protection of collective interests.

Organizations are, by definition, arbitrary human inventions which, as presently designed, channel energies of their members toward organizational goals. If broader societal needs are important, we need to design a *system of dual control*, both organizational and professional. With a system of dual control (in which the professions would become as important as organizations in the evaluation process), the present narrowness of organizational concerns might be breached.

This approach assumes that individuals are socialized professionally to behave in socially desirable ways; that professional values can be infused in the socialization process in such a way that other systems of control become less necessary; and that professional socialization is preferable to other means of organizational control.

There is also the problem of adjudicating conflicts between clients and organizations, between professions and other professions, between larger collective interests and the narrower interests of clients, organizations, and members of organizations. The scheme requires institutions that are able to resolve such disputes particularly when the disputes require technical and professional knowledge.

How much planning is desirable? We know that centralized planning has utility in those areas of social life where quantification is feasible and desirable and has little side effect on the qualitative dimensions of organizations. The design therefore needs to rely on a very limited form of planning. For example, in education, planning would be limited to the total budget and the total flow of students but would not plan the quality or content of the education provided. Such decisions would be left to professional discretion in decentralized units.

How would such a scheme affect organizations? The elimination of the consequences of articulation errors should lead to the elimination of control errors. By eliminating excessive fear we would eliminate the consequences of fear, specifically the defensive strategies or games described in the first part of this book.

Scheme of the Last Two Chapters

The last two chapters discuss these three main ideas. Chapter twelve deals with the first two. We discuss the Soviet experience with centralized planning and examine the way control errors are generated in this kind of social system. Basically our purpose is to highlight the fact that planning has limited utility. Too much planning can be dysfunctional. Having discussed the Soviet experience with centralized planning, we turn to the other alternative — the idea of simplifying social life. We discuss a number of recent proposals and schemes for turning toward "small is beautiful." This time we want to show that while social life may become simpler, there are limits to this approach also.

Chapter thirteen is utopian. It presents a detailed account of a scheme to reduce fear by providing redress for the consequences of articulation errors and to eliminate or stabilize marginal, commons, and control errors. I have gone to considerable length in presenting this material not because I suggest such a scheme as a possible "solution" to the current bureaucratic crisis but to illustrate the complexity of the approach.

As mentioned previously, all three ideas are going to have some effect on the ways bureaucracy will change in the future. There will be more planning — certainly in the non-socialist countries. There will be conscious attempts to simplify social life and to invent more "humane" technologies. There will be some new social inventions along the lines of the scheme described in chapter thirteen — but these will be gradual and probably never as comprehensive as I have described them.

* *
*

twelve

Socialism versus Small Is Beautiful

We begin this chapter with a discussion of centralized planning in socialist economies. We contrast this approach with the market economy and examine how control errors are generated in both systems. In the second part of the chapter we present ideas about the desirability and possibility of creating less complex social systems where environmental uncertainty is reduced because smaller units of production, distribution, and consumption are self-sufficient.

Errors in Socialist Economies

Centralized socialist planning is a reality. In theory, at least, it provides a way to reduce articulation errors by central planning of the most important economic decisions. Commons errors also can be eliminated. In the mid-sixties important reforms were instigated in the Soviet Union. These reforms were intended to give organizations greater freedom in planning. Firms were allowed to retain a larger share of their profits; they were also allowed to finance expansion through bank loans in addition to government budget allocations. But these reforms did not alter the overall importance of planning. Central planning institutions still prescribe targets for all key economic indicators: production, sales, and "profits" (Ryavec 1975, Schroeder 1976). In the Soviet Union planning is intended to reduce uncertainty by eliminating articulation errors *before* they can happen.

Centralized socialist planning is of particular interest because the means of production and distribution are controlled by the state. We can therefore imagine such an economy as a single immense organization, the sub-units of which are coordinated by centralized planning which is enforced because the implementation of the plan is tied to rewards. The 1965 economic reforms permit Soviet firms to make profits and to pay bonuses to workers out of these profits. But the profits are planned. The plan specifies targets for production and prices. If these targets are met, certain profits will be achieved and bonuses can be paid. Therefore, there are direct controls to assure plan implementation. This approach differs from the capitalist economies in which rewards are not directly tied to plan implementation.

Planning reduces uncertainty by eliminating articulation errors ahead of time. But a dilemma emerges. To function correctly, a centrally planned economy requires extensive discipline. If articulation errors are to be eliminated, people and organizations have to obey the plan directives. If the plan specifies that ten thousand engineers per year have to be trained, controls are needed to ensure that ten thousand and not six thousand or twenty thousand are in fact trained. This means that flexibility is eliminated: once the plan is tied to rewards, rigidities have been introduced. Turning the problem around, planners reduce uncertainty *when they plan correctly*. But in a large social system there are always innumerable unforeseen events that take place, including changes in the needs of clients and of organizations and the emergence of commons errors. The rigidities imposed by tying rewards to the plan mean that organizations are caught between the changed needs of their clients, their own changed needs, and the directives of the plan. This conflict results in control errors. The reforms of 1965 were intended to provide more flexibility. But it appears they did not or could not go far enough. A centrally planned system cannot afford to relax central control unless other means of reducing uncertainty are introduced.

Similarly, commons errors are corrected, if and when planners take them into account. But the logic of the situation is to forget about them unless they become so visible and widespread that the center must attempt some remedy.

Dual System of Control

There are significant differences between organizations in socialist economies with central planning and those in capitalist countries with limited forms of planning. First, in socialist economies there are no stockholders and hardly any private sector; all organizations are part of the government bureaucracy. In capitalist countries firms in the private sector make many independent decisions; they finance their activities from profits, by borrowing, or by attracting private investors. In the Soviet Union, firms make far fewer independent decisions; they finance their activities largely from government budgets, but also from profits and from loans. There is therefore some degree of choice, though much less than in the West. But the most significant difference between the two systems is that an individual in a socialist country, working in a government-controlled organization, has little fear of unemployment; nevertheless, other fears prevail as a result of the relationship between planning and rewards as well as of the existence of a dual system of controls inside organizations.

The typical Soviet organization is similar to its American counterpart. There is the organization as we know it in the West, with its hierarchy of directors, management, workers, etc. The organization (a factory or department) controls the behavior of its members. The organization is controlled by a department of a ministry. Within the ministry and within the organization, there are personnel boards which provide rewards and punishments: bonuses, promotions, transfers to better locations, etc. But there is an important difference. There is also a second system of control which coexists with the first. This is the political party. The party is an organization that parallels all the organizations of the ministries and operating agencies from the central directing committee in the capital down to the party *apparat* in each work unit. The party apparat intervenes directly or indirectly in personnel review procedures and appointments. Thus two systems of control operate. But in contrast to our utopian scheme in chapter thirteen, the second system is political and centralized instead of professional and decentralized. Members of the party apparat are not professionally oriented. To be sure, party officials are sometimes also trained in a profession and are able to address themselves to technical issues, but even if they are not rusty (Azrael 1966, p. 168), the party responds to political considerations where finer technical points or professional concerns do not prevail.

In this situation, some professions are weakened and, at times, are in direct confrontation with the political apparat. The party maintains ideological conformity and, in so doing, provides the underlying mechanism of integration of the entire social system. Those professionals who agree with the political apparat tend to be selected for leadership roles. Dissension is therefore lessened, possibly at the expense of innovation.

Planning provides the overt instrument of articulation. In the Soviet Union, planning is controlled by party directives. In addition, the plan is tied to the rewards and punishments provided by organizations. Workers receive bonuses based on the fulfillment of plan targets.

Articulation and reduction of uncertainty are achieved through a continuous, constantly updated national planning procedure which starts from the bottom (in factories, bureaus, communes, etc.), reaches up to the center, and goes back again to the bottom in the form of directives for implementation.

Articulation of supply and demand is a gradual process of aggregation and coherence maintenance. Plants, collectives, or bureaus are assigned or suggest targets for production for the next planning period. These are aggregated and confronted with broad development objectives, first at local (or district) levels, then at county, regional, or republic and national levels. This process of aggregation and coherence maintenance is done in light of party directives. Planners attempt to foresee all the needs for raw materials, energy, labor, and semi-finished and finished goods, and to integrate these needs with known plant capabilities. Ultimately, complex sets of targets are established and prices are set in conformity with them. These targets are issued in the form of directives from the center back to regions, counties, districts, down to plants, collectives, bureaus, etc. Once the directives are issued, they serve to orient the actions of members of organizations. Workers, plant managers, etc., and entire organizations are evaluated in terms of performance in reaching these targets.

We will not attempt to survey the advantages that these systems enjoy. It will suffice to mention that they are able to handle important articulation errors such as unemployment. But they also suffer from other problems, which are caused by the interlocking of planning with the evaluation process and with rewards and punishments.

Articulation errors are eliminated by planning *to the extent that planners are able to predict, measure, and target correctly.* Planners may eliminate some errors, but they also generate new ones. In practice, socialist planning creates rigidities because individual and organizational rewards and punishments are tied to the targets of the plan, without much leeway, even after the 1965 reforms, to deal with innovations, changes, or unforeseen events.

When important unforeseen events take place in the periphery, a ponderous effort of redirection is required at the center. We are not dealing with small, flexible units that are able to adapt continually to changing demands of their environment; we are dealing instead with a national system that sets a well-defined course, that rewards individuals and organizations for implementing pre-selected targets, and that cannot easily adapt to rapid changes.

The system does not facilitate innovations nor does it pay much attention to commons errors unless the center is alerted and the changes are part of the plan. The typical plant manager wants to meet specific production targets in the hope of obtaining projected profits out of which plant bonuses are paid to employees. Innovations usually require additional financing, reorganization, or retooling, which takes time. Therefore, most innovations delay bonuses, and they tend to be rejected unless there are self-evident and immediate gains to be made. Similarly, correcting commons errors such as pollution means diverting resources for this purpose, and organizations will not initiate such remedies unless they are budgeted and it is clear that the organization will achieve its projected profits. To be sure, planners, the party, and the central bureaucracy are able to move rapidly when certain changes are wanted at the top. Some innovations — and important ones — can be recognized, understood, and carried out with a diligence that is difficult to match in capitalist systems. This is seen, for example, in the massive expansion of child care that has been achieved in most of the socialist economies. But these achievements are tempered by the fact that many other innovations are delayed or never implemented at all. As for commons errors, they seem to be as prevalent in advanced socialist economies as in the West.

The system creates considerable friction between organizational units, which is well documented in both Western and socialist literature (Azrael 1966; Fallenbuchl 1976; Granick 1955, 1960; Ryapolov 1966). The plan inevitably falls short of exact articulation of proposed outputs with supplies, raw materials, energy, equipment, and other inputs, either because errors have crept into planning, or because needs or availabilities have changed. A part supplier is assigned targets only to discover that a client has changed his specifications. If the supplier attempts to meet the new needs of his client by modifying his product, he may fail in the output, and the plant will be penalized. The management of a plant in a socialist economy is therefore quite complex and uncertain, but for different reasons than in the West. Since bonuses are awarded if the plan is fulfilled, every plant manager is under considerable pressure from the plant party committee, the trade union, the workers, and the supervisory personnel to convince the relevant administrators of the ministry that the plan is being implemented. Changes in scheduling or new demands from consumers will normally be disregarded since they may jeopardize output and bonuses. Organizations that need supplies are therefore constantly scrambling to obtain what they want, because their bonuses are also in jeopardy. A fair amount of friction among suppliers and users takes place, and much effort is devoted by all concerned to looking good and coming out as intended in the plan. In our language we would say that the plan and the reward system are a direct source of control errors.

In this system, controls on plan performance become important, and the cost of controls is also appreciable. Much effort goes into reporting to assure the center that the periphery is performing as expected. This, of course, is the common problem of all centralized systems, but it is accentuated here because reporting is important both for planning and for the reward system. Although the 1965 reforms eliminated excessive reporting, we see that reporting becomes an end in itself:

> Approximately 2,000 different planning and accounting forms, containing more than 3,000 indicators, are used in large electrical engineering plants such as the Elektrosila plant in Leningrad. It is not hard to imagine the size of the work force required to carry out this non-productive task. I have heard from directors of large machine-building plants that about 2,500 different plan-reporting forms are in use in that industry. The forms cover 3,000 indexes, and each form is filled out from 2,000 to 3,000 times a year. Up to a billion numerical entries have to be made annually. These facts were recently repeated by a plant director writing in *Izvestia* (December 20, 1964, p. 2). (Ryapolov 1966, p. 120)

In such a system, falsification of plan implementation reports also takes place and creates new sources of error:

> Plan falsification under the Soviet system is technically simple and always possible because it is done within an extremely limited and trustworthy circle of people. The participants generally include the director, chief engineer, chief bookkeeper, and production shop chiefs. (Ryapolov 1966, p. 122)

The problem is sufficiently important that penalties for such actions have been increased. The USSR Supreme Court recently rendered a decision whereby falsifying plan fulfillment returns is classified as a serious criminal offense with up to three years imprisonment, and when it includes theft of state property, far longer imprisonment is mandated (*Izvestia*, February 18, 1973).

Soviet writers are aware that falsification is related to the reward system:

> It is common for this [falsification] to take place at the end of the accounting period when it is clear that the enterprise has not met the production targets, and therefore workers and employees do not receive bonuses. (*Izvestia,* July 30, 1973)

Let us summarize: in centrally planned socialist systems, planners reduce organizational uncertainty, which is good and desirable; they eliminate ahead of time some articulation errors, which is also good and desirable. But the plan generates its own planning errors, and these are inevitably converted into control errors.

Central Planning versus the Market Economy

In a pure competitive market economy, articulation errors are avoided by the normal operation of the competitive market. If you produce something no one wants, or if you fail to produce something that is wanted, a keener competitor comes and meets the need. If you continue in your error, sooner or later you lose your customers. Articulation is provided by the market; therefore, control is in the hands of clients. They reject the products they find unsuitable and choose those they prefer. The firms that meet clients' needs prosper. Those that fail to respond are eliminated. But pure competition does not resolve control errors. These are generated outside the relations between the organization and its clients. Without government intervention, nothing stops an organization from polluting the atmosphere. The organization deals with its clients, but it also needs to respond to the public interest, and this is why government intervention is necessary even under conditions of pure competition.

Where pure competition does not exist, the laissez-faire market fails whenever clients can no longer exit and buy elsewhere and can no longer influence the organization. Again, regulation to restrain monopolistic practices and control errors is necessary. But monopoly and control errors are not easily regulated. Take one example: if you go to three different chain stores and you are faced with similar products at similar prices, you realize that your options are non-existent. These chain stores appear to compete; yet the laissez-faire market fails to produce choice. Why? Because organizations cannot sustain the uncertainty created by the whims of their clients. If clients have real options and can decide what goes and what does not, the vagaries of the market are too uncertain and threatening. Therefore, organizations control their environment. If everyone produces similar products, each is assured a share of the market. They use advertising; they expand into huge, interlocked super-organizations. In short, they do not let clients choose.

Uncertainty in the laissez-faire market is generated by clients. As a consequence, organizations attempt to control clients in order to reduce this uncertainty. Planning in capitalist economies is only one such control attempt. Planning reduces uncertainty by creating a prior consensus or agreement about the future. But in the capitalist system, rewards are not tied to planning, they are tied to profits. Therefore, planning does not lead to control errors.

In contrast, in socialist systems with central planning, the uncertainty generated by clients continues to exist to the extent that the plan fails to capture the changes that are possible and desired. These planning errors become the source of control errors. As a result, the bureaucratic process in the Soviet Union is similar to and shares the same pathologies as the bureaucratic process of Western Europe, Japan, India, and the American continent. They all operate in an organizational culture where fear prevails. In one, it is fear of losing one's job, fear of not making a profit, fear of spoiling one's career — of being in the wrong place at the wrong time. In the other, it is fear of misunderstandings and poor evaluations, fear of not meeting production goals, fear of being accused of not contributing to the socialist effort. In both systems, these fears encourage inept bureaucracy.

The central conclusion of this book is that individuals in organizations in both socialist and capitalist systems are subjected to excessive counter-productive controls based on fears. The major pathologies which we described, the games played by individuals or by organizations, are in most instances related to excessive fears. They are protective strategies which are understandable once one understands their causes. In organizational life, the stick is too large and the carrot is too small.

Excessive fear accentuates the quest for power. The kind of power that is available in the world of organizations is not always sought for its own sake. Similarly, corruption is not practiced because people enjoy corruption per se. Power and corruption are related to rewards, and they are therefore related to security and wealth. Is wealth more important than security? In both systems, wealth is intertwined with security, and it is therefore difficult to isolate the effect of one variable on the other. We can ask ourselves if large corporate or government conglomerates are created principally to accumulate wealth or to provide security. It is true that salaries and other emoluments of chairmen and other officers of large conglomerates are somewhat higher than those of smaller organizations, but is this sufficient to explain mergers, acquisitions, etc.? budgets? profits? But what about profits? Is it that conglomerates make larger profits, or is it that their profits are more secure?

In a turbulent environment all organizations have to remain dynamic; if they do not expand, merge, or acquire other organizations, they will be overpowered by larger giants who will acquire their budgets or their markets or their profits. Either the organization plunges ahead, expands, grows, and merges with others or it is destroyed — bought out or controlled by others. But these realities are not necessarily enjoyed on their own merits. It is not necessarily the enjoyment of power that drives organizational empires ahead — it may be the fear of annihilation that hangs over every organization.

To be sure, power and status are enjoyed for their own intrinsic value in every society. But power and status are relative concepts. Does the director have one, two, or three windows in the office? carpet? chauffeur-driven limousine? private dining room for top executives? access to a vacation house? a waiting room with attendant? These are the important and crucial indicators of status differences that are fought for in all bureaucracies.

It is not power or status per se that matters, but relative power or status. In a society with large income differentials, considerable power differentiates the titan of industry from an unemployed worker. In an egalitarian society, minor differences of dress and pay are sufficient to pinpoint the leader. The appetite for power and status is not an appetite that operates in a vacuum. The most dazzling bracelet has no value if no one can admire it. Power and status emerge in the relations of individuals with others. Therefore, the search for power and status does not explain the growth of organizations into solitary giants. If a society wanted to maximize the pleasure of power and status enjoyed by its citizens, it would organize itself in innumerable small organizations. Each citizen would serve in several and have a position of prestige in at least one of them.

The spread of organizations is mainly a response to uncertainty. If the organization grows in size, there is apparently a strong demand for its services; it is going somewhere; something is happening. An organization with stable sales or budget may not last long. The one that is declining in size is on the way out.

What are we saying? Provide more security, and the quest for power may diminish. Provide for decentralization, and the actual enjoyment of power may increase — thus eliminating excesses. But to do these things requires a framework for arbitration of conflict, a basis for collective choices, and — most important — institutions that remedy the consequences of errors.

Let us interrupt this discussion and review the elements of possible futures we have covered. First there is the market economy with government intervention and frequent control errors generated by organizations defending themselves in an uncertain environment. Second, there is the planned centralized economy with frequent control errors generated by the inevitable failures that happen when one attempts to plan for an entire society. What other possibilities are left? Two that we will consider are the economy of self-sufficiency, where errors are avoided because smaller units avoid excessive complexity, and the correcting economy, our utopian model which provides redress for the consequences of errors.

The Economy of Self-Sufficiency

The new literature on the economy of self-sufficiency is probably best summarized by the title of Schumacher's work *Small Is Beautiful: Economics as if People Mattered* (Schumacher 1973). The movement has several characteristics. First and foremost, it opposes economic growth for the sake of economic growth.

> Once we descry the sort of world towards which technological growth is bearing us, it is well worth discussing whether humanity will find it more congenial or not. If, on reflection, we view the prospects with misgivings, we are, at least, freed from the obligation to join in the frequent incantations of our patriotic growth men. More positively, we have an additional incentive to support the policy of reducing industrial investment in favour of large-scale replanning of our cities, and of restoring and enhancing the beauty of many of our villages, towns, and resorts. (Mishan 1967, p. 176)

The advocates of self-sufficiency are concerned with freedom, with dehumanization caused by the machine, with organizational imperialism. The movement is influenced by Rousseau, Thoreau, William Morris, and others; its literature belongs to a long tradition of utopian writings concerned with the simpler life. Authors come from different disciplines: psychology, sociology, history (Fromm 1968; Heilbroner 1976; Illich 1973; Mumford 1970; Nader et al. 1976; Roszak 1975; Stavrianos 1976).

This new literature shares many themes: large bureaucracy is dehumanizing; schools destroy the ability to learn; bureaucratic medicine ignores the poor, creates expensive routine examinations, prescribes unnecessary medicines, and charges too much for hospitalization; people in bureaucracy think they are normal but, in fact, they suffer low-grade psychoses as they acquire an overemphasized attraction to all that is artificial and is not alive.

But it is possible to reconstruct:

> On the terms imposed by technocratic society, there is no hope for mankind except by "going with" its plans for accelerated technological progress, even though man's vital organs will all be cannibalized in order to prolong the megamachine's meaningless existence. But for those of us who

have thrown off the myth of the machine, the next move is ours: for the gates of the technocratic prison will open automatically, despite their rusty ancient hinges, as soon as we choose to walk out. (Mumford 1970, p. 435)

We can summarize the content of this literature by paraphrasing three of its principal concerns:

— Western bureaucratic empires are destroying the West and most developing countries. Many of these nations adopt Western-style development — convert landless peasants and small landowners into migrants to overcrowded cities while agriculture is mechanized and controlled by large conglomerates. Large urban slums house millions of rural poor who do not fit the employment needs of complex international organizations which produce luxuries while the greater part of the population does not have enough to eat or to clothe or shelter itself properly. *But* there is hope. Some countries pursue different strategies: Cuba, China, Guinea-Bissau, Mozambique, Vietnam. In these countries, efforts are made to use technologies that are adapted to the level of economic development so that people are employed, and all forms of unemployment are eliminated. A democratic economy is created in which workers participate in decision-making.

— Consumers in a society of consumption are at the mercy of giant organizations which manipulate the environment, create false needs through advertising, and control demand. These organizations pursue narrow objectives, disregard the health and happiness of the people, and ignore the ecological environment. Consumers are passive, seduced, and uncreative. Life is a meaningless race through ugly cities to acquire unnecessary possessions. In the traditional societies, villagers abandon their elegant ancient designs for the cheap products of the machine. *But* there is hope. Consumers can organize and begin to act as a class against organizations — they can lobby for new laws, dismantle the giants; they can physically block the destruction of desirable natural sites; they can intervene at stockholders' meetings; they can raise consciousness and create a new environment to stop the destructive ability of the giants.

— Modern people are at the mercy of organizations. Short of having their own income, most people have to join organizations to find employment. From the moment they step into the bureaucratic world, they lose their identity and creativity and become servants of technological tools. *But* there is hope. It is possible to select tools that are labor-saving but are not destructive of the human personality, to choose an "intermediary" technology suited to smaller more intimate relationships based on "convivial" tools (Illich 1973, p. xxiv). A new technology can be used by individuals without recourse to organizations:

> To formulate a theory about a future society both very modern and not dominated by industry, it will be necessary to recognize natural scales and limits. We must admit that only within limits can machines take the place of slaves; beyond these limits, they lead to a new kind of serfdom. (Illich 1973, p. xxiv)

Examples are found: presumably, China relies heavily on local initiative, industry, and decentralized provincial planning. The village steel mill still captures the imagination (even if it was not very successful). The Chinese focus on raising living standards before attempting substantial investments in large plants and infrastructure. Of course, whether they really use a different technology is open to debate; some observers seem to think not:

> Not much distinguishes the Chinese from the American or European industrial plant. For producing a given product, industrial plants are everywhere about the same. (Galbraith 1973, p. 130)

In any case, the Chinese have confronted the bureaucratic dilemma. The Great Proletarian Cultural Revolution attacked the bureaucracy. It forced the new elites that had risen to come down and dirty their hands again. But the Cultural Revolution was initiated by Mao, and now Mao is no more. It is not clear whether it is possible to have an effective anti-bureaucratic movement without a very strong charismatic leader.

*
* *

The emphasis of the literature on the economy of self-sufficiency is on the smaller community, on task groups where people know each other, on self-contained and self-sufficient small units such as communes, villages, or small economic areas. It also calls for a return to simpler ways of life, to simpler needs and, therefore, to simpler production, distribution, and consumption systems. It advocates a creative economy, yet a constrained economy, far more austere and far more egalitarian than we now have in Western Europe or the United States.

Not all authors espouse the same ideas, but the call for restraint and for limits on growth is general. It is the call for birth control to stop population growth, for urban re-transformation to stop overcrowding and pollution, for slowing down or reducing consumption of non-renewable resources. It is the call for the creation of small units of production and consumption designed to fit the human spirit. It stresses lost values: to have time not to think of time; to see what is around and recognize what is beauty and truth; to create and be able to see what one has created; to sing and laugh; to feel, touch, smell men and women, children, animals, plants, and things, in that order of importance.

Some, like Illich and Nader, hope that the enlightened people can rise to the occasion. Illich awaits the impending general crisis from which reconstruction through political participation might follow. Nader is far less dogmatic and is willing to intervene in the immediate present. Others, like Stavrianos, await new historical times — the new dark age which will have the same relationship to the twentieth century that the dark ages had to the fall of the Roman empire, a vision of times of reintegration and disintegration, an age that holds the promise of creative new values and new institutions.

A Brief Critique of the Economy of Self-Sufficiency

First, it is difficult to conceive how the current or projected world population can be clothed, fed, and housed without use of sophisticated technology requiring large industrial complexes. Illich calls for austere life styles using "human" technology. His austerity may be so austere that there is little left to life. Reduction of consumption excesses is undoubtedly possible; people in the wealthier countries will have to adjust to much lower standards of housing, less consumption of certain foods, far less consumption of energy, etc., but even with these reductions, it is unreasonable to assume that the current world population could survive without modern technology.

Second, if one accepts the need for technology, one is inevitably discussing the complexities presented in chapter one. We are back to discussing the problems of articulation, the tragedy of the commons, exit and voice, uncertainty, etc. These writers (except for Nader) have little to say about these problems.

Third, the values espoused in this literature clearly evoke sympathies that are widely shared in many circles in the wealthier and more complex societies. On the other hand, there seems to be no way to implement these values short of proposing to eliminate a large portion of the world population.

Fourth, a good deal of the emphasis on the models of revolutionary Third World countries disregards the fact that all revolutionary movements go through an initial phase when ideological commitment provides the necessary motivation to make other organizational controls less necessary. Once the goals of the revolution are achieved, once power is transferred from an elite to the people, the people face the same bureaucratic problem. It is discouraging to assume that bureaucratic pathologies can only be corrected through constant revolutionary turmoil.

Fifth, with the exception of Nader, who is pragmatic and oriented to corrective measures, the strongest criticism to be made of this literature is that it does not confront the success of organizations. Organizations are efficient; they control members and environment. Power is held and kept and not given away readily. Therefore, the ideology of self-sufficiency has to wait for changing values to alter human behavior in organizations.

To conclude, will human values change? Undoubtedly. Not for abstract reasons or theoretical arguments but because of underlying changes in social relations. If we are willing to recognize the breadth of changes — we are already witnessing outside organizations in family life, in sexual relations, in the role of women in society — we can readily perceive that changes can also take place in organizations. These will result from a conscious awareness that the defensive strategies or games now played in organizations are not pleasant and not healthy.

Where and how will the ideology of the economy of self-sufficiency or some variant thereof emerge? It will emerge from the costs and pains associated with modern organizational life. The world of work will change when the pleasures of consumption are paled by the tributes paid to organizations, when it becomes possible to reject the assumptions of bureaucracy and create a new system. But for this to happen, prerequisites have to be met: people have to be able to find employment; they have to be able to relax without fear for their jobs, their careers, and the lives of those they care for. If reconstruction is to take place, it requires new institutions suited to the needs of the time. Reconstruction cannot take place in fear because fear engenders the need to control, which means that power is exercised to control, with all the unpleasant consequences this has for those who are controlled.

How do we contrast this book with this emerging literature? We have repeated many similar themes; therefore, this book belongs to the same school of thought. But it is far less hopeful than most of these works because we spend more time uncovering why bureaucracies behave as they do. We are far less sanguine about the possibility of self-sufficiency, far less hopeful about what is happening in some countries of the Third World, far more troubled by the reality of power and control. This book speaks of excessive fear and of the inevitable relationship that goes from fear to the additional quest for power and control to eliminate the causes of fear. Once we analyze the situation, it is not as easy to understand how humankind can disentangle itself from the web. But it is also true that our analysis can blind us to the possibility of change. Maybe we pay too much attention to the past and not enough to the future.

* *
*

thirteen

Reducing the Consequences of Errors

This chapter provides an overview of a set of institutions which we call for convenience the "New System." The New System includes institutions charged to:

(1) protect and evaluate individual careers: the Professional Governors;

(2) protect organizations: the Councils; and

(3) protect clients and the general public: the Professional Courts.

These three protective institutions are controlled by Professional Boards which tax organizations to raise the revenue necessary to operate all the institutions of the New System.

The description is utopian. Its purpose is only heuristic: describing possible solutions of a current problem is helpful in comprehending its various facets. This does not mean that such solutions are practical or even desirable.

Overview of the New System

The New System relies on the professions to pass judgment on what is just service. The scheme is therefore based on the notion that all work activities can be professionalized, and that control and promotion of the quality of services can be achieved by professional bodies once resources are provided for this purpose.

The Professional Governors, the Councils, and the Professional Courts protect, respectively, the careers of members of organizations, entire organizations, and clients and the general public. The Professional Boards adjudicate conflicts between these protective institutions and raise the necessary revenue to operate the New System.

The Professional Governors provide help to individuals in organizations. They are organized by professions. Every employed and self-employed person is a member of a Governor body which monitors his or her career and provides assistance at critical moments — particularly, when individuals are affected by articulation errors they could not foresee.

The Councils provide assistance to organizations when such assistance is requested. The Councils have a client relationship with organizations. Their main function is to recommend to the Professional Boards specific assistance for organizations that have to adjust to rapid and unforeseen changes.

The Professional Courts are specialized. They define the quality of service and process the complaints of clients, of the general public, and of individual members of organizations. They recommend remedies and penalties to the Professional Boards. They are staffed by judges with legal, technical, and professional expertise.

The Professional Boards are elected from the membership of the Governors. They appoint the Councils and the Courts. They raise the necessary revenue for all the operations of the New System. They review some of the recommendations of the Councils and the Courts, and they review the programs of the Governors.

The remedies provided by the protective institutions focus on the consequences of articulation and commons errors (see chapter ten for definitions). The scheme is not designed to limit change, to stultify innovation, or to constrain entrepreneurship. On the contrary, the scheme is designed to increase risk-taking behavior by providing remedies for errors and thus eliminating the fear that restricts such behavior.

The New System is an insurance scheme. Through taxes levied

on organizations, the Professional Boards remedy the consequences of articulation and commons errors and so remove the causes of control errors. In other words, the purpose of the scheme is to eliminate the need for protective strategies — the games described in the first part of this book.

This means the scheme provides a basis for effective decentralization and, therefore, for overlap, duplication, and redundancy. Since the consequences of articulation errors are remedied, organizations no longer need to control their environment, and it is possible to eliminate the phenomenon of organizational spread.

There are real costs associated with these remedies. The increase in innovation, risk-taking, duplication, etc., has costs — most of which are absorbed by the New System. Like all insurance schemes, the system does not remedy all errors, and these costs are therefore kept under control.

Control on costs is provided, in part, by a very limited form of planning which provides a broad outline of the future. Articulation errors are remedied to the extent that organizations adopt the plan. Since the plan leaves much to the discretion of organizations, the idea is to provide relief for errors that emerge in areas untouched by planning or in areas where the plans do not coincide with reality.

Control on costs is also provided by the Governing Boards, who exercise judgment about the extent and scope of the remedies they provide. In the final analysis, the New System works on a rough cost-benefit schema whereby the cost of the remedies provided is far less than the benefits achieved through lessening bureaucratic fear and eliminating control errors.

The Professional Governors

If we assume that organizational health cannot be achieved unless members of organizations have less fear of unemployment and less fear of hurting their careers, we have to devise a system that solves these problems without affecting organizations. The Professional Governors use the concept of matrix employment. Individuals have dual membership in their professional unit and in the organization that employs them. The Governors guarantee their remuneration even when they are unemployed. The reason this is called matrix employment is that it can be represented by a matrix: on one side of a square are listed all the professions, and on an adjacent side are listed all the organizations. Individuals belong to the Professional Governors but work in organizations. For example, doctors, lawyers, engineers, technicians, administrators, foremen, specialized workers, nurses, cooks, etc., upon termination of training or passing an examination, join their Professional Governor. Each Professional Governor evaluates and places its members in positions in organizations. There are local Professional Governors for lower-level jobs (i.e., where the relevant placement market is local), regional for medium level, and national-international for high-level work. The Professional Governors have direct access to information about job openings, and in the public service they are the sole suppliers of trained personnel.

The Professional Governors base evaluations of members on (*a*) the information/evaluations of working organizations plus (*b*) assessment of relevant circumstances in the organizations served — particularly, efforts made to avoid control errors and the extent to which consequences of planning errors affect the careers of individuals. The Professional Governors' evaluations transcend the limits imposed by the goals of organizations. They provide new incentives to pursue the general welfare in areas where there is a widespread professional consensus about desirable professional practices.

The Professional Governors provide help or redress to individuals adversely affected by planning errors. Appeals from members are examined, and the Governors provide retraining, relocation, or whatever remedies might be necessary and are possible within their budget.

Promotions within organizations or through transfer to other organizations require dual sanction: that of the employer and that of the relevant Governor unit. In some instances, the Professional Governors rubber-stamp the recommendations of employers. But in special circumstances or under appeal, they intervene.

All unemployed members are automatically employed by their Professional Governor until a suitable assignment is found. Since

Professional Governors evaluate the performance of individuals, and since they have access to the recommendations of employers, they decide — in certain cases — to advise individuals to change careers or seek different employment.

They remunerate at the same rate as last employment even when assignments are different. The Professional Governors often employ individuals in professional development work — teaching and training others, evaluation, etc. — or, if desirable, they provide paid continuing education and training.

The idea of matrix employment originates in the elite corps of civil or military service where appointments are permanent but assignments and promotions are guided by the corps. For example, the Conseil d'État in France is both the top administrative court of the nation and also an elite corps whose members can be appointed anywhere in the French administration and in international organizations. This is called the *tour extérieur* (outside tour of duty). When they perform the *tour extérieur,* members still hold permanent appointments in the Conseil. They therefore have the prestige of top-level civil servants and have a permanent home.

Before continuing the description of the New System, I will answer questions which clarify some issues raised by this model.

*
* *

Question having to do with the labor movement: Would the labor movement oppose or support these reforms?

Answer: The Professional Governors are not involved in the main thrust of union work — namely, bread-and-butter issues (wages, length of work week, etc.). Yet they do displace unions in professional affairs. This means they are resisted by the more professional unions. On the other hand, the notion of guaranteed employment fits union ideology; therefore, most unions are pressured to support the scheme. Some unions support their Professional Governors and vice versa: they find them a useful ally.

Question regarding the scope of the scheme: I am struck by the dimensions of the endeavor. The idea that national, regional, and local personnel records on every employee are maintained, that millions of professional careers are monitored, that working individuals are evaluated by persons outside their own organization, and that everyone is employed simply sounds improbable — or impossible. Are you attempting to solve bureaucratic problems by creating a huge new bureaucracy which will create a significant additional volume of red tape? Will this bureaucracy second-guess the judgments of employers and, more important, will this be an incentive for anyone who is bored to seek relief from tediousness by training for another job at the expense of taxpayers?

Answer: Let me emphasize, again, that the function of the Professional Governor is to remove uncertainties which surround careers in organizations — in other words, correct for the impact on individual careers of events that have nothing (or little) to do with one's role performance. Thus, the monitoring of individual careers includes two kinds of evaluations: those undertaken normally by employers and, *in selected cases,* those of the Governor's staff. When appeals are made, the Governors monitor the case. This means that annual monitoring affects only a small percentage of careers. The task is not as cumbersome or complex as might appear; the maintenance of a file of personnel evaluations on each individual is possible, given today's technology. These files are accessible to the concerned individuals: they are a protection.

Also, the Governors counsel individuals whose careers have reached a turning point and provide useful employment and/or education — retraining to those who are unemployed. There is no question that such services will be provided by all governments in the future. It is unrealistic to believe that unemployment, as we know it today in the West, will be tolerated in any advanced society of the future, if only because there is no justification — legal, economic, or moral — for *some* individuals to be severely penalized by organizational articulation errors. We know that such government services will be provided and that the cost burden will have to be properly assigned. Furthermore, these costs need not be much higher than present social welfare schemes.

It is true that the Professional Governors have to maintain a large staff of professional counselors whose task is to reorient individuals with obsolete skills. Close ties exist with professional schools in universities and elsewhere. The Governors finance special programs of retraining as needed. Who controls their expenditures? Their budgets are approved by the Boards. Therefore, they have to make hard decisions like every other organization.

Do people use the retraining schemes to avoid boredom? If they are bored, they should be retrained, and anyone who attends these programs knows that they are hard work.

Question regarding the financing of the scheme: Who pays for this?

Answer: It depends. Some services are paid for collectively out of special taxes on organizations; others are charged to users. Interventions that result from changes that have nothing to do with individual performance are paid for collectively. For example, the costs of counseling, short-term work, and paid salaries while retraining are always paid out of the organization tax. This tax is levied on all organizations (both private and public) and is related to the number of employees in each organization. But individuals seeking to improve their life chances or wanting to change employment pay part or all of the relevant costs, depending on circumstances.

Question regarding the Governors: What assurance do we have that the new remedy will not be the new problem? Who will evaluate the Governors?

Answer: A good question. There is no assurance that the Governors will not be just one more bureaucracy. What matters is the service they provide. This service is not available today. Nor are the services of the Councils, the Courts, and the Boards. In any case, even if they were quite inefficient, these agencies would bring about tremendous change in both the public and private world of organizations.

Question regarding the professionalization of everyone: I believe Wilensky once wrote a paper on the professionalization of everyone. Is this what the Governors would be?

Answer: Wilensky did write such a paper (Wilensky 1964) in which he distinguishes between professions. Some professions, such as medicine or science, depend heavily on a universalistic knowledge base, acquired through long training and practice. Other professions, or semi-professions, are much less dependent on a universalistic knowledge base; for example, the "profession" of real estate salespersons. The Governors organize and consolidate all work roles into professions. Obviously, some professions have far longer histories and traditions and can more readily reach a consensus about what is desirable practice. Other professions are emerging from work roles where there are no formal definitions of "good" performance. The Governors transform the world of work by reintroducing the notion of pride of craftsmanship, of standards of quality which are lost today. They counterbalance the excessive tendency of modern organizations to produce mediocre or shoddy services and products.

Question regarding conflict between professions: Already, at present, we see much conflict between professions. For example, the conflict between doctors and nurses or between engineers and technicians. Will the Governors tend to sharpen these conflicts, and — given the facts of organizational life — will these large professional bureaucracies mean that the professions will become stultified?

Answer: Individuals may invent and join new Professional Governors or separate from the existing ones any time different schools of thought or work definitions emerge. You are right in pointing out that the Governors experience conflict, but they do not intensify it. They provide formal structures where differing points of view can be argued. Moreover, the work of the members of the Governors takes place in operating institutions: the Councils which monitor and assist organizations and the Courts which defend the interests of the general public, of clients, and of members of organizations. It is in these operating institutions that definitions of what is "good practice" evolve. You are quite right to point out that these definitions are not arrived at peacefully. On the other hand, there are important differences, since present organizational fears are alleviated. The Councils and the Courts are oriented towards practice and the evolution of practice. The professions are not stultified because the Councils and the Courts have to deal with the problems faced by clients and the organizations they monitor.

But let me stop; we are getting ahead of the description of these institutions. Let us return to the Councils.

The Councils

The Councils assist organizations. The Councils are created by the Boards. Members of the Professional Governors are assigned to serve on Councils which are composed of members of those professions most relevant to the organizations they monitor. Each Council monitors up to twenty organizations, depending on their size. Some Councils operate at local levels; others have regional or national responsibilities, depending on their assignment. From time to time, the Boards dissolve Councils and reassign members.

Each organization is assigned to a Council composed of no more than ten members. In some cases, the Councils are assisted by research staffs financed directly by special taxes on the organizations they supervise. Therefore, very large organizations are taxed directly to support the larger staffs needed to supervise their activities. Since the function of the Councils is to support organizations, they are careful to limit the costs of their work since their clients will have to seek their help if the burden is excessive.

The Council is responsible for overseeing the general activities and planning of each organization under its supervision. They make *recommendations* to the relevant Board of the Professional Governors regarding remedies and other acts which might be taken to alleviate the difficulties that each organization encounters. They are primarily concerned with providing relief from articulation and commons errors.

Interventions of the Council are voluntary. That is, they only intervene when requested by organizations. Each organization is assigned to a Council; each Council monitors activities of their assignee, but they only intervene when requested either by management or by two-thirds of the entire staff.

*
* *

Question regarding the scope of interventions: What do they do?

Answer: Their mandate is to provide relief from important articulation and commons errors and from other large-scale

unforeseen changes. For example, your organization has over-
produced carburetors on the assumption that the targets in the
national automotive plan would be achieved. But car and truck
production is lower than planned. You appeal for relief to your
assigned Council, documenting the basis for past decisions, the
unforeseen changes, and the proposed remedy. The Council may
or may not investigate the appeal and, on the basis of its information, recommend remedies to the appropriate Boards.

Here is another example: Your organization is gradually losing
its market, yet you have a strong organization, well established in
the community. The members of the organization are accustomed
to working together; they have invested in local housing and generally wish to remain with the enterprise. On the basis of a vote
of two-thirds of the staff, an appeal for organizational relief is
made, stating the kind of production for which the organization
might retool and retrain, and the financial needs of the transition
period. The Council examines the appeal; it invites experts to investigate the proposals and ultimately recommends what financial
support might be provided to the organization to help transform
it. Or it finds no plausible new role for the organization and
recommends that each Professional Governor take in hand the
retraining needs of the staff.

Question regarding organizational spread: But will this mean
that the Councils foment organizational spread?

Answer: The Councils are supportive but in the framework of
policies set by their local Boards. The Boards are organized in a
decentralized manner so that they tend to pursue decentralized
policies. The Boards can set directives about limits on size; if an
organization is too large, Council support is postponed until the
organization presents a plan to divide into several smaller, independent organizations. Councils can also help competitors of very
large monopolies and gradually force these larger organizations
to accept a reorganization into smaller units.

Secondly, the Councils are attentive to the work of the Courts.
For example, government bureaus or agencies that proliferate red
tape, provide poor service, and are having difficulty surviving, are
not automatically given support from their Council. Each appeal
is evaluated, and, on the basis of a formal diagnosis, remedies are

proposed to the Board. In some instances, the Board might ask the Professional Court to concur in the recommendations to be sure that the Council is proposing changes that are desirable in light of complaints of consumers.

Question regarding articulation errors: I fail to see how your Councils would ever be able to disentangle responsibility for articulation errors; in fact, how would they avoid fomenting more errors? If I am in business, and I decide to expand my production and misjudge the market, would the Councils come to my rescue? If they did, wouldn't this be an incentive for me to always misjudge upward? If I overproduce and oversell, I make a higher profit. If I overproduce and misjudge the market, the Council absorbs my loss. Therefore, the elimination of risk or, more correctly, the elimination of the negative consequences of taking risks, foments more errors.

Answer: Yes, this is true, and the Councils have to limit their interventions to situations where the decisions of organizations coincide with targets set by the Planning Agency. To correct for articulation errors means to be tied to a formal planning process. If the Planning Agency issues a plan which gives your firm a share of the market, to the extent that you follow the plan, the Councils correct for errors. If your firm believes the planners are wrong or if you decide to go ahead on a venture because you are convinced of success, you do so at your own risk. The Council's intervention depends on circumstances. If you are the general manager, and you keep making huge errors on your own, the Council might recommend a transfer and a retraining course.

Continuation of previous question: That is fine, but you said earlier that planning has to be limited to very few variables. Let us assume that my firm followed the plan; that is, it produced the total number of gadgets we were supposed to produce, but we made changes in our gadgets — changes that were in an area not covered by planning — say, a qualitative change — something we were supposed to judge on our own, and we misjudged the gadget market, and here we are with a huge problem. Does the Council help us?

Answer: The intervention is discretionary. The Councils exercise professional judgments on the desirability of recommending assistance. Obviously, they cannot help all organizations all the time. They are constrained or, more precisely, the Board is constrained by its taxing ability.

The Boards operate a compulsory insurance scheme. While they have the ability to tax organizations, they cannot tax them beyond certain limits which experience and practice determine. The reallocation of resources to remedy articulation errors depends on the dimension of the errors. Some errors are never remedied because the Boards are not able to finance the recommendations of the Councils. But while the Boards may not be able to help all the organizations that appeal for support, the Professional Governors always do so. The formula is that organizations may be destroyed, but that individuals are not penalized when this happens.

Question regarding the viability of the scheme: Are you suggesting this seriously? This scheme of yours is sheer fantasy. Moreover, it sounds quite impractical. You would create more bureaucracy and more red tape. All your examples, so far, have been with small private firms, but what about government bureaucracy and the large corporations? You know very well, given political reality, that government agencies and large corporations will control planners. Therefore, they are going to use the Councils to shore up their own power. Any large government bureaucracy or large corporation can make certain that a control error, perhaps a service no one wants, is included in the plan, and once this unwanted service is included in the plan, the Council will provide automatic relief when the consumers balk. The scheme will create more opportunities for control errors.

Answer: You assume conditions as they exist today. But this utopian scheme assumes that a transformation took place. You still assume that planners are easily corrupted. Under the scheme, they are far less dependent on the powerful *because* of the existence of the Councils which force reluctant organizations to pay attention to their plans. It is not easy for a large government bureaucracy or a large corporation to force a control error into a plan. Today, this is possible because planners depend exclusively on organizations to implement their plans; they have very little power of their own, as *The Politics of Expertise* (Benveniste

1972) amply demonstrates. But in the New System, the existence of the Councils, the fact that Councils intervene and provide relief for planning errors, enhances the prestige and power of the planners *qua* planners. Organizations have to pay attention to the content of the plan because they take excessive risks if they do not. This protects planners against corruption. Also, corruption is much harder to initiate and maintain in a system where individuals are obligated to pay attention to collective interests. Why would you take risks for short-term personal gain if you know that you are monitored, and it means that your career and those of your accomplices will be ended? Why take such risks in a system which is far less uncertain and far less punishing? No. We do not expect our planners to be for sale.

The Professional Courts

The functions of Professional Courts are (1) to arbitrate conflicts, (2) provide remedies, and (3) prepare legislation for submission to the appropriate legislative bodies.

The Professional Court protects members of organizations, clients, and the public at large from the actions of organizations. It rules in litigation and, as a result of experience with existing legislation, proposes new legislation to appropriate bodies.

Each Court investigates its own cases; it has access to confidential information; all scientific or professional evidence is relevant. The basis for decisions is either statutory or the Court's interpretation of desirable professional practice. The Court is often dependent on outside experts. All decisions of the Courts are published, and all the data, analysis, and arguments leading to decisions are published or available to the general public.

The Courts are appointed by the Boards and are created for finite periods with members of the Professional Governors whose careers include exposure to organizations and administration. These individuals are usually supplemented by persons with legal training, or they receive short-term training to prepare for service on the Court.

Appeals for damages are submitted by individuals or groups.

Where existing procedures are available (such as grievance procedures within organizations or ombudsmen employed by organizations), these lines of appeal must first be exhausted before recourse to the Professional Courts is initiated.

The Professional Courts have an appellate or review procedure of their own to ensure consistency of decisions. There are local, regional, and national-international professional courts. Each level can review decisions made at lower levels. The decision about where a case will be considered and whether it may be submitted to a higher court is made by the local court and, in those instances, the local court simply transmits the case to the regional or national court without passing on its merit or dealing with it in any way. Normally, a case involving many consumers or organizations from different parts of a country is decided by a national court.

The financial implications of the remedies recommended by the Professional Courts are subject to ratification by the Boards. In other words, the Boards exercise a veto power when they believe that a decision is unwise because the financial implications go beyond the resources they can provide for remedies.

In those instances when the Board vetoes a judgment of the Professional Court, the Board is obliged to appear before the Court to explain why it is deciding to veto and what remedies it proposes instead. The Court and the Board are then obliged to reach a joint decision.

The Courts often obtain the concurrence of the relevant Council before making decisions, particularly when the remedies proposed cause a burden on the organization, and the Council is expected to provide necessary relief.

*
* *

Question regarding the ideology of the Courts: If the Professional Courts supervise their own investigations; if they have access to whatever information they want to gather, what stops the Courts from becoming instruments of ideological movements? What is meant by "good professional practice"? Anyone can define these terms to fit circumstances. These Professional Courts can have a negative impact on organizational health and become a new source of organizational insecurity. Anyone can become a plaintiff, go to a Professional Court with a claim that poor "professional practice" has been used, and initiate a full-fledged investigation. The judgments will depend on the whims of the Professional Court. Whose interest will the Courts protect? Which plaintiffs will be more important? What stops the Court from looking at the evidence it wants to look at? What stops the Professional Court from favoring some plaintiffs or organizations or penalizing others because of ideological preferences? What stops the Courts from "looking the other way"? In short, what do these Professional Courts have to do with justice?

Answer: The Professional Courts demystify organizations; they bring into the open what has previously been kept secret. Their rules of evidence are closer to those of scientific research. Organizations are able to present counterarguments and data. Therefore, the Professional Courts do consider their evidence. Yes, it is true that the Professional Courts have to choose "desirable" alternatives. The Professional Courts do make policy decisions. But all courts influence policy. Whereas courts now use the language of the law to pursue policy objectives, the Professional Courts would also use the language of the profession.

The Professional Courts have many fewer qualms when dealing with organizational administrative discretion. They do not protect the autonomy of organizations. The Professional Courts accomplish their goals, in part, on the basis of legislated laws (they are party to the drafting of such laws) and, in part, by the application of an evolving doctrine of "good professional practice" which has to be based on a wide professional consensus. This standard obliges the professions to discuss and take a strong stand on certain public issues.

Keep in mind that doctrines of "good professional practice" do not, and cannot, come out of thin air. All Professional Courts have to legitimate their decisions. In practice, the Professional Courts provide a visible and formal institution where a widespread debate of the pros and cons of professional practices takes place.

Finally, the Courts are appointed by Boards, but the Boards are elected. If the Courts get out of hand, the Boards respond to political pressure.

Now, who are bona fide plaintiffs? What are bona fide complaints? The Professional Courts protect the interests of three classes of plaintiffs: (1) members of organizations, (2) clients, and (3) the general public. Obviously, the interests of these three classes can conflict: for example, when actions of organizations benefit members at the expense of clients, or benefit members and clients at the expense of the larger public or of an affected minority. Also, there are conflicts between professions, and the Courts do not intervene directly but attempt to have the elected legislature provide new legislation. In other words, when they confront political choices where no self-evident guidelines exist, they seek political solutions if these are possible and avoid interventions they cannot legitimate.

The Professional Boards

The main functions of the local, regional, national, and international Professional Boards are threefold: (1) they create Councils and Courts and assign organizations to them; (2) they establish annual taxes on all organizations to carry the costs of the Governors, Councils, and Courts; (3) they appropriate funds from their budgets to provide relief or redress as recommended by the Councils and the Courts.

The Professional Boards are decentralized. They tax organizations in their local areas on the basis of the number of employees. Special taxes are also allowed for very large organizations that require complex Council staff research to monitor. Regional, national, and international Boards are financed with twenty to forty percent of the budgets of local Boards. Thus the power of remedy and the power of punishment tends to remain at the local level.

The Boards are primarily concerned with budgets and the "possibility" of the recommendations of the Governors, Councils, and Courts. They are, therefore, a crucial institution.

Board members are elected by the Professional Governors in proportion to their memberships.

*

* *

Question having to do with the democratic dimension of the model: Your model gives strong powers to the Boards. These are elected by the membership of Professional Governors — which I assume to be that portion of the electorate who are employed. Therefore, you are disenfranchising those who are not members of organizations and who are not in the labor market. Isn't your model somewhat undemocratic?

Answer: Each man, woman, and child can be a member of one and only one Professional Governor. There is a Professional Governor of children three to eight years old that protects their "career" in that stage of their lives. Persons who keep house and/or raise children have a Professional Governor which has done a lot to protect and remunerate work in households. Therefore, the Boards are democratic and their membership goes beyond the conventional electorate. The Boards are local. They are limited by size considerations. No Board can have a constituency of more than 250,000. Large urban areas have several Boards. The Boards are important units of government but their responsibility is circumscribed. They deal only with organizations and with the well-being of members and clients. They have a taxing ability based on the number of people they represent. There is a tax equalization scheme which transfers twenty to forty percent of all Board taxes to regional and national Boards for reallocation to Boards and for use by regional and national Courts.

Question having to do with risks and the concept of private enterprise: You describe carrot and stick institutions designed to permit organizations to function effectively, i.e., to achieve organizational health. The Professional Governors assist the careers of individuals in organizations; the Councils, made up of members of the Governors, assist individual organizations. The Professional Courts protect clients against poor service or undesirable practices. The Boards allow the system to function by raising the necessary organizational taxes and by reviewing the recommendations of the Councils and of the Courts. Therefore, this new system is an insurance scheme which defines what is desirable and needs to be continued, what is not desirable and needs to be changed, and how the costs of these changes can be shared across organizations. It reduces risk and uncertainty and remedies errors.

Now then, if you abolish risk, shouldn't you also abolish the notion of private gain? Isn't the New System intrinsically anti-capitalist?

Answer: The New System is not anti-enterprise for the simple reason that it recognizes the importance of innovation. It is not risk that is eliminated but the consequences of certain errors. The model is designed to favor independent actions by many organizations; it favors small organizations because it provides relief for planning errors; it makes organizational articulation less important and the building up of large, private conglomerates unnecessary. The Professional Councils and the Professional Courts are two forceful institutions that interfere in the internal affairs of organizations. On the grounds that "good or bad" professional practices are exercised, private firms are forced to change. The assumption is that if uncertainty and the consequences of risk-taking are greatly reduced, another principle has to replace the corrective mechanisms of the traditional market, and this corrective mechanism is the deliberate public discussion of professional issues in production and consumption. The New System is not a return to laissez-faire. It is a form of voluntary intervention that allows organizations to seek relief from errors if and when they desire to seek such relief; it allows groups or individuals to seek redress from the actions of organizations; and it protects the careers of those who work in organizations.

The New System provides necessary incentives to coordinate the private sector with a limited form of national planning. As such, the New System is less interventionist than a system where planning is used as the benchmark for private-sector control (such as when bank financing is controlled by government and is tied to planning decisions, thus limiting the ability of the private sector to finance projects outside the plan). Here, planning is used to correct for planning errors. This means that private organizations are assured of relief if they adopt the plan and the outcome is unsatisfactory. This does not mean that private organizations *have* to adopt the plan. If an entrepreneur is absolutely sure that the plan is wrong or sterile, the entrepreneur can still take risks, innovate, introduce a new product, and make a fortune. If the individual fails, that is a private problem.

Let me insist again that this model is designed to favor small enterprise and as such it is far more oriented toward private initiative than any scheme that supports large corporate conglomerates that are no more private than government agencies.

Lastly, what about profits? The model does not specify what happens to profits. But in practice the Councils are always under pressure to limit recommendations for relief since they fear the Boards will not support new taxes if the burden of relief is too high. They therefore pay attention to the profit history of corporations. When profits are excessive, the Councils and the Courts usually intervene jointly to determine why a particular corporation is doing so well. Is it exercising control errors? Should it reduce prices? The practice is to allow two-year high profits for new products or service innovations, but beyond that, profits are expected to be aligned with rates of interest found to be necessary to induce sufficient savings. This procedure tends to force corporations to innovate.

Question having to do with the public sector: What can you tell us about the public sector? How might the Boards, the Courts, and the Councils respond to bureaucratic spread? Will they not initiate more social welfare programs by protecting government bureaucracy?

Answer: This model does not touch allocation issues. The decision to have more or fewer social welfare programs is one that the electorate makes through the existing political process. The Boards, Councils, and Courts are concerned with the efficiency and effectiveness of agency performance. The model permits decentralization and this is an important contribution of these institutions. It permits decentralization because it reduces the false need for control which comes from fears of planning errors. Who instigates decentralization in public services? The members of government agencies and their clients who know at first hand the waste that goes into excessive coordination and documented histories. How do they accomplish this? They use the Courts to change existing controls.

The new principle of control is based on professional discretion, and clients are also protected by the courts. The executive branch of government takes legislative allocations and distributes them to task groups which are given an annual budget and asked to perform in accordance with guidelines set by the legislatures. They prepare a single annual report and that is all.

Of course, it means that government units do, in fact, work at cross purposes: what one unit does is destroyed by another unit. But we know that this happens all the time today, and the present means of articulation and coordination, of "going to the top," are not effective. The Professional Courts respond to the needs and complaints of clients. They are often better able to bring this kind of problem to light. The Courts articulate — but "through the bottom," i.e., through the expressed needs of clients. Do the Courts respond rapidly? Certainly as rapidly as conventional bureaucratic channels.

It also means different standards; different approaches are used, and, as a result, some citizens enjoy better services than others. But this is true today. If we disregard inequities due to unequal allocation of government services, we are left with inequities due to the quality of service provided. Decentralization allows for experimentation — it also permits the sharing of experience and the adoption of successful practices.

Question having to do with planning: Do you think your model of the economy and government is more controlled or less controlled than present conditions in Western Europe or the United States?

Answer: We describe a social system with limited quantitative planning (i.e., production targets are quantified — they provide a rough benchmark for all government and private sector activity). The private sector's incentive to respond to the plan is provided by the assurance that relief is automatic when the plan is in error. But the private sector is not bound by the plan. Relief is less attractive than profit. Innovators find opportunities to operate outside of the plan without Council assurance.

Each unit of government has a precise notion of the resources it can count on. Given this set of quantified targets and definition of available resources, the unit is free to carry the task to completion. The Councils and the Courts watch the performance. They are much better able to assess the qualitative dimensions of the task, to pass judgment on successes and failures, than distant organizations or legislative bodies.

Control is tightened, although much more discretion and responsibility are vested in the unit. How is control tightened? Control from above is reduced, but control from below is increased. One can visualize the situation as follows: Today, the people go through their elected representatives who press the executive to lean upon the agency. In the new scheme, people challenge the agency directly in a Court attuned to professional norms. Today, the people have little control over the juggernauts of commerce and industry. In the new scheme, they challenge them in the Court and re-establish small organizations.

Conclusion

Writing futuristic scenarios is a heuristic device. It is not a plan. It is not an attempt to push a cause, to espouse a "perfect" solution to "save" the world. We present the scenario because it unmasks many of the underlying assumptions that guided the writing of this book. Basically, we do not see any justification for production and consumption systems that penalize some individuals as severely as present systems do — given the technological skills and resources available to mankind.

We see a need for change, though we do not know what direction it may take.

The reader will want to think and criticize. Some of our assumptions may be incorrect. We did pay considerable attention to fear and the way excessive fear generates additional need for power to control. One could argue that fear is not a sufficient explanation for power, that there are other sources of power including the intrinsic pleasures derived from its enjoyment.

Have we discussed incentives sufficiently? So much of bureaucracy operates as it does because there does not exist any incentive to act differently. Did we pay enough attention to this aspect of organizations?

We focused on excessive uncertainty. Did we go too far in attributing so much to uncertainty?

Can we really expect organizations to perform more efficiently and effectively if less fear prevails? How much fear would we suggest as desirable?

We placed much emphasis on the role of professions in providing guidelines for good service. But have we paid enough attention to the bureaucratization of professions? Who will control the professions once they have much power?

We discussed three ideas: planning, reducing social complexity, and finding ways to correcting errors after they take place. What other ideas should we think about? What about love and altruism? Have we neglected this potential dimension? What are the ways in which changes can be implemented? How will bureaucracy evolve?

* *
*

References

AIKEN, Michael, and Hage, Jerald. 1968. Organizational interdependence and intra-organizational structure. *American Sociological Review* 33, 912–30.

Alderfer, C. P. 1967. The organizational syndrome. *Administrative Science Quarterly* 12, 440–60.

Altshuler, Alan A. 1970. *Community Control: The Black Demand for Participation in Large American Cities.* New York: Western Publishing Co.

Anderson, S., ed. 1968. *Ombudsman for American Government.* Englewood Cliffs, N.J.: Prentice-Hall.

Appleby, Paul H. 1952. *Morality and Administration in Democratic Government.* Baton Rouge, La.: Louisiana State University Press.

Apter, David E. 1971. *Choice and the Politics of Allocation: A Development Theory.* New Haven, Conn.: Yale University Press.

Argyris, Chris. 1964. *Integrating the Individual and the Organization.* New York: John Wiley & Sons.

———. 1970. *Intervention Theory and Method: A Behavioral Science View.* Reading, Mass.: Addison-Wesley Publishing Co.

Armstrong, John A. 1973. *The European Administrative Elite.* Princeton, N.J.: Princeton University Press.

Arrow, Kenneth J. 1963. *Social Choice and Individual Values.* Second edition. New York: John Wiley & Sons.

———. 1974. *The Limits of Organization.* New York: W. W. Norton & Co.

Azrael, Jeremy R. 1966. *Managerial Power and Soviet Politics.* Cambridge, Mass.: Harvard University Press.

BANFIELD, Edward C., and Wilson, James Q. 1963. *City Politics.* Cambridge, Mass.: Harvard University Press and The MIT Press.

Bannock, Graham. 1973. *The Juggernauts: The Age of the Big Corporation.* Harmondworth, England: Penguin Books.

Barnet, Richard J., and Muller, Ronald E. 1974. *Global Reach: The Power of the Multinational Corporations.* New York: Simon & Schuster.

Baum, Bernard H. 1961. *Decentralization in a Democracy.* Englewood Cliffs, N.J.: Prentice-Hall.

Bayley, David H. 1966. The effects of corruption in a developing nation. *Western Political Quarterly* 19, 719–32.

Becker, Howard S. 1952. The career of the Chicago public school teacher. *American Journal of Sociology* 57, 470–77. Reprinted in part in Barney G. Glazer, ed., *Organizational Careers.* Chicago: Aldine, 1968, 381–87.

Becker, Selwyn W,, and Neuhauser, Duncan. 1975. *The Efficient Organization.* New York: American Elsevier Publishing Co.

Beckhard, Richard. 1967. The confrontation meeting. *Harvard Business Review* 45, 149–54.

———. 1969. *Organization Development: Strategies and Models.* Reading, Mass.: Addison-Wesley Publishing Co.

Bendix, Reinhard. 1949. *Higher Civil Servants in American Society.* Boulder, Colo.: University of Colorado Press.

Bennis, Warren G.; Benne, Kenneth D.; and Chin, Robert, eds. 1969. *The Planning of Change.* Second edition. New York: Holt, Rinehart & Winston.

Bennis, Warren G., and Slater, Philip E. 1968. *The Temporary Society.* New York: Harper & Row, Publishers.

Benson, J. Kenneth. 1975. The interorganizational network as a political economy. *Administrative Science Quarterly* 20, 229–49.

Benveniste, Guy. 1972. *The Politics of Expertise.* San Francisco: Boyd & Fraser Publishing Co. and The Glendessary Press.

Bernstein, Ilene N., and Freeman, Howard E. 1975. *Academic and Entrepreneurial Research: The Consequences of Diversity in Federal Evaluation Studies.* New York: Russell Sage Foundation.

Berg, Larry L.; Harlan, Hahn; and Schmidhauser, John R. 1976. *Corruption in the American Political System.* Morristown, N.J.: General Learning Press.

Bergson, A. 1938. A reformulation of certain aspects of welfare economics. *Quarterly Journal of Economics* 52, 310–34.

Berne, Eric. 1964. *Games People Play: The Psychology of Human Relationships.* New York: Grove Press.

———. 1972. *What Do You Say After You Say Hello?* New York: Grove Press.

Bienen, Henry. 1974. *Kenya: The Politics of Participation and Control.* Princeton, N.J.: Princeton University Press.

Blake, Robert R., and Mouton, Jane Srygley. 1964. *The Managerial Grid.* Houston, Tex.: Gulf Publishing Co.

Blake, Robert R.; Shepard, H. A.; and Mouton, Jane Srygley. 1965. *Managing Intergroup Conflicts in Industry.* Houston, Tex.: Gulf Publishing Co.

Blau, Peter M., and Scott, Richard W. 1962. *Formal Organizations.* San Francisco: Chandler Publishing Co.

Blauner, Robert. 1964. *Alienation and Freedom.* Chicago: University of Chicago Press.

Blum, Fred H. 1953. *Toward a Democratic Work Process.* New York: Harper & Bros.

Blumberg, Paul. 1969. *Industrial Democracy: The Sociology of Participation.* New York: Schocken Books.

Bogulsaw, Robert. 1965. *The New Utopians: A Study of System Design and Social Change.* Englewood Cliffs, N.J.: Prentice-Hall.

Bowers, David G. 1976. *Systems of Organization: Management of the Human Resource.* Ann Arbor, Mich.: University of Michigan Press.

Bowman, Mary Jean, ed. 1958. *Expectations, Uncertainty and Business Behavior.* New York: Social Science Research Council.

Braibanti, Ralph. 1962. Reflections on bureaucratic corruption. *Public Administration* 40, 357–72.

Brasz, H. A. 1963. Some notes on the sociology of corruption. *Sociologia Neerlandica* 1, 111–28.

Brewer, Garry D. 1973. *Politicians, Bureaucrats and the Consultant.* New York: Basic Books.

Brewster, R. Wallace. 1963. The tribunaux administratifs of France: a venture in adjudicative reorganization. *Journal of Public Law* 11, 236–59.

Brooke, M. Z., and Remmers, H. L. 1970. *Strategy of Multinational Enterprise.* New York: American Elsevier Publishing Co.

Bross, Irwin D. J. 1953. *Design for Decision.* New York: The Macmillan Co.

Burke, W. Warner, ed. 1972. *Contemporary Organization Development: Conceptual Orientations and Interventions.* Washington, D.C.: NTL Institute.

Burke, W. Warner, and Hornstein, H. A., eds. 1972. *The Social Technology of Organization Development.* Fairfax, Va.: NTL Learning Resources Corp.

CAIDEN, Naomi, and Wildavsky, Aaron. 1974. *Planning and Budgeting in Poor Countries.* New York: John Wiley & Sons.

Caro, Francis G., ed. 1971. *Readings in Evaluation Research.* New York: Russell Sage Foundation.

Carter, C. F.; Meredith, G. P.; and Shackle, G. L. S., eds. 1962. *Uncertainty and Business Decisions.* Liverpool: Liverpool University Press.

Cartwright, Dorwin, and Zander, Alvin, eds. 1960. *Group Dynamics: Research and Theory.* Second edition. Evanston, Ill.: Row & Petterson & Co.

Chapman, Richard A., ed. 1973. *The Role of Commissions in Policy-Making.* London: George Allen & Unwin.

Child, John. 1972a. Organizational structure, environment and performance: the role of strategic choice. *Sociology* 6, 2–21.

————. 1972b. Organizational structure and strategies of control: a replication of the Aston study. *Administrative Science Quarterly* 17, 163–77.

Churchman, C. West. 1968. *The Systems Approach.* New York: Dell Publishing Co.

Clark, Burton R. 1965. Interorganizational patterns in education. *Administrative Science Quarterly* 10, 224–37.

Clark, James V. 1969. A healthy organization. In Warren G. Bennis et al., eds., *The Planning of Change,* second edition. New York: Holt, Rinehart & Winston, 282–97.

Cohen, Stephen S. 1969. *Modern Capitalist Planning: The French Model.* Cambridge, Mass.: Harvard University Press.

Committee on Education and Labor. House of Representatives. 1967. *Study of the United States Office of Education.* Washington, D.C.: United States Government Printing Office.

Covarrubias, A., and Vanek, J. 1975. Self-management in the Peruvian law of social property. *Administration and Society* 7, 55–64.

Cox, Robert W., and Jacobson, Harold K. 1973. *The Anatomy of Influence: Decision Making in International Organizations.* New Haven, Conn.: Yale University Press.

Crozier, Michel. 1964. *The Bureaucratic Phenomenon.* Chicago: University of Chicago Press.

————. 1965. Pour une analyze sociologique de la planification française. *Revue Française de Sociologie* 6, 147–63.

————. 1970. *La Société Bloquée.* Paris: Éditions du Seuil.

Crozier, Michel, et al. 1974. *Ou Va l'Administration Française?* Paris: Les Éditions d'Organisation.

DERTHICK, Martha. 1974. *Between State and Nation.* Washington, D.C.: The Brookings Institution.

Dill, William R. 1958. Environment as an influence on managerial autonomy. *Administrative Science Quarterly* 2, 409–43.

Dogan, Mattei, ed. 1975. *The Mandarins of Western Europe: The Political Role of Top Civil Servants.* New York: John Wiley & Sons.

Donaldson, Lex; Child, John; and Aldrich, Howard. 1975. The Aston findings on centralization: further discussion. *Administrative Science Quarterly* 20, 453–60.

Dorf, Richard C. 1974. *Technology and Society.* San Francisco: Boyd & Fraser Publishing Co.

Dornbusch, Sanford M., and Scott, Richard W. 1975. *Evaluation and the Exercise of Authority.* San Francisco: Jossey-Bass Publishers.

Duffy, Norman F. 1975. *Changes in Labour-Management Relations in the Enterprise.* Paris, France: Organization for Economic Co-operation and Development.

Duncan, Robert B. 1972. Characteristics of organizational environments and perceived environmental uncertainty. *Administrative Science Quarterly* 17, 313–27.

Dunning, John H., ed. 1972. *Multinational Enterprise*. New York: Praeger Publishers.

Dror, Yehezkel. 1968. *Public Policy Re-examined*. San Francisco: Chandler Publishing Co.

———. 1971a. *Design for Policy Sciences*. New York: American Elsevier Publishing Co.

———. 1971b. *Ventures in Policy Sciences: Concepts and Applications*. New York: American Elsevier Publishing Co.

Durkheim, Emile, 1933. *The Division of Labor in Society*. New York: The Macmillan Co. (First published in French in 1893.)

EDGETT, James D. 1972. *How to Manage Your Way to the Top*. West Nyack, N.Y.: Parker Publishing Co.

Eells, Richard. 1972. *Global Corporations: The Emergency System of World Economic Power*. New York: Interbook.

Emerson, R. 1962. Power-dependence relations. *American Sociological Review* 37, 31–41.

Emery, F. E., and Trist, E. L. 1965. The causal texture of organizational environments. *Human Relations* 18, 21–34.

Etzioni, Amitai. 1961. *A Comparative Analysis of Complex Organizations*. New York: Free Press.

———. 1964. *Modern Organizations*. Englewood Cliffs, N.J.: Prentice-Hall.

FALLENBUCHL, Zbigniew W., ed. 1976. *Economic Development in the Soviet Union and Eastern Europe, Vols. 1 and 2*. New York: Praeger Publishers.

Fantini, Mario, and Gittell, Marilyn. 1973. *Decentralization: Achieving Reform*. New York: Praeger Publishers.

Fesler, James W. 1949. *Area and Administration*. University, Ala.: University of Alabama Press.

———. 1968. Centralization and decentralization. In *International Encyclopedia of the Social Sciences, Vol. 2*. New York: Macmillan, 1968, 370–77.

Fishburn, Peter C. 1964. *Decision and Value Theory*. New York: John Wiley & Sons.

Fisher, John. 1975. *Vital Signs, USA*. New York: Harper & Row, Publishers.

Forbes, Jean, ed. 1974. *Studies in Social Science and Planning*. New York: John Wiley & Sons.

Fordyce, J. K., and Weil, R. 1971. *Managing with People*. Reading, Mass.: Addison-Wesley Publishing Co.

Foulke, William Dudley. 1919. *Fighting the Spoilmen: Reminiscences of the Civil Service Reform Movement*. New York: G. P. Putnam's Sons.

Franklin, Jerome L. 1973. *Organization Development: An Annotated Bibliography.* Ann Arbor, Mich.: Center for Research on Utilization of Scientific Knowledge, Institute for Social Research, University of Michigan.

Freedeman, Charles E. 1961. *The Conseil d'Etat in Modern France.* New York: Columbia University Press.

French, W. L., and Bell, C. H., Jr. 1973. *Organization Development.* Englewood Cliffs, N.J.: Prentice-Hall.

Friedlander, Frank, and Brown, Dave L. 1974. Organization development. *Annual Review of Psychology* 25, 313–41.

Friedmann, John. 1973. *Retracking America: A Theory of Transactive Planning.* Garden City, N.Y.: Anchor Press.

Friedmann, Karl A. 1974. *Complaining: Comparative Aspects of Complaint Behavior and Attitudes toward Complaining in Canada and Britain.* Beverly Hills, Calif.: Sage Publications.

Friedrich, Carl J. 1972. *The Pathology of Politics.* New York: Harper & Row, Publishers.

Fromm, Erich. 1968. *The Revolution of Hope: Toward a Humanized Technology.* New York: Harper & Row, Publishers.

Furstenberg, F. 1969. Workers participation in the Federal Republic of Germany. *Bulletin of the International Institute for Labor Studies* 6, 94–147.

GARDINER, John A. 1970. *The Politics of Corruption: Organized Crime in an American City.* New York: Russell Sage Foundation.

Gardiner, John A., and Olson, David J., eds. 1974. *Theft of the City: Readings on Corruption in Urban America.* Bloomington, Ind.: Indiana University Press.

Galbraith, John Kenneth. 1967. *The New Industrial State.* Boston: Houghton Mifflin Co.

———. 1973. *A China Passage.* Boston: Houghton Mifflin Co.

Gelhorn, Walter. 1966. *Ombudsmen & Others: Citizens Protectors in Nine Countries.* Cambridge, Mass.: Harvard University Press.

Gittell, Marilyn, et al. 1973. *School Boards and School Policy: An Evaluation of Decentralization in New York City.* New York: Praeger Publishers.

Glaser, Barney G., ed. 1968. *Organizational Careers.* Chicago: Aldine Publishing Co.

Glueck, Eleanor. 1936. *Evaluative Research in Social Work.* New York: Columbia University Press.

Goffman, Erving. 1961. *Asylums.* Garden City, N.Y.: Anchor Books, Doubleday & Co.

Golembiewski, Robert T. 1972. *Renewing Organizations: The Laboratory Approach to Planned Change.* Itasca, Ill.: F. E. Peacock Publishers.

Gonzalez, Richard F., and Negandhi, Anant R. 1967. *United States Overseas Executive: His Orientations and Career Patterns.* East Lansing, Mich.: Michigan State University, Graduate School of Business Administration.

Goodman, Robert. 1971. *After the Planners.* New York: Simon & Schuster.

Granick, David. 1955. *Management of the Industrial Firm in the USSR: A Study in Soviet Economic Planning.* New York: Columbia University Press.

———. 1960. *The Red Executive: A Study of the Organization Man in Russian Industry.* Garden City, N.Y.: Doubleday & Co.

Grémion, Pierre. 1976. *Le Pouvoir Péripherique: Bureaucrates et Notables dans le Système Politique Français.* Paris: Éditions du Seuil.

Gross, Bertram M., ed. 1967. *Action under Planning: The Guidance of Economic Development.* New York: McGraw-Hill Book Co.

Guttentag, Marcia, and Struening, Elmer L., eds. 1975. *Handbook of Evaluation Research, Vols. 1 and 2.* Beverly Hills, Calif.: Sage Publications.

HARE, Paul A., Borgatta, Edgar F.; and Bales, Robert F., eds. 1965. *Small Groups: Studies in Social Interaction.* Revised edition. New York.: Alfred A. Knopf.

Hart, David K. 1972. Theories of government related to decentralization and citizen participation. *Public Administration Review* 32, 603–21.

Hayek, Friedrich A. 1944. *The Road to Serfdom.* Chicago: University of Chicago Press.

Hayes, Samuel Perkins. 1959. *Measuring the Results of Development Projects.* New York: UNESCO Monographs in the Applied Sciences.

Hayward, Jack, and Watson, Michael, eds. 1975. *Planning, Politics and Public Policy: The British, French and Italian Experience.* Cambridge: Cambridge University Press.

Heidenheimer, Arnold J., ed. 1970. *Political Corruption: Readings in Comparative Analysis.* New York: Holt, Rinehart & Winston.

Heilbroner, Robert L. 1974. *An Inquiry into the Human Prospect.* New York: W. W. Norton & Co.

———. 1976. *Business Civilization in Decline.* New York: W. W. Norton & Co.

Heller, Walter W. 1967. *New Dimensions of Political Economy.* New York: W. W. Norton & Co.

Heydebrand, Wolf V., ed. 1973. *Comparative Organizations: The Result of Empirical Research.* Englewood Cliffs, N.J.: Prentice-Hall.

Hicks, J. R. 1939. The foundations of welfare economics. *Economic Journal* 49, 696–700, 711–12.

Hill, Michael J. 1975. *The Sociology of Public Administration.* New York: Crane, Russak & Co.

Hirschman, Albert O. 1967. *Development Projects Observed.* Washington, D.C.: The Brookings Institution.
———. 1970. *Exit, Voice and Loyalty.* Cambridge, Mass.: Harvard University Press.
Hitch, Charles J., and McKean, Roland N. 1961. *The Economics of Defense in the Nuclear Age.* Cambridge, Mass.: Harvard University Press.
Holmberg, A. R. 1958. The research and development approach to the study of change. *Human Organization* 17, 12–17.
Hoos, Ida R. 1972. *Systems Analysis in Public Policy: A Critique.* Berkeley, Calif.: University of California Press.
Horn, John D. 1964. *How to Become Head of Your Firm before Forty.* New York: Coleridge Press.
Hunnius, G.; Garson, G. D.; and Case, J., eds. 1973. *Worker's Control.* New York: Random House.

ILLICH, Ivan. 1973. *Tools for Conviviality.* New York: Harper & Row, Publishers.
International Bank for Reconstruction and Development. 1960. *Some Techniques of Development Lending.* Washington, D.C.: IBRD.
International Union of Local Authorities. 1971. *Citizen Participation and Local Government.* The Hague, Netherlands: n.p.

JACQUEMART, Denis. 1957. *Le Conseil d'État, Juge de Cassation.* Paris: Librairie Générale de Droit et de Jurisprudence.
Jacoby, Henry. 1973. *The Bureaucratization of the World.* Berkeley, Calif.: University of California Press.
Jewkes, John. 1948. *Ordeal by Planning.* London: Macmillan & Co.
Jun, Jong Sup, and Storm, William B., eds. 1973. *Tomorrow's Organization.* Glenview, Ill.: Scott, Foresman Publishers.
Jurkovich, Ray. 1974. A core typology of organizational environments. *Administrative Science Quarterly* 19, 380–94.

KALDOR, N. 1939. Welfare propositions of economics and interpersonal comparisons of utility. *Economic Journal* 49, 549–52.
Katz, Daniel, and Kahn, Robert L. 1966. *The Social Psychology of Organizations.* New York: John Wiley & Sons.
Katz, Daniel; Gutek, Barbara A.; Kahn, Robert L.; and Barton, Eugenia. 1975. *Bureaucratic Encounters: A Pilot Study in the Evaluation of Government Services.* Ann Arbor, Mich.: Survey Research Center, Institute for Social Research, University of Michigan.
Kaufman, Herbert. 1973. *Administrative Feedback: Monitoring Subordinates' Behavior.* Washington, D.C.: The Brookings Institution.
Kefauver, Estes. 1951. *Crime in America.* New York: Doubleday & Co.
Kessler, Marie-Christine. 1968. *Le Conseil d'État.* Paris: Cahiers de la Fondation Nationale des Sciences Politiques, Armand Colin.

Keynes, John Maynard. 1964. *The General Theory of Employment, Interest, and Money, First Harbinger Edition.* New York: Harcourt, Brace & World.

Kimble, George H. T. 1962. *Tropical Africa. Volume I. Land and Livelihood.* Abridged edition. Garden City, N.Y.: Anchor Books, Doubleday & Co.

Kindlegerger, Charles P., ed. 1970. *The International Corporation.* Cambridge, Mass.: MIT Press.

Kirkhart, Larry, and White, Orion F., Jr. 1974. The future of organization development. *Public Administration Review* 34, 129–40.

Klaw, Spencer. 1961. Two weeks in a T-group. *Fortune* 64, 114–17.

Knight, Frank H. 1921. *Risk, Uncertainty and Profit.* Boston: Houghton Mifflin Co.

Kochen, Manfred, and Deutsch, Karl W. 1969. Toward a rational theory of decentralization: some implications of a mathematical approach. *American Political Science Review* 63, 734–49.

Komarovsky, Mirra, ed. 1975. *Sociology and Public Policy: The Case of Presidential Commissions.* New York: American Elsevier Publishing Co.

LANDAU, Martin. 1969. Redundancy, rationality, and the problem of duplication and overlap. *Public Administration Review* 29, 346–58.

Landesco, John. 1968. *Organized Crime in Chicago.* Chicago: University of Chicago Press.

Landsberger, Henry A., ed. 1970. *Comparative Perspectives on Formal Organizations.* Boston: Little, Brown & Co.

Lange, O. 1942. The foundations of welfare economics. *Econometrica* 10, 215–28.

La Porte, Todd R., ed. 1975. *Organized Social Complexity.* Princeton, N.J.: Princeton University Press.

Lautman, Jacques, and Thoenig, Jean-Claude. 1966. *Planification et Administrations Centrales: Études Sociologiques.* Paris: Centre de Recherches de Sociologie des Organisations.

Lawler, E. E.; Hackman, J. R.; and Kaufman, S. 1973. Effects of job redesign: a field experiment. *Journal of Applied Social Psychology* 57, 467–71.

Lawrence, Paul R., and Lorsh, Jay W. 1967. *Organization and Environment.* Boston: Harvard Business School.

Lee, Eugene C. 1960. *The Politics of Nonpartisanship.* Berkeley, Calif.: University of California Press.

Lesieur, Frederick G., ed. 1958. *The Scanlon Plan.* Cambridge, Mass.: The Technology Press of MIT.

Levine, Robert A. 1972. *Public Planning, Failure and Redirection.* New York: Basic Books.

Levy, Frank; Meltsner, Arnold J.; and Wildavsky, Aaron. 1974. *Urban Outcomes: Schools, Streets and Libraries.* Berkeley, Calif.: University of California Press.

Levy, Frank, and Truman, Edwin M. 1971. Toward a rational theory of decentralization: another view. *American Political Science Review* 67, 172–79.

Likert, Rensis. 1967. *The Human Organization: Its Management and Value.* New York: McGraw-Hill Book Co.

Lindblom, Charles E. 1965. *The Intelligence of Democracy: Decision Making through Mutual Adjustment.* New York: Free Press.

Lippitt, G. L. 1969. *Organizational Renewal.* New York: Appleton-Century-Crofts.

Luce, R. Duncan, and Raiffa, Howard. 1967. *Games and Decisions.* New York: John Wiley & Sons.

Lund, Herbert F. 1973. *The Real Official Executive Survival Handbook: How to Stay in Office Politics.* New York: Dial Press.

MAAS, Arthur, ed. 1959. *Area and Power: A Theory of Local Government.* Glencoe, Ill.: Free Press.

Maher, J. R. 1971. *New Perspectives in Job Enrichment.* New York: Van Nostrand Reinhold.

Mainzer, Lewis C. 1973. *Political Bureaucracy.* Glenview, Ill.: Scott, Foresman & Co.

Mannheim, Karl. n.d. *Man and Society in an Age of Reconstruction.* New York: Harcourt, Brace & World. (First published in German in 1935; translated, revised, and considerably enlarged in 1940.)

———. 1965. *Freedom, Power, and Democratic Planning.* London: Routledge & Kegan Paul. (First published in 1951.)

Marris, Robin, ed. 1974. *The Corporate Society.* New York: John Wiley & Sons.

Marrow, Alfred J.; Bowers, David G.; and Seashore, Stanley E. 1967. *Management by Participation.* New York: Harper & Row, Publishers.

Mayntz, Renate, and Scharpf, Fritz W. 1975. *Policy Making in the German Federal Bureaucracy.* New York: American Elsevier Publishing Co.

Mayo, Elton. 1924. Revery and industrial fatigue. *Journal of Personnel Research* 3, 273–81.

———. 1933. *The Human Problems of an Industrial Civilization.* New York: Macmillan & Co.

McGill, Michael E. 1974. The evolution of organization development: 1947–1960. *Public Administration Review* 34, 98–105.

McGregor, Douglas. 1960. *The Human Side of Enterprise.* New York: McGraw-Hill Book Co.

———. 1967. *The Professional Manager* (edited posthumously by Warren G. Bennis and Caroline McGregor). New York: McGraw-Hill Book Co.

McMullan, M. 1961. A theory of corruption. *Sociological Review* 9, 181–201.

Meltsner, Arnold J. 1976. *Policy Analysts in the Bureaucracy.* Berkeley, Calif.: University of California Press.

Meyerson, Martin, and Banfield, Edward C. 1955. *Politics, Planning and the Public Interest: The Case of Public Housing in Chicago.* New York: Free Press of Glencoe.

Meynaud, Jean. 1963. *Planification et Politique.* Lausanne: Études de Science Politique.

Michael, Donald N. 1968. *The Unprepared Society: Planning for a Precarious Future.* New York: Basic Books.

Miles, Raymond E. 1964. Conflicting elements in managerial ideologies. *Industrial Relations* 4, 77–91.

———. 1965. Human relations or human resources. *Harvard Business Review* 43, 148–56.

Miles, Raymond E., and Ritchie, J. B. 1970. An analysis of quantity and quality of participation as mediating variable in the participative decision making process. *Personnel Psychology* 23, 347–59.

Miller, S. M. 1965. Evaluating action programs. *Trans-action* 2, 38–39.

Millett, John D. 1947. *The Process and Organization of Government Planning.* New York: Columbia University Press.

Mindlin, Sergio E., and Aldrich, Howard 1975. Interorganizational dependence: a review of the concept and a re-examination of the findings of the Aston group. *Administrative Science Quarterly* 20, 382–92.

Mishan, Ezra J. 1967. *The Costs of Economic Growth.* New York: Frederick A. Praeger, Publishers.

Moore, Wilbert E. 1966. The utility of utopias. *American Sociological Review* 31, 765–72.

Mumford, Lewis. 1970. *The Pentagon of Power.* New York: Harcourt Brace Jovanovich.

NADER, Ralph; Green, Mark; and Seligman, Joel. 1976. *Taming the Giant Corporation.* New York: W. W. Norton & Co.

von Neumann, J., and Morgenstern, O. 1953. *Theory of Games and Economic Behavior.* Princeton, N.J.: Princeton University Press.

Newhouse, John. 1973. *Cold Dawn: The Story of SALT.* New York: Holt, Rinehart & Winston.

Nias, J. 1972. "Pseudo-participation" and the success of innovation in the introduction of the B.E.D. *Sociological Review* 20, 169–83.

Niskanen, William A., Jr. 1971. *Bureaucracy and Representative Government.* Chicago: Aldine and Atherton.

Novick, David, ed. 1965. *Program Budgeting: Program Analysis and the Federal Budget.* Cambridge, Mass.: Harvard University Press.

Nye, J. S. 1967. Corruption and political development: a cost benefit analysis. *American Political Science Association* 61, 417–27.

OSBORN, Richard N., and James G. Hunt. 1974. Environment and Organizational effectiveness. *Administrative Science Quarterly* 19, 231–46.

Ozga, S. Andrew. 1965. *Expectations in Economic Theory*. Chicago: Aldine Publishing Co.

PAPE, Ruth H. 1964. Touristry: a type of occupational mobility. *Social Problems* 11, 336–44. Excerpted in Barney G. Glazer, ed., *Organizational Careers*. Chicago: Aldine, 1968, 388–97.

Paul, W. J.; Robertson, K. B.; and Herzberg, F. 1969. Job enrichment pays off. *Harvard Business Review* 47, 61–78.

Pavalko, Ronald M. 1971. *Sociology of Occupations and Professions*. Itasca, Ill.: F. E. Peacock Publishers.

Perrow, Charles. 1967. A framework for the comparative analysis of organizations. *American Sociological Review* 32, 194–208.

———. 1972. *Complex Organizations: A Critical Essay*. Glenview, Ill.: Scott, Foresman & Co.

Peter, Lawrence J.; and Hull, Raymond. 1970. *The Peter Principle*. New York: Bantam Books.

Popham, James W., ed. 1974. *Evaluation in Education*. Berkeley, Calif.: McCutchan Publishing Corp.

President's Commission on Law Enforcement and Administration of Justice. 1967. *Task Force Report: Organized Crime*. Washington, D.C.: United States Government Printing Office.

Primack, Joel, and Von Hippel, Frank. 1974. *Advice and Dissent: Scientists in the Political Arena*. New York: Basic Books.

Proxy, George. 1969. *How to Get Your Boss's Job: The Secrets of Executive Success*. New York: Funk & Wagnalls.

Pugh, D. S.; Hickson, D. J.; and Turner, C. 1968. Dimensions of organization structure. *Administrative Science Quarterly* 13, 65–105.

Putnam, Robert D. 1973. The political attitudes of senior civil servants in Western Europe: a preliminary report. *British Journal of Political Science* 3, 257–90.

RAIFFA, Howard. 1968. *Decision Analysis: Introductory Lectures on Choices under Uncertainty*. Reading, Mass.: Addison-Wesley Publishing Co.

Rein, Martin. 1972. Decentralization and citizen participation in social services. *Public Administration Review* 32, 687–700.

Rendel, Margherita. 1970. *The Administrative Functions of the French Conseil d'Etat*. London: London School of Economics and Political Science.

Reutlinger, Shlomo. 1970. *Techniques for Project Appraisal under Uncertainty*. Baltimore: Johns Hopkins Press.

Roemer, Michael, and Stern, Joseph J. 1975. *The Appraisal of Development Projects*. New York: Praeger Publishers.

Roethlisberger, Fritz J., and Dickson, William J. 1939. *Management and the Worker.* Cambridge, Mass.: Harvard University Press.

Rolfe, Sidney E., and Damm, Walter, eds. 1970. *Multinational Corporation in the World Economy.* New York: Praeger Publishers.

Rosengren, William R., and Lefton, Mark, eds. 1970. *Organizations and Clients.* Columbus, Ohio: Charles E. Merrill Publishing Co.

Rossi, Peter H. 1967. Evaluating social action programs. *Trans-action* 4, 51–53.

————. 1969. Evaluating educational programs. *Urban Review* 3, 17–18.

Roszak, Theodore. 1975. *Unfinished Animal.* New York: Harper & Row, Publishers.

Rowat, Donald C., ed. 1968. *Ombudsman: Citizen's Defender.* Second edition. Toronto: University of Toronto Press.

Ryapolov, Gregory. 1966. I was a Soviet manager. *Harvard Business Review,* Jan.–Feb., 117–25.

Ryavec, Karl W. 1975. *Implementation of Soviet Economic Reforms: Political, Organizational and Social Processes.* New York: Praeger Publishers.

SAROFF, Jerome R. 1974. Is mobility enough for the temporary society? Some observations based upon the experience of the Federal Executive Institute. *Public Administration Review* 34, 480–86.

Savitch, H. V., and Adler, Madeleine. 1974. *Decentralization at the Grass Roots: Political Innovation in New York City and London.* Beverly Hills, Calif.: Sage Publications.

Scanlon, J. N. 1948. Profit sharing under collective bargaining: three case studies. *Industrial and Labor Relations Review* 2, 58–75.

Schlesinger, Joseph A. 1966. *Ambition and Politics: Political Careers in the United States.* Chicago: Rand McNally & Co.

Schmandt, Henry J. 1972. Municipal decentralization: an overview. *Public Administration Review* 32, 571–88.

Schmuck, R. A.; Runkel, P. J.; Saturen, S.; Martell, R.; and Deer, C. B. 1972. *Handbook of Organization Development in Schools.* Palo Alto, Calif.: National Press Books.

Schroeder, Gertrude E. 1976. Post-Khrushchev reforms and Soviet public financial goals. In Z. M. Fallenbuchl, ed., *Economic Development in the Soviet Union and Eastern Europe, Vol. 2.* New York: Praeger Publishers, 348–67.

Schultze, Charles L. 1968. *The Politics and Economics of Public Spending.* Washington, D.C.: The Brookings Institution.

Schumacher, E. F. 1973. *Small Is Beautiful: Economics as if People Mattered.* New York: Harper & Row, Publishers (Perennial Library).

Schumpeter, Joseph A. 1947. *Capitalism, Socialism and Democracy.* Second edition. New York: Harper & Brothers Publishers.

Scitovsky, Tibor. 1973. Notes on the producer society. *De Economist* (Amsterdam) 121, 225–50.

Scott, James C. 1969. The analysis of corruption in developing nations. *Comparative Studies in Society and History* 2, 315–41.

———. 1972. *Comparative Political Corruption*. Englewood Cliffs, N.J.: Prentice-Hall.

Scott, William G., and Mitchell, Terence R. 1976. *Organization Theory: A Structural and Behavioral Analysis*. Homewood, Ill.: Richard D. Irwin.

Scriven, Michael. 1969. Evaluating educational programs. *Urban Review* 3, 20–22.

Seashore, Stanley E., and Bowers, David G. 1970. The durability of organizational change. *American Psychologist* 25, 227–33.

Segal, Morley. 1974. Organization and environment: a typology of adaptability and structure. *Public Administration Review* 34, 212–20.

Selznick, Phillip. 1966. *TVA and the Grass Roots: A Study in the Sociology of Formal Organizations*. New York: Harper & Row, Publishers. (First published in 1949.)

Sethi, S. Prakash, and Holton, Richard H. 1974. *Management of the Multinationals: Policies, Operations and Research*. New York: Free Press, a division of Macmillan Co.

Shackle, G. L. S. 1952. *Expectation in Economics*. Cambridge: Cambridge University Press.

Sherman, Lawrence, ed. 1974. *Police Corruption: A Sociological Perspective*. New York: Anchor Press.

Simon, Herbert A. 1957. *Administrative Behavior: A Study of Decision-Making Processes in Administrative Organization*. Second edition. New York: The Macmillan Co.

———. 1960. *The New Science of Management Decision*. New York: Harper & Row, Publishers.

Simpson, Richard L., and Gulley, William H. 1962. Goals, environmental pressures, and organizational characteristics. *American Sociological Review* 27, 344–51.

Siroka, Robert W.; Siroka, Ellen K.; and Schloss, Gilbert A. 1971. *Sensitivity Training and Group Encounter*. New York: Grosset & Dunlap.

Smelser, Neil J. 1964. Toward a theory of modernization. In Amitai Etzioni and Eva Etzioni, eds., *Social Change, Sources, Patterns and Consequences*. New York: Basic Books, 258–74.

Stacey, Frank. 1971. *The British Ombudsman*. Oxford: Oxford University Press.

Stavrianos, L. S. 1976. *The Promise of the Coming Dark Age*. San Francisco, Calif.: W. H. Freeman & Co.

Stenberg, Carl W. 1972. *The New Grass Roots Government? Decentralization and Citizen Participation in Urban Areas*. Washington, D.C.: Advisory Commission on Intergovernmental Relations.

Stewart, P. A. 1967. *Job Enlargement*. Iowa City: University of Iowa College of Business Administration.

Stewart, Richard B. 1975. The reformation of American administrative law. *Harvard Law Review* 88, 1669–1813.

Stinchcombe, Arthur L. 1974. *Creating Efficient Industrial Administrations*. New York: Academic Press.

Strauss, George. 1966. Participative management: a critique. *ILR Research* 12, 3–6.

Suchman, Edward A. 1967. *Evaluative Research*. New York: Russell Sage Foundation.

Suleiman, Ezra N. 1974. *Politics, Power and Bureaucracy in France*. Princeton, N.J.: Princeton University Press.

Sutermeister, Robert A., ed. 1963. *People and Productivity*. New York: McGraw-Hill Book Co.

TAYLOR, Frederick W. 1911. *Scientific Management*. New York: Harper Publishers.

Terkel, Studs. 1974. *Working*. New York: Avon Books.

Thoenig, Jean-Claude. 1973. *L'Ère des Technocrates: Le Cas des Ponts et Chaussées*. Paris: Les Éditions d'Organisation.

Thompson, James D. 1967. *Organizations in Action*. New York: McGraw-Hill Book Co.

Thompson, Victor. 1961. *Modern Organizations*. New York: Knopf.

Timbergen, Jan. 1958. *The Design of Development*. Baltimore, Md.: Johns Hopkins Press.

Trist, E. L.; Higgin, G. W.; Murray H.; and Pollock, A. B. 1963. *Organizational Choice*. London: Tavistock Publications.

Turk, Herman. 1969. Comparative urban studies in interorganizational relations. *Sociological Inquiry* 38, 108–10.

———. 1970. Interorganizational networks in urban society: initial perspectives and comparative research. *American Sociological Review* 35, 1–19.

Turner, Louis. 1971. *Invisible Empires: Multinational Companies and the Modern World*. New York: Harcourt Brace Jovanovich.

Tyler, Gus, ed. 1962. *Organized Crime in America: A Book of Readings*. Ann Arbor, Mich.: University of Michigan Press.

UNITED Nations, 1958. *Manual on Economic Development Projects*. New York: UN Document 58.II.G.5.

United States Department of Labor, Bureau of Employment Security, 1965. *Dictionary of Occupational Titles*. Volume I, Third Edition. Washington, D.C.: United States Government Printing Office.

VANEK, Jaroslav. 1971. *The Participatory Economy*. Ithaca, N.Y.: Cornell University Press.

Vernon, Raymond. 1972. *The Economic and Political Consequences of Multinational Enterprise: An Anthology.* Cambridge, Mass.: Harvard Business School.

Vroom, Victor. 1960. *Some Personality Determinants of the Effects of Participation.* Englewood Cliffs, N.J.: Prentice-Hall.

―――. 1964. *Work and Motivation.* New York: John Wiley & Sons.

WACHTEL, H. 1973. *Worker's Management and Worker's Wages in Yugoslavia.* Ithaca, N.Y.: Cornell University Press.

Waldo, Dwight, ed. 1971. *Public Administration in a Time of Turbulence.* Scranton, Pa.: Chandler Publishing Co.

Waline, Marcel. 1961. *La Competence Jurisdictionnelle du Conseil d'État et des Tribunaux Administratifs.* Paris: Librairie Générale de Droit et de Jurisprudence.

Warren, Roland L. 1967. The interorganizational field as a focus for investigation. *Administrative Science Quarterly* 12, 369–419.

Warwick, Donald P. 1975. *A Theory of Public Bureaucracy: Politics, Personality and Organization in the State Department.* Cambridge, Mass.: Harvard University Press.

Waterston, Albert. 1965. *Development Planning: Lessons of Experience.* Baltimore, Md.: Johns Hopkins Press.

Weeks, Kent M. 1973. *Ombudsmen around the World.* Berkeley, Calif.: Institute of Government Studies, University of California.

White, Orion F., Jr. 1969. The dialectical organization: an alternative to bureaucracy. *Public Administration Review* 29, 32–42.

―――. 1971. Social change and administrative adaptation. In Frank Marini, ed., *Toward a New Public Administration.* Scranton, Pa.: Chandler Publishing Co., 59–83.

White, Orion F., Jr., and Gates, Bruce L. 1974. Statistical theory and equity in the delivery of social services. *Public Administration Review* 34, 43–51.

Wiener, Norbert. 1948. *Cybernetics.* New York: John Wiley & Sons.

Wilczynski, J. 1970. *The Economics of Socialism.* Chicago: Aldine Publishing Co.

Wildavsky, Aaron. 1964. *The Politics of the Budgetary Process.* Boston: Little, Brown & Co.

―――. 1975. *Budgeting: A Comparative Theory of Budgetary Processes.* Boston: Little, Brown & Co.

Wilensky, Harold L. 1964. The professionalization of everyone? *American Journal of Sociology* 70, 137–58.

―――. 1967. *Organizational Intelligence: Knowledge and Policy in Government and Industry.* New York: Basic Books.

Wilkinson, Rupert, ed. 1969. *Governing Elites: Studies in Training and Selection.* New York: Oxford University Press.

Williams, Walter. 1971. *Social Policy Research and Analysis.* New York: American Elsevier Publishing Co.

Wraith, Ronald, and Simkin, Edgar. 1963. *Corruption in Developing Countries.* London: George Allen & Unwin.

Wyner, Alan J., ed. 1973. *Executive Ombudsmen in the United States.* Berkeley, Calif.: Institute of Government Studies, University of California.

ZIMBALIST, Andrew. 1975. The dynamics of worker participation: an interpretative essay on the Chilean and other experiences. *Administration and Society* 7, 43–54.

Zimet, Melvin. 1973. *Decentralization and School Effectiveness: A Case Study of the 1969 Decentralization Law in New York City.* New York: Teachers College Press.

Zink, Harold. 1930. *City Bosses in the United States.* Durham, N.C.: Duke University Press.

Znaniecki, Florian. 1965. *The Social Role of the Man of Knowledge.* New York: Octagon Books. (First published in 1940.)

Index